THE FATE OF
IBM

THE FATE OF
IBM

Robert Heller

LITTLE, BROWN AND COMPANY

A *Little, Brown* Book

First published in Great Britain in 1994
by Little, Brown and Company

Copyright © Heller Arts, Ltd 1994

The moral right of the author has been asserted.

A CIP catalogue record for this book
is available from the British Library.

ISBN 0 316 90742 1

Typeset by M Rules
Printed and bound in Great Britain by
Clays Ltd, St Ives plc

Little, Brown and Company (UK) Limited
Brettenham House
Lancaster Place
London WC2 7EN

To Matthew and Shelley

Contents

IV Silicon Valley Steals the Show

V IBM's Armour: The Fateful Cracks

VI The Winning War of the Clones

VII The Resistible Rise of Japan

VIII The Trouble with Mainframes

IX The Many Reinventions of IBM

X The Nadir of the Nineties

Acknowledgements

For his help in the conception and writing of this book, I would like to thank my friend Jean-Claude Solera, a veteran of 30 years with IBM. Although the views expressed in the book are mine, my many discussions with him have been very helpful in developing my understanding of the industry in general and IBM in particular. If his own early warnings about the fate of IBM had been heeded, the story told in these pages would have been very different, and I eagerly await the completion of his own book, *The IBM Way Revisited – The Gravediggers of IBM*.

Among the many sources I have used in piecing together the story of IBM, I owe a particular debt to *Blue Magic* (Grafton Books, 1989), in which James Chposky and Ted Leonsis, while largely (and brilliantly) recounting the astonishing story of the IBM Personal Computer, provide in the process a most vivid and well-researched account of the corporation. Their bottom-up insights form a counterpoint to the equally remarkable view from the top given, in *Father, Son, and Co.* (Bantam Books, 1990), by the former and outstandingly successful chairman, Thomas Watson, Jr.

His book's frank and fair-minded account of IBM's greatest days, and of its author and his extraordinary father, places it in the very front rank of business books, let alone business autobiographies. Interestingly, though, its bibliography does not include three of the other books on IBM that I found illuminating, indeed, indispensable: *Blue Magic, IBM* by Robert Sobel (Truman Talley, 1981) and *Big Blue* by Richard Thomas DeLamarter (Dodd Mead, 1986).

Their accounts of IBM were written at the apogee. The subsequent ups and (mostly) downs of this great business have been charted by the journalists working for *Business Week, Fortune, The Wall Street Journal, The New York Times,* the *Financial Times,* and many other journals – including the specialist computer press, whose standards are wholly admirable. My debt to other papers, and to several of the individual writers, is gratefully acknowledged in the text: Jack Schofield, computer editor of the *Guardian,* has been a consistently valuable guide, while among IBM watchers, none excels William F. Zachmann, president of Canopus Research.

Among more general management sources, Charles H. Ferguson made a particularly stimulating contribution to the debate on America's electronic future in the *Harvard Business Review.* Everybody interested in management should read *The Fifth Discipline* by Peter M. Senge (Doubleday, 1990: Century Business 1992), which is essential to understanding the general principles which worked through into the particular fate of IBM. I have had the priceless opportunity of discussing the case with many friends, including Peter Drucker and Michael J. Kami, whose depth of knowledge and insight have been invaluable.

My understanding of the technological issues owed much to my work on *Culture Shock* (Hodder & Stoughton, 1990), whose sources are acknowledged in that book. The BBC, with *The Dream Machine,* produced not only an example of TV science fiction programming at its best, but an enthralling book of the series, by Jon Palfreman and Doron Swale (BBC Books, 1991). Also, *Fumbling the Future,* by Douglas K. Smith and Robert C. Alexander (Morrow, 1988), is a wonderful account of how Xerox invented the personal computer and, in missing its fantastic potential, simply exemplified Large Company Disease.

The paradox is that, within the huge organisations showing that disease's awful symptoms, labour men and women of the highest integrity, ability and achievement. Over the years, I have met many IBM executives, and admired them all – notably Edward Nixon, who so ably led IBM (UK) for many years. For obvious reasons, I have not mentioned them all by name. It is equally obvious that the IBM performance in recent years has not reflected the contributions of these truly excellent managers and the no less outstanding technologists and scientists on whom they depend.

In great business organisations, the whole can all too easily become much less than the sum of its individual parts. In trying to explain how this happened to IBM, I have inevitably been (I hope) fair in my judgements and reporting, but unfair in that, in a warts-and-all portrait, the blemishes catch the eye: the clear skin does not. This is the place to record my deep admiration for what IBM has achieved, and is achieving, along with my sorrow that its success turned so sour. For the sake of those still working and being recruited by the company, I wish nothing more fervently than the return of the sweet smell of success.

The book also owes a great deal to articles commissioned by the editors of *Management Today*, *Business Solutions*, and *Business Life*, to whom I owe many debts of gratitude. I benefited from the friendly and constructive criticism of Truman Talley, the distinguished New York publisher; and from the admirable efficiency of my secretary, Elli Petrohilos. My thanks go to them, and to a host of other friends and helpers.

Introduction:

Who Killed IBM?

This book is a detective story, a Whodunnit. On a day in February 1992, the old International Business Machines died. The world's most prodigious money machine reported an enormous $2.8 billion loss. The inexorable profitability had vanished; so had the reputation for unbeatable superiority; and so might the corporate structure on which both had rested. A few weeks before, the management had committed itself to radical change, towards fragmenting the mightiest of the monoliths.

A year later, in March 1993, the doctors certified the death. Chairman John F. Akers lost his job, the first IBM chief executive to do so. Louis V. Gerstner Jr. took over, coming from travel and financial services (American Express) via tobacco and food (RJR Nabisco). It was another first – the first outsider to head IBM. In yet another breach of tradition, a posse of other outsiders joined the new boss. All the herds of sacred cows were eligible for slaughter.

The result? 'Chaos,' said one senior executive that May. Significantly, he's German. Other giants, in oil and automobiles particularly, have spread irresistibly worldwide. But nobody had market shares on IBM's transcendent scale – up to four-fifths of sales – in every market. From Duluth to

Frankfurt, Japan to the old Soviet Empire, Australia to Norway, IBM was synonymous with 'electronic data processing' – the arid name for the scintillating computer technology that was changing the world.

Bestriding that world like the colossus it was (and is), IBM could expect everlasting growth in its industry. Most of that endless expansion had to come its way. True, the computer market had become cyclical as the 'dream machine' became universal and saturation points approached or even appeared. But new markets were constantly being born as others aged. The trouble for IBM was that the new births challenged its old superiority.

But if the market was the murderer, it needed accomplices – managers inside IBM who missed the changes in the environment, or reacted ineptly to their effects. Yet this was for long the Most Admired Corporation in America – selected year after year by its peers as leader for quality of management and for almost every other attribute of excellence. Either the peers were fooled, or IBM truly was the best-managed corporation. If so, its demise has profound consequences for American capitalism. If the best-run business in the most modern industry, a competitor feared even by the Japanese, can fail, what of lesser champions? What of General Motors?

What, indeed. For in 1991, GM reported losses twice as great as IBM's. To anyone with eyes to see, the large American corporation was in crisis. Eyes began to open, even in boardrooms where blindness had been most harmful. The GM board, weirdly tolerant during the long, disastrous reign of Roger B. Smith, rounded on Robert C. Stempel, its own poor choice as successor.

Stempel, first publicly humiliated by removal of powers, was shortly forced to resign – an obvious precedent, and read as one, for IBM. With his salary slashed and performance savaged, Akers suddenly seemed – and was – vulnerable. Many boards, for the first time in decades, began to question not only the competence of chief executive officers, but the stupendous monetary rewards heaped on these CEOs (by, of course, their boards).

Excessive 'compensation', unmatched by any unusual or even necessary economic contribution, played some part in the decline of big-time corporate performance. Like the bacterial infection which complicates a viral attack, the pay scandal seriously undermined the patient's condition. But overpayment was a pernicious symptom rather than an underlying cause.

So who did kill Cock Robin? Given that IBM's morbidity wasn't unique (several other giants, including American Express, lost CEOs in similar circumstances), the hunt is on for a serial killer. But 'kill' needs to be carefully defined. It's the old IBM that died, the brilliantly commercial, supposedly benevolent corporation, whose jobs-for-life employees occupied an internal world controlled as effectively as its external markets. Another IBM, with an unbeatable customer base, myriad patents, brilliant laboratories, fine factories, great product lines, superb branding, and massive sales firepower still existed. But to exploit those assets with renewed success, a new IBM was needed. The only issue was (and is) what kind of IBM to create.

This investigation can hope to find the murderers. It can't prove that an IBM Phoenix will rise from the ashes to reclaim its lead in reputation and achievement in new ways. The task before IBM, and American big business as a whole, is massive – as one hard fact shows. The best performers in US capitalism have faced least foreign competition in general, and least Japanese competition in particular: food and drink companies, for instance, service businesses and drug manufacturers. Many of these markets are highly competitive at home. But the competitors all play by the same rules, and their sheer size has been protective. In its own heyday, IBM faced only ineffective competition, mostly from other large US companies. All foolishly attacked a far more powerful army head on. You probably need a three-to-one advantage to win in frontal assaults. Since IBM had this superiority, and its attackers didn't, their defeat was inevitable.

Foreigners made much the same mistake. And the Japanese, short on technology and crippled by an impenetrable language, were sidelined – maybe for ever, the optimists thought. But small competitors did by necessity what large rivals had failed to do: they went round the side. Outflanked in apparently peripheral markets, IBM became a Gulliver: little people crawled all over its giant carcass, tying it down, inflicting pinprick wounds that cost too much blood.

When the Japanese overcame their disadvantages and joined battle, they faced an IBM weakened by attacks around its fringes. The three-to-one advantage had dwindled and frontal assaults now stood a chance. None of this happened overnight, though, and none of it went unheralded or unremarked. IBM had been created by a prime expert in assassinating competition. It had marched in the same aggressive mood for decades. How did it fail to meet a whole series of threats with the same old, comprehensive finality?

That's the same question: Whodunnit? The answer points not only to the future of America's greatest industry (which still leads the electronic revolution), but to the fate of the whole US corporate economy. The challenge to IBM is a national challenge – and, given its even larger position outside the US, a challenge for the entire West.

Peter Drucker saw the decline of the major corporations coming from a long way off. He said in early 1992 that 'The *Fortune* 500 is over' – meaning, in the magazine's words, that big businesses must 'slowly and painfully transform themselves into a new kind of creature'. How slow? How painful? How new?

The answers look important even in the context of a $5 trillion economy. The 500 account for $2.2 trillion of sales (more than the gross domestic product of a united Germany) and employ twelve million people. That's four million fewer people than at the start of the Eighties, and is one stark measure of absolute decline – in which IBM has fully shared. Millions of the 500's employees and billions of dollars of their sales lie outside the US. That makes the numbers worse, not better, for the bulk of the cutbacks have come at home. 'With curious serendipity,' wrote *Fortune*, 'the start of the decade coincided with a new set of imperatives for American industry – to review the mistakes and excesses of the past, or to make fundamental changes and to gird for the fiercely competitive times ahead.'

You could argue (of IBM, the 500 and the US economy) that the cutbacks at the beginning of the Nineties, by lowering the cost base, had set the stage for a rousing recovery in profits as economic recovery came. But that could be illusory, like the rebound in British corporate profits that was prematurely celebrated after the Thatcher recession of 1979–80.

Later events proved that getting 'leaner and fitter' *à la* Thatcher, by closing plants and slashing workforces (essentially the 500's recipe), was not the fundamental change required to turn past failures into future successes. That 'new set of imperatives' for American industry, after all, had been obvious throughout the Eighties. If essential action had been dodged earlier, what were the chances of much the same managements (those guilty of 'the mistakes and excesses' of the past) leading a true corporate revolution? Raking over the past is pointless, in economics as in personal life, however, unless investigation leads to action.

To understand why the old IBM died, you have to delve back into the past, to discover the motives and identify the actions of the principal characters. The conventional view as the Akers regime drew to its painful close was to approve his strategy; IBM was on the right road; breaking up the colossi into smaller, focused units was the new way, the method of combining the power of sheer size with the swiftness of the relatively small.

The issue is more than whether IBM's turnaround man, Lou Gerstner, will (as suggested shortly after his accession) reject this received wisdom. It's whether the giants are capable of total transformation; whether men like those in charge as IBM was humbled can build a new society. What died on that February day in 1992 was an old society, one of the most successful in history. Something will replace it. The search for the new IBM starts with the responsibility for the death of the old.

I
THE AGONY OF JOHN F. AKERS

1

Growth Everlasting: The 100 per cent Error

'The fact that we're losing market share makes me goddam mad . . . Everyone is too comfortable when the business is in crisis . . .' Within hours, the anger of John F. Akers, the fifth chairman of International Business Machines since the great Thomas Watson Sr, had sped round the company – and then round the world. Akers meant his broadside to be private, confined to a few senior managers. Like many of this chief executive's good intentions, it miscarried.

The incident is an epitome of the fate of IBM, the quintessential American corporation of the mid-twentieth century. The distance IBM had fallen, dropping like Icarus out of the sky, can be measured by what Frank Cary, who tapped Akers for eminence, had said a few years before. Asked about the chances of IBM sustaining its success, Cary had rated them as '100 per cent'. In 1991, the year of Akers' attack, the company lost $7.75 million a day: in 1992, $13.4 million.

Even the way in which his words burst upon the world explains much of what happened in the interval between Cary's 100 per cent and Akers' enormous losses. A well-meaning executive, impressed by the boss, wanted his own staff to share the message. He distributed the memo via electronic mail, forgetting that the system is worldwide and instantaneous.

The metaphor is unmistakable. A world market that IBM once tied up like a Christmas parcel has become wide open. The wonder of electronic mail is only one part of a technology that has burgeoned – and is burgeoning – at breakneck pace. The speed of change has outstripped IBM's capacity to respond and its ability to control. The overwhelming question is, What happens next? The answers aren't easy – as Akers found time and time again.

IBM's fall will be indelibly associated with his name, however unfairly. Until Akers quit under pressure, each chief executive had named his own successor. It's a rotten tradition, not least because the outgoing leader, consciously or subconsciously, may well pick an inferior who won't steal the predecessor's thunder. The tradition appeared to work wonders at IBM – but then, during the years of market dominance, everything worked. Certainly no king could have hailed his heir more rousingly than John R. Opel. After crowing about how IBM was surpassing all its goals for the Eighties – on productivity, profits and quality – Opel declared that 'John Akers will bring his own brand of leadership to the momentum we have achieved. He is remarkably well qualified in every major aspect of the business. His record of past accomplishment foretells the brightest of futures.'

The fault lay less with Akers, perhaps, than with his stars. Inadvertently, the outgoing Opel put his finger on the problem that was to swamp Akers and blacken IBM's bright future. 'In IBM,' said Opel, 'the transition from one CEO to another recalls the adage that the more things change, the more they are the same.' But things were changing more than ever and would never be the same again

The 'common culture, rooted in IBM's unchanging beliefs' was fine for unchanging times: but the beliefs included untested notions that the company truly did provide the 'very best in customer service', achieve 'excellence in every task we undertake', and show 'respect for the individual'. John Akers was tailor-made for the role of curator of this tradition. Only fifty when he replaced Opel, Akers potentially had a decade ahead as sixth CEO. The house magazine, *Think*, pictured a quintessential 'Organisation Man', not one for 'intimidation or harshness', and possessed of an 'unquenchable optimism'. At thirty-nine, he had badly needed this buoyancy when a crucial promotion, to head up the Data Processing Division, IBM's largest domestic unit, coincided with economic recession.

Akers later recalled that 'It's a good thing we didn't know how bad things were supposed to be, or maybe we wouldn't have enjoyed ourselves so much.' DPD had two exceptionally good years, and Akers was a made man. A former carrier pilot, Akers had left the Navy in 1960. He found the inside track at Armonk, IBM's head office, twenty miles north of New York City, early on. He worked for Frank Cary as administrative assistant shortly before the latter became IBM's president. Akers' own verdict ('I didn't understand a lot, but I got the exposure') sounds a fair summary.

By his early forties Akers was a vice president, working on plans and control for a powerful figure named Paul Rizzo (a member of what is, not altogether jokingly, known as IBM's Italian Mafia). Akers joined the élite in 1978, taking charge of the Data Processing's marketing group before becoming its boss: two years later, he got the newly formed Information Systems and Communications Group. 'We had development, manufacturing, the personal computer, the typewriter business', said Akers. 'It was a great job for me. I would have loved to do it a lot longer than I did.'

It's churlish to point out that the PC business subsequently recorded one of the most precipitate losses of market share in history; while the typewriter operation's future was so ill-guarded that later IBM sold off this one-time world leader – with Akers presiding over the sale. But he was only two years in the post before he became president of the corporation. His own account illustrates a pell-mell rush to the top: 'I had five years running two different

11

groups, two years now as president, and I have been involved in all parts of the business.'

Nothing in this all-parts experience had tested his ability to command a major corporation, not for a short spell, but a whole decade. His career had epitomised the centripetal nature of management in the great American corporation. As all power gravitates inwards, its exercise falls to those most adept within the hub. Akers was superbly qualified to manage the Armonk hub: but IBM's needs, and its problems, were flooding in from outside. If the board of directors had been able to stand back, and throw away IBM's traditions (as they did in March 1993), they might have considered a different paradigm: somebody who had created or recreated a highly successful business and managed it over time, through the vicissitudes of growth, transition and challenge. Two to three years in jobs whose parameters have been laid down by other people is not enough preparation for the maelstrom into which Akers was plunged.

As IBM's profit margins declined and its cash mountains dwindled to foothills, IBM faced tough problems familiar enough to the large rivals it had massacred in the past. But hard economic facts are only the skeleton of the crisis of a corporation. The flesh is human. Great organisations like IBM develop rich and deep cultures, lifestyles which are sanctified by success and consecrated by conceit.

The attack by Akers on his own company – the shot heard round the world – was aimed at these human targets: inevitably, it was aimed at himself. The smoke signals rose almost from the moment when this square-jawed IBMer took charge. Down below him, and in the market place, insiders and customers had been telling tales of woe for years before the Akers outburst. In July 1992, Akers appeared on the cover of an issue of *Fortune* magazine from which he could have learnt many of these home truths. For example, large corporate customers were 'fed up with the mediocrity of IBM's marketing', and thought its sales people had a poor 'knowledge base', and couldn't get the solutions they wanted. Worse, a software developer found that the company's approval process formed 'giant pools of peanut butter we have to swim through'. Since these biting criticisms were in the cover story, the cover star presumably read them.

The comfort was just as cold in *Business Week*. There, a top IBM saleswoman (quoted in an article alongside Akers himself) said that, because it's 'politically incorrect' to query development plans, what customers really wanted didn't penetrate – even if it did, slow reactions meant that 'by the time our product is out, my customers will already have a competitor's product in place'.

The tirade to his managers indicated that Akers was in a mood to accept the criticisms. But could he cure the diseases? Recent history at both IBM and GM (and many other large companies) says otherwise: the chief comes out with ringing declarations of intent; reorganisations and redundancies are eventually ordained; and inadequate outcomes appear – a couple of years too late.

The management cycle merely reflects (and explains) what happens in products. Spectacularly late into personal computers, IBM made a spectacular entry – only to be equally late into laptops. Its product arrived in spring 1991, when the market had already passed $5.5 billion in annual sales. Like many large companies, IBM has a matrix organisation. Having one boss can be bad enough. But if functional, national and product bosses all have fingers in your pie, it takes a long time to cook.

IBM was not among the giants (ten picked out of dozens) named by Harvard professor John P. Kotter for achieving effective long-term cultural change in the Eighties. General Electric, led by Jack Welch, was among the number. But GE, unlike IBM or GM, is a conglomerate without a core; Welch could (and did) move in and out of businesses at will. Akers could (and did, with typewriters) sell the odd peripheral activity, but the bulk of IBM's assets is inalienable. Inalienable, and not amenable to easy treatment, either. As Keith H. Hammonds remarked in *Business Week*, 'The restructuring, the cost-cutting, the new message can be effective for starters, but it takes follow-through to make sure they're more than skin-deep.' So what was the answer for IBM?

The magazine turned to six sources of wisdom and won some very strange replies. A former IBM non-executive director thought unhelpfully that, since the company had the 'horsepower' and 'the science', you only needed 'to get right in there and rattle the cage'. The boss of Nucor, a relatively small steelmaker much loved by devotees of open management, wanted Akers to 'nag' managers into cost-effectiveness by one-to-one or small meetings – great for lesser Nucor, but a non-starter for giant IBM.

Irving S. Shapiro thought that IBM should emulate Du Pont, the company he once chaired, which 'took a generation' after its nylon triumph to learn the competitive frame of mind. But IBM doesn't have a generation, or even a decade, to spare: not when its industry is in a state of chronic technological convulsion. Anyway, Du Pont isn't much of a role model. Once pre-eminent, the Wilmington company is now just one of the chemical boys, beset with giant problems of its own.

In March 1992, the *Wall Street Journal* summed up the worst of those problems as follows: 'Despite spending of more than \$13 billion . . . over the past 10 years, Du Pont's 5,000 scientists and technologists were a technological black hole. They sucked in money, but, company officials concede, didn't turn out a single all-new blockbuster product or even many major innovations.' To crack its problems, Du Pont needed 'to restructure a bloated bureaucracy'. The group's chief executive since 1989 seemed to echo Akers: 'Du Pont needs a top-to-bottom overhaul,' said Edgar S. Woolard Jr.

As noted in the introduction, IBM's malaise of the Nineties was not peculiar to itself, but symptomatic of an illness affecting many giant corporations in the US – and possibly in the

West as a whole. Certainly, they have defects in common. For example, one top PC manager said in 1990 that IBM would never worry him: he had spent an entire career in PCs, while his IBM counterparts were just passing through – *en route* to their next mission. That's the way leviathans love it. At Unilever, for instance, high fliers are put through several different functional, product and geographical posts, often rotating every two or three years. At least the Anglo-Dutch combine falls naturally into distinct, branded businesses: having cultures of their own, they are better equipped to withstand all the chopping and changing.

Once IBM briefly enjoyed such a business, when the PC people, tucked away in Boca Raton, Florida, and given their heads, exceeded their remit and presented their sponsor with a world-beating product in little more than a year. Eventually, the corporacy closed in, and the usual tale of delays and deadbeat moves began (witness the laptop). IBM never took the true lesson of Boca Raton to heart, even though the moral – independence breeding incandescent triumph – was trumpeted forth at the time by the group's publicity machine. Had the model been followed, Akers might never have needed to moan – and would still be CEO. The PC really did point the way to cure elephantiasis.

In theory, the remedy lies in internal break-up, break-out or buyout. You reduce headquarters to a supervisory and long-term strategic role, and you give full power to autonomous business teams which are free to create their own cultures and battle plans. Under this disposition, head office doesn't preside over multi-layered cakes. On the contrary, it might very well pressure the business bosses into laying off the layers themselves.

Very few of the men who climb the highest summits, though, have the courage or common sense to dismantle the apparatus which establishes their own importance (and self-importance). The 'everyone' who was 'too comfortable' at IBM must have included Akers and the other senior executives. Colossal scale creates cosy chairs in which over-cosseted captains try to manage the unmanageable by remote control. It can't work: which makes it far from surprising (to everybody but the captains) if their companies don't work, either.

2

Last Laugh to
the Trustbusters

IBM's history is strewn with litigation. Other great businesses
have fought lawsuits, some of them crucial – like the anti-trust
action that broke up AT&T and created all the Baby Bell telephone companies. But no business has pursued and been
pursued by so many lawsuits over so many fronts and years.
And none has had more stunning success.

IBM has actually beaten its legal opponents more emphatically than the competitors in its markets – although the two
were mostly one and the same. IBM's commercial practices
have been a barrier to competitors' progress, an obstacle at
least as important as the champion's technological prowess.
So, to attack those practices was a rival's natural response. The
record shows, in terms of commercial results, that what's natural can be sinful. Time and again, IBM came out of its legal
battles in triumph.

To senior IBMers, the explanation was simple. The corporation was not guilty, and never would be. A strict code of
conduct guaranteed that IBM would never break the law, or
even stretch it. Even the guilty verdict and prison sentence
passed on Thomas Watson Sr in 1912 for his illegal activities at
National Cash Register had receded into exculpation. His son
wrote that, 'Dad did not understand the illegality of what he

was getting into' – and, of course, 'the case was appealed and no one ever served time'.

In later years, IBM did lose the occasional case, but victory was again snatched from defeat. A celebrated instance is the suit brought by Telex, a maker of 'plug-compatible' tape and disk drives. These and other 'peripherals' depended on the capacity to plug the devices (cheaper than IBM's own products) into an IBM mainframe. Their success was among the factors leading IBM to launch the notorious Operation SMASH. This consisted of slashing its lease prices, coupled with threats not to renew licensing agreements.

To protect its interests, Telex launched its anti-trust suit in January 1972. Eighteen months later Judge Sherman Christensen gave an uncompromising verdict. SMASH was directed 'not at competition in an appropriate competitive sense, but at competitors and their viability as such'. Treble damages of $350 million were imposed on IBM. Against that, Telex had to pay only $22 million for breaches of IBM patents. Even more important were the restraints laid on IBM's future conduct.

From IBM's point of view, a still greater threat lay in the many other suits filed and foreshadowed: 'I think,' said one contender, 'almost any company in the computer industry has got to be thinking about bringing suit against IBM.' Winning the appeal was thus of overwhelming importance for Armonk. Even IBM's lawyers, though, must have been surprised by the victory that followed. It was of Desert Storm proportions. In 1975, Christensen's judgement was completely overturned. Worse still for Telex, its financial position had been shattered by SMASH, and now it was facing an $18.5 million adverse judgement from the Court of Appeal. Since it couldn't afford to seek justice from the Supreme Court, it had no option but to settle out of court. 'The case was appealed and nobody ever served time': the original Watson anti-trust result reverberated down the years.

Robert Sobel has an arresting image for IBM's minor anti-trust troubles: 'It was as though some huge whale were beset by schools of sharks.' These litigants, though, felt that IBM was the shark: a super-Jaws which threatened their very lives, and whose legal teeth proved to be painfully sharp. As IBM itself blandly reported: 'We have completed six trials, and we have won them all. Ten Federal judges have ruled completely in our favour.' The case was one 'that turns on the same issues that we have won time and again'.

But these cases, potentially lethal in themselves, were only the preliminaries to the main event; for while the Telex litigation was going through the courts, the Federal case, aiming at nothing less than a break-up of IBM (which would have made the Telex charges irrelevant) was at last getting under way. No better account of this action exists than that of its central figure: Thomas Watson Jr. With exemplary fairness, he explains in *Father, Son, and Co.* why the suit was brought – because IBM's sheer size, allied to its policy of 'total system sales', covering all aspects of computing, created an uncompetitive industry. Watson describes the case rightly as 'comparable to the one in 1911 when the US took apart Rockefeller's Standard Oil Trust'.

IBM's tactics had always been to head off the trustbusters, and to sign consent decrees 'that gave IBM plenty of room to grow'. The argument on which the Watsons rested their case was that 'the competition IBM faced was strong and increasing thanks to the constant evolution of technology, on which nobody had a monopoly'. That was truer, as subsequent events proved, than IBM knew. But the Justice Department's hand had been forced to some extent by Control Data (whose lawyers worked in close co-operation with Justice).

Watson rightly describes Control Data as the most important of the half-dozen litigants 'all claiming we'd tried to do them in'; and also as 'the worst thorn in my side' he had to endure 'in all my years of management'. It's a curious observation, given that CDC's founder, William Norris, and his genius designer, Seymour Cray, never mounted a serious challenge to

IBM's heartland – the large corporate customers – and only had $60 million of sales, a mere fraction of IBM's, at the time of the suit.

What rankled was Cray's skill at producing supercomputers, top-of-the-range machines that attacked IBM's birthplace: the big number-crunching uses in government and the universities. In fact, the brilliance of Norris and Cray was aided and abetted by IBM's ineptitude (including Watson's own), but that only made the sore place worse. In 1961, a huge machine named STRETCH came in late and 40 per cent under specification. The failure drove a 'disappointed and irate' Watson to savage publicly not only the price (he announced a cut from $13.5 million to $8 million), but the performance of the engineers.

His own 'grievous mistake' (Watson's words) understandably put the engineers off large computers for two years. In the interim, Cray perfected the 6600, launched in August 1963 at a million dollars below the cost of the cut-price and abandoned STRETCH, and with three times its power. Watson's temper moved on from irate to 'furious'. The famous 'janitor memo' resulted, getting its name from his acerbic comment that Control Data's laboratory employed only thirty-four people, 'including the janitor'.

Watson noted that Norris' contingent included fourteen engineers and four programmers, one of whom was the only PhD. 'Contrasting this modest effort with our own vast development activities, I fail to understand why we have lost our industry leadership position by letting someone else offer the world's most powerful computer.' It was a complaint that his successors could well have echoed. IBM never caught up in supercomputers, and was consistently and badly beaten at the other end of the scale when the personal computer age got under way. 'Industry leadership' meant customers, not technology, at IBM, and the reaction to the Cray design, which (says Watson) 'IBM was never able to beat' (why not?), was not to attack the unbeatable design but the customers.

As Watson carefully says, the 'moves IBM made in response to my anger were too close to the limits of the law'. In April 1964, the company announced plans for a new supercomputer that would easily surpass Control Data's 6600. The wonder existed only on paper, but the tactic was 'exactly the kind of thing I'd told our salesmen to be careful about because of IBM's great size'. It worked like a charm: the 6600 order book dried right up. Hence the anti-trust suit.

Eventually Watson swallowed his pride and decided that IBM should leave supercomputers to other, smaller firms. Such specialised machines, he now argued, would be incompatible misfits with the main product range. In truth, this reflected the decision to stay with a restrictive architecture, rather than any inherent problems to do with IBM's size. But in the meantime Watson's burst of temper had helped to create a fast-growing legal monster.

Ironically, the supercomputers that sparked the case intensified the pressure on IBM. Norris used his machines to crunch through 80,000 key documents – reduced from millions upon millions. Watson notes that this enabled Control Data to codify 'no fewer than thirty-seven different ways in which we had supposedly abused our market power'. He fairly observes that without its partner's efforts, the Justice Department, with only twenty-five people on the case, couldn't have made much, if any progress.

Control Data, however, was over-matched by IBM. To get the heaviest possible artillery, Watson went to the top – to Senator Robert Kennedy. According to Watson, the two men were at the Watson ski lodge in Stowe, Vermont, when Bobby said, 'You've done a lot for the Kennedys, Tom. Is there anything we can do for you?' Watson says his response was intuitive rather than planned. 'Bobby's team at the Justice Department was disbanding, and he had brilliant men.' The only two men who Kennedy would recommend, Nicholas Katzenbach (his successor as attorney general) and Burke Marshall (the civil rights head of Justice), both went on the

IBM payroll – Marshall at once, Katzenbach after a few years. Using their inside knowledge of Washington, they spearheaded an enormously expensive defence effort with great success. One of Marshall's most important contributions, however, lay in discovering that, for all IBM's protestations of innocence, on important issues its position was indefensible.

Watson's own remark about the trustbusters – 'We tried to mollify them by cleaning up our act voluntarily' – makes no sense unless something was unclean. Marshall saw that IBM must lose the case unless it abandoned its time-honoured practice of 'bundling': that is, you couldn't buy or lease just an IBM computer – you also had to pay, willy-nilly and expensively, for IBM software, engineering help, maintenance and training. What IBM saw (not so innocently) as helpful, others understandably viewed as a surefire method of barring competition – customers were hardly going to pay twice for the same thing. Six months after Justice filed its suit, and under heavy pressure from Marshall, the reluctant IBMers unbundled. Like the consent decree that settled an earlier anti-trust suit in 1956, the retreat permanently changed IBM's competitive environment.

The 1956 decree, which forced IBM to sell as well as rent, opened the door to companies that leased computers at prices lower than the manufacturer's. The decree also forced IBM to license its patents, thus strengthening the hands of competitors. Now, after unbundling, the latter were free to attack specific parts of the IBM bundle. Proliferation became endemic in the industry: no major, across-the-board competitor could emerge because of IBM's gigantic, highly protected customer base – instead the giant was steadily nibbled away by many mice.

In 1972, though, the only mouse that mattered was Control Data. The lawyers advised an out-of-court settlement. The vast expense shows how vital it was to get Norris out of the legal way. The $15 million cost of paying Norris' legal fees was negligible compared to the other payments – cash and IBM contracts in a package which totalled $101 million. In addition, Watson handed over IBM's service bureau business at a giveaway price. It made Control Data the largest supplier of computer services – which (another irony) formed its only viable business twenty years later, when the computer side, now ailing unto death, was hived off.

Even more crucial than removing Norris from the courts was obtaining his anti-IBM documentation, the 'index', which was 'the master link in all the other anti-trust suits against IBM', including the government's. It now fell into Watson's hands and he was promptly urged to destroy the lot. Legally, the index had not been put in evidence and belonged to IBM, which could do with the papers whatever it wished. Watson had them burnt at once, though 'it made me feel uneasy'.

Part of the unease was that the act *felt* illegal, even if it wasn't. Also, Watson had a more than sneaking sympathy with the merits of the Justice Department's complaint: 'IBM was clearly in a commanding position in the market, and some of our tactics had been harsh.' He blames an over-zealous judge, David Edelstein, for the delays in the twelve long years of legal process. IBM, he says, would otherwise have settled much earlier for a consent decree.

The terms he mentions, though, are as mild as skimmed milk: holding back from 'announcing our machines until we were a little further along with their development', loosening 'our grip on the educational market', and so on. The account glosses over two things: first, the ferocity with which IBM fought the case, including a highly unusual attempt to have Edelstein removed; and, second, how far IBM would go to avert the fate of being broken up like Standard Oil.

'At the beginning I was willing to split IBM in two' – large machines and the rest. His sticking point was the trustbusters' wish to bust IBM into seven separate billion-dollar segments. Ranged against 'the most powerful corporation in the world', which 'fought tooth and nail for the continuation of that power' as it 'spent lavishly on its defence', the government trial team, wrote Richard Thomas DeLamarter, was 'never able to match' that spending. The trustbusters felt themselves to be leading an underarmed crusade.

DeLamarter was one of the crusaders. His book *Big Blue*, published in 1986, is a unique study from the inside of an anti-trust case brought against a major corporation. To quote his subtitle, the crusade was against 'The use and abuse of power'. A senior economist in the Justice Department team, DeLamarter believed that 'IBM was, and still is, the most powerful corporation in the world', and that, to sustain that power, IBM knowingly abused it. In his view, indeed, 'it was not IBM's excellent management or its superior products that made it successful: rather it was the clever ways in which the company has exploited an exclusive position of power'. That had enabled IBM to ensure that 'all its competitors, large and small' existed 'entirely at its sufferance' in what was 'arguably the most important industry in the world'.

This preternatural and threatening dominance was achieved despite the fact that, 'Like its competitors, IBM is at times poorly managed, its products inferior, its customers unhappy, and its actions ruthless, if not illegal.' How, then, was the monopoly maintained? By abuse of monopolistic power. IBM played a 'cat-and-mouse' game with the anti-trust laws, 'coming as close as possible to illegality without risking its commercial advantages'.

Changing metaphors in midstream, DeLamarter talked about Big Blue's 'carefully choreographed dance' around the edges of the law. The crusaders thus faced a certain difficulty: if the dance never crossed that boundary, how could IBM be found guilty? That didn't stop them from feeling, and expressing, fierce indignation when, on 8 January 1982, their thirteen years of hard work went for nothing; 'the Reagan Administration's assistant attorney general in charge of the Anti-trust Division, William Baxter, walked away from the case.' What really stung was his view that 'our work was without merit'. As the book, based on the court proceedings and IBM's own documents, makes abundantly clear, the work was certainly meritorious. No other corporation has ever had its inner workings and commercial secrets exposed so relentlessly – and the trustbuster's marshalling of the evidence is seldom complimentary to IBM. But writing a powerful critique is different from proving a case in law.

If IBM's legal choreographers had done their highly paid work efficiently – and this efficiency is one aspect of the corporation's success that nobody has ever challenged – the case might well have failed in court, like all its forerunners. IBM was far more strongly armed than the crusaders: its huge team was led by a vice president and general counsel, Katzenbach, who had been deputy attorney general when the enquiry into IBM began. As for Baxter, his President had no love for crusades against big business – and Baxter had none for this case.

Long before, he had written to another incoming Administration that 'the IBM case should never have been brought'. In any event, DeLamarter, in an eloquent and worrying passage, admits that the US antitrust laws under which his colleagues laboured are an unsure defence against monopoly of the kind exercised at the time by IBM – a monopoly that rested, not on the traditional overweening size of market share, but commercial and technological practices. What DeLamarter – and for that matter Watson – failed to spot was that those very practices were undermining the quasi-monopoly (that being a more accurate description of the reality of the mid-Eighties). The author began his analysis with 'a few facts about IBM' that make strange reading today:

1   IBM was 'the most profitable company in the world'.

2   'IBM continues to dominate the computer business and is well on its way to dominating everything that is connected to and/or operates with these computers.'

3   'IBM faces no significant domestic or foreign competition that could threaten this dominance.'

4 'The anti-trust laws, designed to police such unequal competition, are of little use.'

Half a dozen years later, only the last of these points is still valid, but wholly irrelevant – given that IBM's profits, after degenerating into multi-billion losses, show no sign of ever regaining, or even approaching, the 13 per cent margins of 1985; given that its market shares in most major product lines, and its overall share of the computing market, have fallen dramatically; given that competition, both foreign and domestic, has burgeoned at every point.

The ultimate defence of Watson and other IBM potentates to anti-trust charges was always that they faced formidable and growing competition. Once highly debatable, that argument became more agonisingly true than the defenders ever feared. IBM exercised its commercial and technological powers to sustain the quasi-monopoly and its profits, and in so doing fatally weakened its ability to cope with a vortex of change among competitors and customers alike.

The final irony is that, had DeLamarter and his fellow crusaders had their way, a broken-up IBM's constituents, left to fight their own ways through the vortex, might well have competed far more effectively. By the end of 1991, indeed, IBM was moving towards internal break-up, under the latest reorganisation promoted by John F. Akers. Whatever his successors decide, in 1993 the wise money was betting that the thwarted trustbusters would enjoy the last laugh, that break-up of some kind would inevitably result.

Lord Acton wrote that, 'All power corrupts, and absolute power corrupts absolutely.' IBM, 'the most powerful company in the world', never had absolute power. It had more than enough power to corrupt its own competitive ability.

3

Recovery Is Just
Around the Corner . . .

Time and again, as John Akers struggled with the mounting
problems of his troubled giant, the word was reassuring. The
problems weren't mounting, but receding as the latest top
management strategy began a handsome pay-off. But time and
again the hopes proved forlorn. Usually there was good reason
or excuse – notably the recession that made the whole computer industry a pained example of economic decline in the
early Nineties.

More than recession explained the losses. At both Compaq
and IBM, precipitate falls in prices hit companies suffering
from runaway costs. Yet IBM, a byword for pernickety controls
over spending, had been attacking costs ever since John Opel
became chief executive in 1981. His successor, Akers, had been
slashing away far more severely since pressure on profits intensified in the mid-Eighties. What explains the sluggish response
to so much energy?

In part, IBM offset staff savings and other economies by
heavy 'strategic' spending on development projects and investments, much of it misplaced. Moreover, when unit prices are
falling, the overhead ratio becomes a moving target. The cure
can also precipitate a new disease. Thus, Lee Iacocca condemned Chrysler to a grave new model shortage by sacking

thousands of engineers to cut payroll costs. In this case, the need for sheer survival made retrenchment inevitable, however awful the consequences – or, to use a medical metaphor, the secondaries.

While Akers told his senior management that the business was in crisis, the urgency was less acute than Chrysler's. Yet the cutbacks had a real impact on capability – as one account executive complained to Akers. His headcount had dropped from twenty-two to sixteen, and the executive connected the cuts with a fall in revenue from $35 million to $25 million. That prompted an outburst from the boss: 'For Christ's sake, you don't need sixteen people to drive $25 million!' You don't if the process driven by the people has been improved, both to accommodate a 27 per cent reduction in numbers and to avoid counter-productive 'secondaries'. Otherwise, you do. The instance exemplifies the common management fault that MIT's Peter M. Senge calls 'shifting the burden'. That means treating symptoms rather than the disease, and thus worsening the latter. It's one of eleven 'laws' of *The Fifth Discipline* (the title of his excellent book). The fifth discipline is that of thinking about the whole, interrelated system, not just the problem that immediately confronts you.

The full list of laws is as follows:

1   *Today's problems come from yesterday's solutions:* witness Chrysler's shortage of new models.

2   *The harder you push, the harder the system pushes back:* witness the IBM account executive cutting back on numbers to cut costs and then losing revenue.

3   *Behaviour grows better before it gets worse:* misguided policies (as above) will show good initial results.

4   *The easy way out usually leads back in:* if the first round of job cuts doesn't work try another (see IBM *passim*).

5 *The cure can be worse than the disease:* which was worse, drinking alcohol or the organised crime created by Prohibition?

6 *Faster is slower:* why do so many high-growth start-ups run into high-octane trouble?

7 *Cause and effect are not closely related in time and space:* manufacturing problems may not arise in the plant at all – but in design, marketing or somewhere else.

8 *Small changes can produce big results – but the areas of highest leverage are often the least obvious:* e.g. changes in reporting systems can radically improve management performance.

9 *You can have your cake and it – but not at once:* as the Japanese have shown, low cost and high quality aren't incompatible, but actually go hand-in-hand – eventually.

10 *Dividing an elephant in half does not produce two elephants:* artificial boundaries between functions and departments cause all parties to underperform.

11 *There is no blame:* as noted at the start, the recession which 'caused' IBM's problems wasn't something independent of Akers and his organisation – everybody's in the same boat.

Senge certainly helps to explain the IBM saga. All eleven laws were amply demonstrated after Akers took command. Story after story told of his sweeping, radical changes. In November 1988, the *Wall Street Journal* headline read 'Campaign To Cut Bureaucracy, End Insularity Starts To Pay Off'; this was 'history's second great experiment in *perestroika* and *glasnost* . . . showing results that the other *perestroika*'s architects would envy. IBM's earnings will be up about 14 per cent this year and probably at least that much in 1989.'

A year later, in November 1989, the *Journal* told a much different tale. Falling prices had forced Akers to incur $2.3 billion in 'restructuring' expenses to save $1 billion in annual costs. Another 10,000 people were to go . . . and that 14 per cent earnings growth dissolved into a 40 per cent slump. But there's a curious correlation. When employment peaked at 405,000 in 1984–85, so did earnings. As jobs fell by 12 per cent to 1991, the earnings trend also declined, culminating in the $2.8 billion loss in that year. At the same time, IBM's share of the market (defined by the Gartner Group as all computer hardware, software and services) fell from 40 per cent in 1984 to 23 per cent. And still observers were caught by surprise. The *Journal*, in March 1991, reported that the company 'dropped an earnings bomb', thanks (or no thanks) to problems affecting most product lines and most of the world, 'which arose so quickly they stunned analysts' – and Akers.

A couple of months later, in the famous leaked diatribe already reported, he was berating managers for losing market share and for a host of hair-raising (or hair-tearing) defects. The symptoms hadn't responded to treatment, which must mean that the disease, too, hadn't improved. The patient may well have deteriorated. This wouldn't surprise Senge, who provides acute analysis of why managements get into trouble – and how to avoid it.

Every company, he points out, works in a 'limits to growth' structure. When growth halts, or goes into reverse, the limits have been reached. So far, so very obvious. What's less clear, and demands extra-careful analysis, is why? Where and what are the true limits? If the company has stimulated lagging demand by progressive price cuts and discounts, for example, management will tend to stimulate sales by more of the same – again, an expedient to which IBM kept on returning, like some hooked junkie.

This may have a short-run effect. But what if the explanation is different? What if the company's service and product range are at fault? Then, the costly price cuts won't affect the underlying, adverse situation. Similarly, if excessive costs arise from sloppy processes, cutting jobs cuts the wage bill, but overall costs stay stubbornly and disappointingly high. Worse still, the sloppiness may increase, because excessive numbers are often needed to make inefficient processes work (witness the complaining account executive mentioned earlier).

Mass cutbacks in staff, moreover, are seldom selective, save in an unintended and unwelcome way. The best employees, who will most easily find new and better jobs, are the quickest to seize their money and run. Encouraged by over-generous provisions for early retirement, that certainly happened at IBM. Departure of the brightest and best will intensify any service and sales problems, especially since morale is inevitably damaged by large-scale redundancies.

That applies doubled and redoubled in a company that, like IBM, has long prided itself on guaranteeing jobs for life. The lifetime guarantee did great financial damage, since the promise delayed and strung out the necessary cutbacks. It was also symbolic of a larger and graver hang-up. The guarantee belonged to a past that had fled. By clinging to the past, IBM was crucifying itself in the present.

Its history of amazing success rested on two prime strategies. Its favourite was sewing up a market through closing off alternatives. Buyers of the old punch card machines also had to buy the immensely profitable IBM cards. In the computer age IBM went to great lengths to ensure that buyers had only two choices – IBM or IBM. Where this was impossible (and rapid evolution of technology made IBM's task increasingly difficult), the second strategy was applied: cutting prices.

That strategy was undertaken in full confidence that greater scale and efficiency would win. That theory, too, has been undermined, partly by the technology, again, and partly by the fact that IBM's self-image of quality, efficiency, technological leadership and customer-orientation was self-delusion.

31

The delusions surfaced in an aim of 'growing with the industry' that was plainly impossible – IBM was coming up against its 'limits to growth'.

If the 40 per cent market share of 1984 had been maintained the company would have reached *over double* its actual 1991 sales. The additional sales then required to reach its original target ($180 billion by the mid-Nineties) were equivalent to eight Hewlett-Packards or Digital Equipments – a blatant absurdity. The strategy of 'growing with the industry' was bound to fail, and should never have been attempted.

Loss of market share is hard for any management to tolerate. But unless causes are properly understood, intelligent responses cannot be achieved. Rather than seek out and adopt new strategies, IBM's managers persisted with the mixture as before – the very medicine that had conspicuously failed. Rather than mocking their stupidity, it's important to note that this reversion to type is common among companies (and individuals – look at all the fat ex-dieters and recidivist smokers).

Senge blames the 'mental models' held within all firms. The surefire way to destroy your career is to offend against some traditional precept of corporate life. Instead, you will continue to respond to the stimulus of that precept long after it has become a pernicious threat to stability and survival. In 1991, for instance, the chief executive of one of Europe's largest supermarket groups called on IBM to discuss an order for over 1,000 personal computers, modified to meet his chain's particular needs. The IBM executive concerned was delighted – until his visitor explained that he just wanted a cup of coffee: the order had already gone to Nixdorf. When the chain had first aired its needs, it only wanted a few hundred machines – and IBM had refused to make the modifications for so small an order. The 'mental model' is that, below a certain economic scale, IBM wouldn't meet customer requirements that were regarded as inconvenient. For the individual executive, turning away business is safer than accepting deals that will earn criticism as well as revenue.

What Senge calls the 'inertia of deeply entrenched mental models' applies widely at IBM. Sadly, it could have followed the quite different model of its own, already described. Bureaucracy and insularity had been triumphantly defeated ten years before the crisis of 1991. The small group at Boca Raton launched the personal computer after a crash programme whose speed still seems unbelievable: one year and a month. That was only achieved by giving the group total autonomy, which included total freedom to buy in outside designs and components. Those risks, however, were only taken because lifetime sales were put at a piddling 250,000. Soon the quarter-of-a-million lifetime target was being chalked up *every month.* In IBM's mental model, the division then becomes too important to keep the freedoms which had brought about that importance. They were removed, and the subsequent PC errors are as legendary as the initial success.

A decade later, Akers was attempting to recreate the Boca Raton experiment in the corporation as a whole, dividing it into self-contained businesses subject to less central control. But without changing those mental models, nothing can be achieved by such reforms. For example, IBM is not tolerant of mistakes. In any of the innumerable meetings, managers fearful of error, or genuinely disagreeing, can 'non-concur', to use the corporate lingo. The decision then rises to the next appropriate level – which could mean the CEO himself adjudicating on some trivial issue.

That kind of problem can't be solved by specific action – only general reform will remove the difficulty. What about the set of problems listed below? Would you describe them as symptoms or systemic?

1 'Filtering' of instructions and intentions from on high, so that they never penetrate to lower levels of management, or do so in diluted form.

2 Plenty of good excuses for bad results (Field Marshal

Montgomery memorably defined this process as 'belly-aching or 'inventing poor reasons for not doing what one has been told to do.').

3 An internal perception of quality as excellent which is not echoed by the customers.

4 Too many meetings at all levels of management.

5 Too little urgency and too much 'waiting to be told what to do'.

6 Low priority to issues of operational performance.

7 Lack of focus on each distinct business.

8 Toleration of low performance and low performers.

9 Excessive numbers of people in key areas.

These failings, to which all organisations are prone, were singled out by Akers in his diatribe. None of the areas described is a self-contained system: all are symptoms of the breakdown of a wider system whose defects have been exposed by the limits to growth. IBM's dramatic loss of market share, in Senge's language, is a 'balancing process', bringing the company's sales into line with its true ability to serve the market.

The old system, in which growth seemed limitless, was quasi-monopolistic. For that happy condition, a centralised bureaucracy with endless internal checks and balances was appropriate. At its peak of success, the system matched the market, for that consisted mainly of larger organisations and hinged on a single product. The 360 family of mainframe processors covered virtually all data processing needs.

In a market of multitudinous suppliers, multiplying needs, innumerable segments, different leaders in nearly every segment and customers of all shapes and sizes, a totally different system is mandated. The route to that system doesn't lie through reshuffling the organisation (though that may be a necessary adjunct). The true road runs back from the customers to rethinking the way the company operates within the industry structure – whatever form that takes.

The 'just-around-the-corner syndrome', in which promised renaissance is always postponed, is a sure sign that Senge's laws are at work. IBM was striving to bring down its expense ratios. But it wasted billions to give the public what it didn't want – a proprietary alternative to Microsoft's Windows that would bind customers to IBM. The company was seemingly driven not only by its obsolete lust for tied markets, but by jealousy of Microsoft, whose very different management culture was much better matched to the new marketplace.

Changes in culture are inseparable from changes in the way people work. All the Akers reinventions centred less on changing behaviour than on demanding changed results. To quote the *New York Times*, the 'new IBM' was trying to push 'the lessons of entrepreneurial capitalism down to the level not just of managers . . . but also to sales people, researchers and factory workers.'

What were the lessons? 'Everyone is a two-legged profit centre, selling to each other and to outsiders. That mentality is nurtured by constantly measuring performance and customer satisfaction, and rewarding the teams of workers and individuals who do the best.' In Akers' own words, 'We are clearly putting competition into the IBM system.' The only problem is that collaboration, rather than competition, is the effective method of changing culture.

Take the *Times* example of the new IBM in action. Breakdown of the IBM system at a WalMart hypermarket in Dallas threatened to be the last straw that broke the company's lucrative business with the country's biggest retailer. The local account executive, William Almon Jr, took a number of obvious steps (like assigning service people to a group of stores, round-the-clock), and 'in a real break with the IBM of old, the thirty-six-year-old Mr Almon and his staff devised and executed the plan on their own, without endless rounds of reviews, committee meetings and hand-wringing at corporate headquarters in Armonk, NY.'

So far so good. But this and other examples don't add up to a cultural revolution, or anything like it: a regional manager in Southern California allowed more freedom to set prices and cut costs; a software developer in North Carolina throwing away the 'Red Book' that used to govern and hamstring her group's work; a business development director in Austin, Texas, hustling IBM technology to win more workstation business; a senior assembly specialist, also in North Carolina, leading a 'learning center' – a small worker team whose role is to get its members to 'buy into' the new IBM. These examples were no great leap forward for IBM's mankind, only the first steps along a path that management teachers have marked out for more than a decade. IBM's lag in innovation has been more serious in management than in products.

In its crisis, the company didn't turn to its people for help, but in certain respects turned against them. The rapid succession of organisational upheavals, job cuts and transfers had destabilised the system. Nothing had been put in its place. Internal revolt, in the shape of declining morale and productivity, helps to explain the disappointing results of the reorganisations. IBM is not alone. Senge's laws are universal, and other big companies have suffered likewise. Massive reductions in operations and employment have allegedly been followed up by programmes of empowerment and participation. But appearance and reality aren't necessarily the same in management.

Retrenchment, reorganisation and re-equipment were the 'Three Rs' of IBM's recovery effort. Hardly any of the assaults on the IBM system had sought to discover what its people – all its people – could do if set free to exercise their own initiative and intelligence in an atmosphere of collaboration freed from fear. On the contrary, fear and anxiety were among the weapons with which Armonk hoped to wrest better performance from hundreds of thousands of people from Austin to Tokyo, Greenock to Boca Raton.

'We're always running scared here,' said the manager making personal computers at the North Carolina plant, where 'learning centers' were trying to indoctrinate workers in the spirit of the new IBM. The fear was that of being asked to leave in the continuing shake-out of numbers. The product development director at Austin, Lucian Bifano, sounded a similar note. Under pressure to build his business, and quickly, he told a visitor, 'If this doesn't succeed, you won't be talking to me a year from now.'

The whip and the carrot alike are old-fashioned management tools. They are as obsolete as the 360 family of mainframe computers with which IBM consolidated its fortune, management style and corporate cultures. In January 1972, the hero of the 360 saga, T. Vincent Learson, then in his brief rule as chairman and CEO, said this: 'I'm seriously disturbed by the signs of bureaucracy, especially in times like these. Here's an assurance I want to give you: in this new year, I'm going to do all I can to fight this problem . . .'

Twenty years on, John F. Akers was saying much the same thing. So had the two intervening chairmen. However hard these four men pushed against the system, the harder the system pushed back. The corporation required a new system, founded not on its products, but on its people. That required managers at all levels who were capable of brand-new thinking and brand-new action. That almost certainly meant brand-new managers at the top: hence the belated arrival of Lou Gerstner and his team to replace the Akers regime.

John Kotter of Harvard Business School writes perceptively about cultural transformation and large companies. In *Fortune*'s words, he 'concluded that corporate insiders like Akers can seldom transform an organisation beset by inertia'. To Akers' credit, he invited Kotter to discuss his research with top IBM executives at the annual corporate strategy session. Kotter 'confronted them with some really tough stuff', but Akers 'came up to me afterward and said, "You've done exactly what I wanted today".'

Those who (like me) have engaged in similar exercises will recognise the remark. It's what they nearly always say. The overriding, burning, all-encompassing issue is not what they say, but what they, and all those cascading down the system, will do to change the system by deeds, not words – no matter what the cost to themselves, their privileges and their authority. There's the rub, and there lie the roots of failure.

II

IN SEARCH OF
IBM'S 'EXCELLENCE'

4

Armonk Takes Off
the Gloves

Many visible signs of common culture imposed by Thomas
Watson Sr, including the once ubiquitous objects bearing the
founder's watchword, 'Think', were much less conspicuous by
the Eighties. But the typical IBMer still bore the founder's
stamp, and that included John Opel, one of the most successful executives in all IBM's years – to judge by the published
record.

That record covers the pivotal era. When Opel took over
from Frank Cary, IBM was on the threshold of a new age. To
his great and lasting credit, Cary spotted some of the crucial
changes that were sweeping over management – above all, the
new emphasis on quality. But Opel didn't truly understand
quality. He didn't connect quality of product and service with
quality of management. Nor did he appear to sense the external and internal conflicts that, over his half-decade in power,
began to tear IBM's sinews apart.

Opel was a self-confessed Corporation Man, white-shirted,
dark-suited and stripe-tied in true Watsonian style. This CEO
shunned, rather than sought, publicity for himself. In the tradition of IBM's top men, Opel was no technologist. A business
graduate, he started work by selling for IBM in his own home
town, Jefferson City, Iowa. He passed through eighteen more

jobs on his journey to the top. Only one involved manufacturing.

Nothing on the record indicated or apparently prepared the way for his succession to a *de facto* position of American technological leadership. Rather, his crucial spell was spent in the private office of Tom Watson Jr. That was another IBM tradition. John Akers spent time at the right hand of Frank Cary, shortly before the latter rose to president; that spell pointed the young man in the right and upward direction.

Opel had, however, developed apparently unconventional ideas of his own. Rising up the hierarchy towards the centre of power, he turned against centralisation. As a riding-high CEO, Opel said that, 'You have to have people free to act, or they become dependent. They don't have to be told, they have to be allowed.' Did this imply a new spirit of democracy and *laissez-faire*? Any such idea should have been dispelled by another dictum: 'No matter what I had in my jurisdiction, I typically felt I was more competent to deal with it than anybody else. And that wasn't conceit, it was just simple laws of nature.'

The competent and confident Opel became CEO on the first day of 1981. He heralded his arrival with a letter to employees in the January/February issue of *Think*, the IBM house magazine. His message was shot through with hyperbole: 'In IBM we are always geared up to do better, no matter how well we have done in the past . . . IBM people have always responded magnificently to challenge . . . You are a group of men and women with no parallel in or out of the business world.'

Exaggeration is inevitable in clarion calls. Even so, the high-flown language indicates the high conceit and arrogance which the successes of the Seventies had reinforced. Opel was absolutely right, though, in telling his troops that they faced 'a market that is without apparent limits, one that is driven by technologies that show no end of promise'. His formula for exploiting the 'great opportunities that we see before us' was also coherent and seemed to fit the unfolding decade.

In its final 1983 version, Opel's manifesto set out four goals:

1   To grow with the industry.

2   To exhibit product leadership across the entire product line – to excel in technology, value and quality.

3   To be the most efficient in everything we do, to be the low-cost producer, the low-cost seller, the low-cost administrator.

4   To sustain our profitability, which funds our growth.

The bizarre truth is that throughout Opel's apparently successful reign IBM was heading for abject failure on nearly all these crucial counts. It was to lose market share, however measured, on an unprecedented scale; to be beaten time and again on technology and value; to be unveiled as the highest-cost producer, seller and above all administrator; and in consequence to see its vaunted profitability drain away into heavy loss.

Lack of vigour wasn't to blame. Opel immediately launched a worldwide quality improvement programme. It was 'absolutely essential that we build satisfaction into the product before it leaves the plant'. On technological leadership, he warned that, 'It's not enough to be the first with the newest: what counts is to be the first with the newest and the best.' That meant first in price/performance, technology and function and 'first with the best in quality of product'.

'Quality' began to usurp the old position of 'Think'. Posters and slogans popped up all over IBM's world. 'Do it right', 'Quality is free', 'Quality comes first', they crowed. The so-called 'Excellence Program' soon began to generate a rich crop of success stories. At East Fishkill, for example, the error rate of semiconductor masks had been cut from 7 per cent to 1 per cent; at Lexington, one department had reduced scrap more than tenfold and raised productivity by 24 per cent.

A Quality Institute was opened in the autumn of 1982 to train senior managers in quality concepts and practices. The 'clear-cut' aim was to tie 'the quality principle, in both theory and practice, into everything we do'. Across the corporation over 2,000 flowers bloomed – quality circles and improvement teams. The remit was uncompromising: to ensure that every new product bettered its predecessor and the competition; and to use design to ensure that products could be manufactured and serviced to the same high quality standards.

In contrast to quality pioneers like Motorola, however, IBM had not grasped a central point. Quality is above all a new way of managing. Its results are won by improving processes of all kinds – and doing so incessantly. The effort must be led from the top, by example and effort, rather than exhortation. Its success will be measured, not only in fewer defects per unit manufactured, but in savings of time and cost as operations speed up. IBM's quality drive was an add-on, not a fundamental, long-range rethinking of its business methods.

The distinction was highlighted by a visit paid to IBM Europe in autumn 1983 by Joseph M. Juran. He is one of the two doughty veterans of quality preaching and practice (the other being W. Edwards Deming) whose American ideas have revolutionised Japanese – and thence Western – practice. Juran listened politely to his IBM hosts as they proudly explained what their company was doing. Nobody suggested that (as Ford Motor did later, to famous effect) IBM should use Juran's services. As he was being driven back to the Hotel Concorde in Paris, the great man delivered his verdict: 'IBM understands nothing about quality.'

As early as the start of 1983, however, Opel was stirred to new hyperbole. The emphasis on quality had convinced him that 'we are capable of achieving higher levels of performance than we ever thought possible'. Savings were already estimated in 'the hundreds of millions'. More: IBM had 'learned that error-free performance is not some impossible dream. It's attainable; it's achievable; it's something we can and should expect . . .'

These stirring sentiments had been encouraged by events. One record year succeeded another. The 20.4 per cent growth in earnings per share in 1982 encouraged Opel to say, 'That speaks for itself.' What did it say? To Opel the word was that mainframe dominance had been fully sustained; that 'despite some earlier difficulties' with the 3380 disk file, the same was true in direct access storage; that the gross profit and expense/revenue ratios had 'done very well', with profitability growing faster than revenue. And the personal computer had been launched. For the first time since the 360 mainframe range, IBM had shaken the industry with a wholly new product that was already changing both computing and the company. And there was another landmark event that Opel wanted to celebrate – the withdrawal of the anti-trust case on 8 January 1982, a year and a week after Opel had taken office. As Opel assured his people, IBM had prevailed 'first and mostly, because we were blameless'.

The Government had been unable to show any violation of IBM's 'first principle', which was never to tolerate 'unfair or unlawful conduct anywhere in this business'. That being said, IBM would 'continue to compete aggressively, as we always have'. The second part of his message was received more clearly than the first. Freed from the anti-trust shackles, IBM went for every jugular in sight. As noted earlier Tom Watson Jr was moved to admit, in the wake of the legal victory, that IBM's 'tactics had been harsh'. They became no softer.

The aura of success was intensified by assiduous public relations and spiky reactions to outside criticism. In the autumn of 1984, Opel expressed some ire at one news magazine's statement that 'IBM is not renowned for technological innovation'. Another journal quoted a competitor who said that 'nobody has accused IBM of being innovative'. To Opel the idea that 'because IBM is a big corporation, we are slow and not innovative' was an 'irksome, purely fictional myth'.

Unfortunately, the myth was founded in some awkward realities. IBM *was* sluggish, unresponsive and bureaucratic. Opel knew that his ideal of a corporation based on openness and 'personal two-way communication' diverged from day-to-day experience. 'Sometimes, given the specialisation we now have in so many functions and divisions, it's not easy to know how to get information to the right place or to get the right answer . . . Despite all the checks and balances we have built into IBM, we are occasionally caught by surprises that might have been avoided if only a single voice had been raised.'

The checks and balances were part of the disease, rather than its cure. They exerted a far more powerful influence on people and events than the many communication channels, including those designed for 'single voices'. 'Speak Up' guaranteed any IBMer a reply to any point raised. 'Open Door' allowed an IBMer's concerns to work right up the corporation, all the way to Opel. But the layers of bureaucracy prevented a 'single voice' from being listened to, as opposed to merely heard – unless the single voice was at the top.

Legend has it that only Cary's anguish at finding IBMers using Apples ('they're stealing the hearts and minds of my executives!') had given life to the idea of launching a personal computer. That was years after the market opportunity had appeared. Opel, whose protection was vital in turning the PC plan into brilliant reality, could diagnose the illness as well as spot the symptoms. IBM needed to 'stem the tide of bureaucracy'. In 1982 he noted that an employee needed thirty-one approvals before he could buy a much-needed piece of equipment; that another had to order 100 typewriter ribbons, wanting only one, because his stockroom didn't carry the item; that these weren't isolated examples. Opel believed that, following the reorganisation instituted on his promotion, 'much of the bureaucracy that had accumulated in the company was swept away and we were off for a fresh start'.

His antidote was to lay down as few rules as possible, delegate more authority to people, and hold them 'accountable for their own judgements, rather than straining to relieve them of the need for ever having to make a decision'. If all this failed, 'question the practice' and take the question up the line: in other words, through the very bureaucracy that had caused the problem in the first place.

For all the encouragement of 'bottom-up' communication, IBM was a top-down company by nature – what else could be expected from the Watsonian tradition? As the British writer Rex Malik observed in 1975, at IBM 'power is as widely distributed as is power in the Kremlin'. As in the old Russian model, rules existed for everything. In human relations, for example, the rules ranged from setting pay to 'the contract' – the guarantee of lifetime appointment. This produced some weird contortions. To fill three personnel jobs in the mid-Eighties, the British company had to move thirteen to fifteen people. Internal jokes underlined the bureaucratic snake in IBM's vaunted Eden – a snake which Opel had spotted, not scotched. As the next decade began, for instance, simple journalistic requests that one PR person could have handled in most large companies passed through at least three pairs of hands.

One senior European IBMer liked to tell audiences of how seriously IBM took Opel's boast that 'we are always geared up to do better', meaning better not only than its own past standards, but better than anybody else at anything. So a rowing man promptly bet that IBM (UK) couldn't beat Oxford University at rowing. The company accepted the challenge, trained a crew with its customary thoroughness, and was thoroughly beaten. Realistically, IBM accepted that you couldn't command success on a first outing. So it challenged the weaker Cambridge crew and got beaten again, almost as badly. IBM Europe ordered a thorough multi-disciplinary analysis of the loss. The team attributed the defeat to a single fact: while the two universities used one man to steer and eight to row, IBM had one man rowing and eight men steering.

The report was sent to Armonk, which studied the findings

and gave its orders: change the rower. The fable reflects deep problems inside the corporation. They surfaced, not only in stories of petty bureaucracy, but in the debates about IBM's technical direction. To hear Opel, addressing his employees in 1983, the crew was being steered brilliantly and rowing hard: 'Our labs are going full speed ahead on every front important to our future.' He claimed (untruthfully, given IBM's late entry into digital computing) that 'From the very start of this industry IBM has been in front, breaking new ground with significant technological developments . . .' He selected a list of impressive achievements to back his claim: 'We were first with the vacuum tape drive, first with a large family of compatible computers, first with monolithic main memory, first with mass production of 64k-bit memory chips.'

The debatable validity of IBM's technological claims is examined in more detail later. In this context, however, two points leap out. First, IBM had most certainly not led in the technology of the personal computer – every single major development had come from other hands, or brains. Second, the words indicate a mounting hubris that Opel himself had begun to query – at least in public – on the unarguable grounds that, 'success often leads to complacency. And complacency can lead to trouble'.

This 1984 warning noted that many of IBM's 'past critics became our biggest boosters . . . Yesterday they said we were phlegmatic and bureaucratic. We were not. Today they say we are perfect and omnipotent. We are not.' Opel warned solemnly of the danger of letting 'all this applause we've been getting turn our heads, make us arrogant or overbearing'. This ignored one relevant fact. The applause hadn't sprung unbidden from the audience.

On the contrary, IBM had spent much effort and cash to convey the image of a company that was nearing omnipotent perfection. Freed from legal threat, Armonk had taken off the gloves. The energies released by the anti-trust settlement were rushing through the corporation in an unstoppable flood. To deliver this message, the powerful PR machine at Armonk had been reinforced by executives seconded from other activities (secondments for special purposes are a feature of the IBM system). The newspapers and magazines, responding to this stimulus, had unwittingly become IBM's claque. They were applauding its achievements to signals sent from the company itself.

How could Opel expect his people to shun arrogance? He was simultaneously assuring them that IBM led the world in technology, that 'as good as we were', IBM could get better still – and was doing so. Wasn't he applying to the corporation the same judgement that he had formed of his own superior abilities? And that, remember, 'wasn't conceit, it was just simple laws of nature'.

The laws of nature seemed to have worked triumphantly in the micro-computer market. There IBM had taken on, not the mainframe rivals known as the Seven Dwarfs – mostly large corporations of lumbering tendencies – but light-footed newcomers. There IBM had attacked, not the large corporate market which was its home, but the widest field of business usage. There it had recovered from a late start to reach market dominance even faster than at the dawn of the computer era.

Opel could certainly take much credit for the PC – the wonder product had come to market in his tenure and under his personal aegis. There, IBM had seemed to demonstrate that when its people were 'free to act' and didn't 'have to be told', but rather 'allowed', they could achieve mighty deeds. The results were overwhelming. In a four-year spell sales soared from $26 billion to $45.9 billion. Net income of $6.6 billion, the highest in America and thus the world, represented a 14.3 per cent return on sales and 24.9 per cent on stockholders' equity – phenomenal figures for a company of any size.

In 1984, numbers of PCs sold actually trebled – an amazing performance. Yet the achievements of those twelve months, Opel's last year as CEO (he stayed on as chairman), marked the high tide in IBM's affairs. It would never be glad, confident morning again. The hubris which Opel feared, but which he had encouraged by word and deed, vitiated IBM's efforts to cope with its greatest crisis. Ironically, that crisis was precipitated by its greatest success: the PC.

5

The Boys from
Boca Raton

The origins of the IBM personal computer, the little machine
that changed the world, are tantalisingly obscure. Three men
certainly played lead roles in this famous genesis, providing
respectively impetus, sponsorship and execution. John R.
Opel, as CEO, played sponsor. He must have determined that
IBM should enter the low end of the computer market; he
strongly endorsed the creation of an Independent Business
Unit, of a kind foreign to IBM, to undertake the mission; he
extended indispensable protection to the unit until its mission had triumphed.

Stimulus at all points came from William C. Lowe. As manager of the Entry Level Systems Unit in Boca Raton, Florida,
and then laboratory director for the site, Lowe became sure
that an IBM PC had to be built. In July 1980, he made an historic proposal. At headquarters in Armonk, where he was a
well-known visitor, Lowe advised the Corporate Management
Committee (CMC) that IBM should enter the personal computer market. He added that, to judge by past disasters, this
couldn't be done within IBM's own culture. The task would
have to be executed with heavy external aid. It was Lowe,
too, who conceived the general outline of an IBM personal
computer; who assembled thirteen planning engineers for

'Project Chess' (they entered legend as the 'Dirty Dozen'); who nursed the Chessmen along as they assembled the prototype; who had it approved for further development by the CMC in August 1980; and who took it through the October 1980 'checkpoint' at which the CMC gave Project Chess the go-ahead.

It was also Lowe who, correctly anticipating his own departure for higher things in IBM, lined up Philip 'Don' Estridge to take over the execution. That choice was as decisive as Lowe's other moves, for Estridge, the right man at the right time in the right place, provided the charismatic leadership that made victory possible. The irony of that smashing success is that, had top management foreseen the triumph, it might never have happened.

'The corporation had the insight to turn us loose,' said Estridge later. 'They let us act like we were a venture capital investment of IBM's. This freed us from a number of time-consuming reviews and clearances so we could move at our own speed.' That speed was blistering by anybody's standards, let alone those of a multi-billion dollar multinational. One year and one month after Armonk gave its go-ahead, IBM started shipping the first PCs.

Since the expectation was that only 250,000 units would be made over the entire life of the project, IBM was at risk for no more than $14 million – which the corporation took a mere five hours to generate – if the project flopped completely. With so little at stake, IBM could afford to put pace before procedure. But who was responsible for this decision – fundamental, as it turned out?

All these events, including the superlative handling of the management and the technology by Estridge, have been most ably chronicled by James Chposky and Ted Leonsis in *Blue Magic*. They tell *how* the PC got to market at such lightning speed. But *why* were impossible deadlines set? Who found this project so compellingly urgent? In retrospect, the urgency, as so often in management, created much of the excellence.

Under time pressure, and because of it, the team took decisions that, in a more leisurely atmosphere, would neither have been considered nor approved. Within the programme's fiendish constraints, IBM's traditional, time-consuming system of approval couldn't be accommodated. For instance, the heresy of selling through non-IBM retailers couldn't have survived months of opposition from the vested sales interests in IBM. But there was no time to mount the opposition. Nor was there time to manufacture the PC, like all other IBM products, in-house. As Lowe foresaw, IBM had to go outside.

The equally heretical idea, not just for IBM, but for the entire computer industry, was to shun the proprietary route. The architecture of the system would be 'open' – that is, outsiders would be able to enter the design without infringing IBM patents. Again, the time constraint was decisive. To quote *Blue Magic*, the machine 'could not make it to market in a tight time-frame unless the hardware and software development were performed independently.'

The first software packages would be worked on by specialist firms outside IBM while the hardware was still being perfected. This stroke of genius eventually opened the floodgates to imitators. But the clones could never have surged through so easily save for the extraordinary deal IBM struck with a twenty-five-year-old programming genius from Seattle, Bill Gates. The decision to buy the essential operating system outside IBM was, yet again, necessitated by time pressures. Presumably enough software talent existed in IBM, but the talent certainly couldn't have been mobilised in time.

IBM's first choice blew the opportunity. Its boss missed the appointment, and his stand-ins wouldn't sign the usual mandatory non-disclosure agreement that protected IBM's secrets; nor would they agree to modify their operating system to suit IBM's needs. The team went on to Microsoft; Gates cancelled another meeting to be there and actually wore a suit. The IBMers decided that the tiny West Coast concern should write the BASIC programming language for the unnamed personal computer.

That wasn't too daring – Microsoft had made its young name with BASIC. But the IBM group also mentioned the need for an operating system, which by then was becoming urgent. Here, Gates had considerable disadvantages – no experience and, therefore, no system. He overcame both by buying an operating system from a local firm; providentially, it had been designed for the sixteen-bit technology chosen by IBM. For $50,000 the Seattle Computer Products Disk Operating System, or SCP-DOS, became the basis of the Microsoft Disk Operating System, or MS–DOS.

The later gibe is that DOS really stood for Dirty Old Software. The system had inherent disadvantages with which millions of users and thousands of designers have wrestled since it became the 'industry standard'. It wasn't an IBM standard, though. The open architecture has often been blamed for the cloning that destroyed IBM's market share. The clones would have been hamstrung, though, but for Bill Gates.

As one West Coast rival put it, Gates 'worked out a deal that had Microsoft working with IBM to develop an operating system that Microsoft then turned around and sold to IBM's competitors. I can't believe it.' The unbelievable eventually created a scarcely credible fortune for Gates. Heads he won, if IBM sold its PCs, every one containing MS–DOS: tails he won, too, if an IBM-compatible vendor, also using MS–DOS, stole the sales.

The deal took away IBM's last line of defence against imitators. The Gates bonanza resulted partly because only limited sales were expected, but also because of the inexorable deadline. That driving urgency bears the stamp of chairman John Opel. Project Chess expressed two of his major strategies: that IBM should offer a full range of computers, catering for every need; and that the corporation would experiment with new, decentralised, liberating methods of working.

Such methods, to use the metaphor of Opel's predecessor, Frank Cary, might 'teach an elephant how to tap-dance'. The PC task force answered both Opel's strategic demands. They boldly went outside IBM for almost all components, seeking only those that were already proven. If IBM companies wanted to bid, they had to stand in line, cap in hand, and meet the team's requirements – or lose the work. The requirement included fixed prices. That was another heresy in a culture where margins were customarily added to costs.

The culture still influenced decisions to some extent. The team rightly adopted the faster and more powerful 16-bit architecture (against the 8-bit used by Apple and other players). But it baulked at going beyond Intel's 8088 microprocessor to a newer chip. Its power might be uncomfortably close to other IBM products. Fear of cannibalisation, of robbing Peter's sales to achieve Paul's, was to bedevil the future of the IBM PC.

The 8088 still served excellently as the core of the design. That was an imaginative combination of originality (like allowing for expansion of the memory by slotting in extra boards) and playing safe (like enlarging the dimensions to keep the off-the-shelf components further and more conveniently apart). Working to their own architectural rules to keep the design coherent, the task force members strove through long working days and strenuous arguments to keep the design solid and simple.

Almost everybody involved was an engineer. Estridge had graduated in electrical engineering. He had worked for IBM on both the SAGE early warning radar system and the Apollo moon mission before being moved to the opposite end of the scale – 'entry level systems'. Symbolically, that title persisted deep into the microprocessor era. At IBM, PCs were where computing beginners came in. These customers would, as their needs developed, trade up to bigger, more powerful – and more profitable – machines.

To Estridge's engineers, personal computing was an end in

itself: the end generated the means, and the triumph. As with all successes, that of the PC casts a retroactive glow over their every decision. They deserve their myth. For a start, they broke down IBM's notorious insularity. Outsiders like retailers Computerland (its president, Ed Faber, was a former IBM salesman) made important contributions. The people at Boca Raton had plenty to learn about PCs – and everything to learn about mass merchandising.

In their innocence and haste, the Estridge group stumbled on what in the Nineties became a highly fashionable management approach: synchronicity. Not only was the software under development before the hardware was perfected, but the 'communications' plan for advertising, public relations, etc. was commissioned before confirmation of the vital facts about the machine and its market. A few months before the plan was unveiled, the man responsible, Jim D'Arezzo, was one of several administrators for IBM's advertising, operating in the Office Products Division. Now he was presenting his campaign for the all-powerful Corporate Management Committee's approval. The hero of what is still computing's most famous ad campaign, Charlie Chaplin, was craftily slipped before the CMC almost as an afterthought.

That was how the task force worked. People plucked from other IBM jobs seized total responsibility in their areas and exercised it with full freedom from the familiar corporate constraints. It wasn't a garden party. Anybody who couldn't keep up with Estridge's demands was rapidly removed. Nor did individualism run riot – Estridge invented democratic, informal Saturday morning meetings so that the 'inner circle' could stand clear of day-to-day pressures and pull the project together. There was no time for slow decisions, indecision or second-guessing. Wrong decisions were simply corrected. Estridge didn't like – or have time for – the contentious style of argument which dominated IBM. According to technical overlord Joe Sarubbi, his boss 'would stop everyone and say, "Wait a minute. What is it we have to do? What do we have to provide?" Then he'd make us stick to the point until we agreed on what we had to do and when . . .'

This is another demonstration of later management fashion, that of 'consensus'. The most effective demonstration of the group's cohesion came when a too close tolerance raised the threat of electric shock for anybody who touched the PC's casing. The launch demonstration at Sears Roebuck was only eighteen hours away, so a task force was flown to Chicago by private jet to put insulation in every machine.

Estridge knew how to generate the invaluable morale behind such endeavours. He gave team members a small red rosette to show they belonged to 'the finest, most professional and most loyal team that's ever been assembled in the history of IBM'. From time to time he staged a mass 'pep rally', including one in which 1,000 staff filed into a college auditorium to the strains of rocked-up classical music. That was in January 1983, early in a new era which saw the morale gradually ebb away. Until the launch, the project had been driven by the timetable. Now the business was being driven by demand – pent-up, bursting, insatiable demand. After its New York launch, dead on the deadline, complete with eight software programs, the PC took off into a sunrise of media approval.

The boys in their dingy headquarters at Boca Raton had assembled not only the wonder product of the micro-computer age, but a blueprint for the future of the entire corporation. They had shown what energy and power could be let loose by 'turning loose' – and the publicity machine was quick to exploit the implications. The publicists had a flying start from the product itself, launched to what one business reporter styled 'more hoopla and excitement over a product than I've seen in years'.

Entering long years after Apple, Tandy/Radio Shack and others, IBM was obviously a serious contender, but the industry took as sober a view of prospects as Armonk, according to *Business Week*: 'The IBM computer may initially cut into sales of competitors Apple Computer, Commodore and Tandy, but its long-term impact will be to expand the market.' The magazine went on to quote Tandy's financial vice-president: 'There is nothing that IBM has presented that would blow the industry away.'

He was wrong: the IBM product blew up a storm. Orders outstripped trade forecasts ninefold. Boca Raton fell stupendously short of need. Production couldn't come anywhere near the demand. The 13,553 units shipped in the first four months were a mere trickle compared to the tidal wave of orders. The new machine was on allocation to dealers all through 1982, despite hectic efforts to boost production. By the first five months of 1983, though, Boca Raton was making 600 per cent more PCs every day.

IBM's ability to cope in unfamiliar marketing territory, with products sold in higher volumes at lower prices, was no longer in doubt. Tandy and Apple had welcomed IBM's entry as a seal of legitimacy on their industry (Apple even publicised its welcome with some famously cheeky ads). But IBM had not so much stimulated the market as recreated the industry by providing the missing, crucial factor: a standard.

Publishing the PC's technical specifications in full, showing how the machine was built and operated, was a profound deviation from IBM practice. It was justified by the need to get software writers to collaborate – as one IBMer observed, 'The decision to publish the design was fundamental to our success'. But in fact IBM had recreated a 360 dilemma in even more virulent form. Plug-compatible became IBM-compatible. Soon hundreds of companies, using the same Intel microprocessor and the same Microsoft operating system, were marketing machines that could run most applications developed for the IBM PC.

To stress that compatibility, these rivals were forced to advertise IBM in their own promotional material. That didn't answer IBM's long-term need to retain customer loyalty and seize the bulk of new buyers. Its problem was the lack of fundamental technical difference between the PC and its rivals.

There was a non-technical difference: the magic letters IBM. Now was the time for all those years of brilliant design and image-building to prove their worth.

But the company's tradition was one of crushing competition, not fighting on equal terms. It couldn't tie up PC customers with proprietary software or peripherals – the only weapon seemed to be price. As its share of a booming market soared (from 17 per cent in 1982 to 26 per cent in 1983), IBM began reducing prices, starting with a 20 per cent cut. The host of small manufacturers seemed doomed, just like the myriad lesser car firms forced out by Ford and the other Detroit giants. Without the IBM sales volumes, how could the minnows compete on costs? And if they couldn't match IBM's costs, how could they cope with its prices?

The economic pressure which IBM applied was severe and continuous. By April 1985, the price of a typical PC package was just over $2,000 – representing an overall decline of 72 per cent. Yet still the competition refused to die. It even prospered. Compaq Computer was launched in the teeth of the IBM storm. Rod Canion, its president, warned that 'You have to offer something else. Playing the price game is dangerous.' Compaq's 'something else' was portability (you could carry the first Compaq about, if only just).

But others even stayed in the price game. IBM's margins still left plenty of room in a business which, unlike the car industry, was not manufacturing-intensive. If you're buying in components from outside (as IBM was itself) and simply assembling them in your own configuration, economies of scale are less significant. The biggest buyer gets the lowest prices, but the benefit can quickly be offset by mammoth overheads – and IBM's vastly exceeded those of its micro-competitors.

Their survival would have been an irritant in any circumstances, but the very success of the PC had made that survival a threat to IBM's central strategy. The smashing breakthrough of the PC reinforced the conviction that IBM could do no wrong; that the computer age had taken a new turn, and was heading full-speed in IBM's direction. Instead of supplying mainframes with passive terminals, the company would get a PC on every desk in every organisation which was already served by IBM.

New customers would choose the IBM PC in preference to any other product, and from that choice the newcomers could be upgraded, in the time-honoured manner, to bigger, better and much dearer installations. The flaw in this otherwise powerful theory was that IBM had no proprietorial position apart from its logo. Having created an open industry standard, the company was powerless to insist that its customers bought from IBM and nobody else.

They actually might have done better to stick to IBM. Purchases of micro-computers ballooned out of hand, festooning offices with many makes of machine which, while they might use the same software, couldn't communicate at all. In his book *Big Blue*, Richard Thomas DeLamarter shows how strongly IBM played the communication hand in dealing with its large customers, 'many of whom were uncertain how to deal with the wildfire proliferation of PCs throughout their organisations'.

Data processing managers, eager to retain control, loved to be told how to remove the risk of 'data processing anarchy' by sticking with IBM. In this context, it didn't matter that the actual connections were very limited in their power. Technological backwardness apart, DeLamarter believed that 'IBM had little commercial interest' in making its PCs work together too well, for that would lead its largest customers to install them instead of other 'relatively high-profit' products.

In any event, IBM soared to an astonishing 80 per cent of the corporate PC market – a domination every bit as strong as its peak penetration in mainframes. But there was a worrying discrepancy (which apparently didn't worry IBM) between this overwhelming strength among corporations and the reaction of the stand-alone purchaser. In this market, IBM's share was no more than 32–35 per cent, despite the brilliant Chaplin campaign. DeLamarter's interpretation of the gap is damning: 'When it cannot use the threat of changing interfaces to limit customer choice, IBM's products must stand on their own merits, and those merits often fail them against technically superior products from relatively tiny competitors.'

Yet that criticism can't be levelled at the first PC. It was, without question, the best in specification and in quality on launch day and for long afterwards. Here Estridge and his team can hardly be faulted. The task facing them, however, had wholly changed. It was no less formidable. Then, they had been stretched to meet a near-impossible deadline. Now, they had to raise production and employment by leaps and bounds, and to extend the PC family, amid all the pressures of runaway success. Many of the pressures were exerted from within IBM. The Estridge group had shown the world that part of the elephant could indeed tap-dance like Fred Astaire. Now, the paths of the elephant and the hoofer were converging fast. The result of their collision could never be in doubt.

6

The Accolade of
Tom Peters

The IBM of the early Eighties was a place of inexhaustible pride. Like the Roman Empire at its zenith, IBM was rich with the fruit of past conquests and supremely confident of new victories. To admirers, inside and outside the empire, its actions and ideas seemed to fit together with an innate perfection, like some vast Swiss watch. Only, the days of IBM triumphant, like those of the clockwork timepiece, were numbered.

In both cases, downfall developed from apparent supremacy. The Swiss had produced the ultimate breakthrough in timekeeping: the electronic quartz movement. IBM had shown with the PC, that leviathan could take on the brightest and best of the long-haired intellectuals, the maverick millionaires, the freebooting innovators of Silicon Valley. It could beat them at their own sport. The myth of IBM was no myth, but a demonstrated reality.

The gospel of invincible excellence spread far beyond IBM's own borders. It lodged most famously in the New York office of McKinsey and Co, the highest profile management consultants. *Business Week* had published a short article on McKinsey's analysis of corporate excellence. Thomas J. Peters had since led a sometimes unsteady effort to complete a book on this high-powered theme; another McKinsey man, Robert Waterman Jr, had been recruited into the project – and as the team worked to support their thesis with examples, IBM often came to the rescue.

In Search of Excellence, the fruit of their labours, had twenty-six references to IBM, all glowing. At its zenith, the IBM Empire did seem to enshrine many of the Excellent virtues:

1 A bias towards action.

2 Simple form and lean staff.

3 Continued contact with customers.

4 Productivity improvement via people.

5 Operational autonomy to encourage entrepreneurship.

6 Stress on one key business value.

7 Emphasis on doing what they know best.

8 Simultaneous loose-tight controls.

The Peters-Waterman view, though, was external. Outside opinions of organisations are notoriously fallible, but a few clear-eyed insiders knew that IBM was seriously deficient on perhaps half of the eight counts. Overall, the verdicts of *Excellence* proved ill-judged in three-quarters of the chosen exemplars – a low batting average, even by the weak standards of such exercises.

Occasionally an outsider with unusual powers of analysis and observation spends enough time inside an organisation to form a far more accurate picture – as Peter Drucker did with his pathfinding study of General Motors, *Concept of the Corporation*. Interestingly, the leaders of GM, including Alfred

P. Sloan, its virtual creator, disagreed with Drucker's conclusions – which doubtless proved him right.

To see ourselves as others see us is rarely a comfortable experience. But inside IBM self-regard chimed harmoniously with the view from McKinsey. No effort was spared to capitalise on the image of excellence, to project it into the marketplace where it could reinforce the sales message: IBM is best. The Big Story was that of how a colossus, freed from the shackles of the anti-trust action, had burst into a new era of creative success, in which the PC was both cornerstone and conclusive evidence.

The PR message was, and remained, far too successful for IBM's own good. Over the Eighties, each successive failure and disappointment was strongly countered by well-massaged stories that used the media to trumpet reassurance: no, the barbarians have been routed, yes, Rome is itself again – proud and triumphant. There was always plenty of triumph to salute. How many chief executives, in a seventeen-year span, have trebled employment, moved HQ twice, added an entire factory and raised revenues by 3,455 per cent – from £45 million to £1,600 million? Edwin Nixon did that in one satrapy of the empire – the UK.

Here, IBM lacked its all but universal market dominance. First, the Hollerith patents on punch card machines had been vigorously exploited by another company: The British Tabulating Machine Co. Without its usual customer base, Nixon recalled, 'we were completely unknown' and had to explain what IBM was 'nine times out of ten'. Second, Britain had pioneered electronic data processing, both in theory and application.

Alan Turing, a tortured, brilliant individual, conceived the idea of the digital computer, and several Britons made vital contributions in turning concept into reality. Weirdly enough, a company famed for tea-shops and cakes, J. Lyons, pioneered the development of a computer called Leo, and sold it for business use long before IBM had mastered the new technology. The evolution of the British industry was mostly a history of trial and too much error, but IBM, confined to a third or so of the market, always had to contend with strong local opposition.

The PC, though, seemed to crack this mould. The main opposition, International Computers Ltd (like IBM, a lineal descendant of the old punch card companies), had no worthwhile position in this fastest growing of markets. Nixon had won the PC 'mission' for his Greenock plant. In 1983 its exports had already reached £160 million – and Scotland had a prime role in an unfolding prospect of endless growth, placing a PC in all the workstations which every desk worker would have by 1994.

The PCs would, naturally, come overwhelmingly from IBM, which saw their sales supporting, and being nourished in turn by, the sales of large systems. The company was wrong about the pace of the revolution, very wrong about its own share of the market, wrong about the future of large systems – but in 1984 none of this was suspected. Of course, there were problems, and IBM's executives had identified many of them, mostly correctly. Moreover, policies had been formulated and implemented (at least in theory) to provide solutions.

In 1980, Nixon had looked at the prospects to 2005 and concluded that 'everything that's happened is irrelevant to what's going to happen' – and he was dead right. Armed with 'a blank sheet of paper', Nixon rethought IBM (UK) from scratch – people, resources, products, the lot. This was the *Excellence* ideal in action: a country manager, 3,000 miles from Armonk, responding to a correctly assessed challenge by taking the initiative, all within the framework of a master plan understood by all.

To IBMers, their multinational system was superior to any, with marketing organised nationally; research and development, globally; and manufacture on a continental basis. In Nixon's era, his two plants fitted into an integrated network of fourteen European factories. They manufactured components and sub-assemblies, and assembled final products for the whole non-US world (save Japan and some of Latin America). The fourteen plants didn't overlap. 'Missions', such as Nixon's PC victory, were concentrated in specific plants to achieve optimum economies of scale.

The role of the national manager was to achieve maximum penetration of the local market and, in competition with other European managers, to obtain the maximum slice of the rich European cake for his factories and other facilities. To get the high-tech support centre for European software, Nixon had to promise that the building would be ready in twelve months – and to lobby to achieve government approval 'in ten days flat'. Otherwise, the mission would have gone to one of Nixon's major competitors – 'my colleagues in IBM France, Germany, and Mexico'.

Exactly the same philosophy of internal competition inspired the development work at the UK's Hursley laboratories. The object was to 'develop something with the largest possible product range and which gives the highest possible added value'. This, Nixon was convinced, had given his limb of the colossus a position in the 'massive potential' of terminals that couldn't be shaken.

This ideal world had its tensions – the Havant plant's loss of the largest computers to Montpelier in France still rankled – but they were internal tensions, not external ones imposed by competition. The internal tensions, though, weren't confined to battles over missions. Country managers were restricted by many more bonds than the detailed budgeting and planning controls. The latter would be expected in any major corporation – and are no less necessary for minor ones.

In IBM's process, the Europeans related, not to Armonk, but to Paris. Every one of his top executives reported, not to Nixon alone, but to somebody with an equivalent functional responsibility in Paris. So did Nixon. He was able to say that, 'I speak to my boss in Paris rarely – sometimes we go for weeks without talking'. That mightn't have been true of his senior people, whose allegiance to the country boss was limited in one very important sense: he didn't appoint them. The idea of somebody running a £1.6 billion company, yet unable to select his own team, would sound bizarre in most places outside IBM. A thick book, however, reserved this and many other powers to Paris. If Nixon, as he said, 'hadn't looked at the book for ten years', that was because the system it enshrined permeated every aspect of a senior manager's life.

Every summer Paris gave the national companies the targets and guidelines needed to construct two-year plans, one year firm, the other relatively sketchy. By September, a function-by-function operating plan was back in Paris for co-ordination with all the other European plans. That took a month – then the Parisian comments went back with the plans to the national companies. After a few weeks incorporating the comments, the nationals batted them back to Paris for a final round of consolidation.

The complete European plan next travelled to Armonk for final approval. European managers then got the approved and blessed budget in the nick of time for the start of the new year. Looked at analytically, this system was heavily geared towards the short-term and the operational. By the time the anointed budget got back to Nixon, his company was already deeply committed to actions and policies that would largely determine results for the first half of the coming year – if not the whole year.

The two-year time horizon was very short by most multinational standards. Yet this wasn't a period when technological changes were forcing the pace – not on the surface. Beneath the surface, though, the pace was working up to excruciating speed. This was the kind of issue that should have been caught by the five-year strategic plan, drawn up every April. Whether strategy and tactics were satisfactorily combined is another matter – for the pressure on the national companies was tactical, not strategic.

Relations between Paris and London were smooth nearly

all the time. When friction and difficulty did arise, poor results were the usual cause – like those which followed the British devaluation of 1968. The way to keep Paris off your back was to hit or exceed your targets. The traditional IBM yardstick of return on sales still reigned, but in 1984 a new 'prime focus' on asset management had started to develop because of the fundamental change to IBM's business engendered by the PC.

From making low volume, high-priced products with high margins – the source of IBM's riches throughout its history - the corporation was moving to high volume, lower-priced products with lower margins. From unique dependence on its own sales force, IBM now had to sell through dealers – for the first time in its life. From a mainframe culture, homogenous and highly controlled, it was moving into a multifarious marketplace where dominance was still sought. The ideal situation was that 'nobody else can get in'.

That exclusion became far more difficult to achieve. A single, closely related business, with one management and one measurement system, was changing to different businesses with different systems. Each of them was expected to make a profit in its own right. But did IBM know how to run such a company? By 1984, Nixon already had thirteen separate business areas under his command.

One, however, was very much more equal than the others: mainframes. For the first time IBM could claim to cover the waterfront. Wherever technology could be brought to bear on information, in the office, factory, telephone exchange, shop, bank, etc., etc., the company had a machine or machines to compute, type, print, communicate, reproduce, display, design, and so on. Yet only in mainframes was the old dominance guaranteed – not to mention the old profits.

All the pundits expected growth in mainframe sales to slow – to perhaps half the 30 per cent per annum (doubling every two and a half years) expected in other areas. 'What do we do?' cried an IBMer. 'It would be very foolish to ignore the opportunity to sell a large machine for a million pounds.' That posed an obvious contradiction, for 'part of the job is to stop the focus on large systems'. Not only had that focus made IBM's fortunes, it was built into the ethos and the corporate system.

That gave reason to hope that capitalising on the large system strengths would continue almost by osmosis. That was the natural order of things; in contrast, the other businesses required IBM to learn entirely new marketing skills. From relying on 200 key customers, heavily invested in information technology systems and in IBM hardware and software, the company now had to focus on thousands of potential, undoctrinated purchasers.

To reach these, IBM had to master yet another culture – that of dealer organisations, where it had little understanding. To get more, in another acute break with tradition, IBM opened its own retail stores – an unhappy and costly operation over which history has kindly drawn a veil. So the need for sweeping change was clearly enough recognised, and frightened nobody. Didn't the *Excellence* ethos hold that IBM was uniquely good at mastering and managing change?

In the sense of accommodating growth, introducing new products and starting new activities, this was certainly true. If you envisage the corporation as a giant railroad system, starting with one trunk line, then adding branch line after branch line, modernising the rolling stock, improving the signalling and marshalling, opening new stations, bringing in new people to replace and grow business – at all this IBM had become superbly effective, excellent indeed.

It remained the same system, managed by the same people in the same way. If the need was for an entirely new transportation system manned by different people in a different way, IBM's excellence was not only doubtful but untried. Moreover, the nature of the changes sweeping the world was misunderstood. In 1984, a senior British executive, in charge of development and manufacturing, firmly believed that the future of the PC lay with information storage, not microcircuits: 'Silicon,' he said flatly, 'is no longer the driving force.'

IBM was spectacularly wrong in this perception; it was the 386 silicon chip that enabled Compaq to make a vital techno-logical leapfrog. IBM's own reduced instruction set computing (RISC) and other microcircuitry inventions also created the industry's next phases. Not only that, but IBM was also wrong in believing that in information storage (which it thought had the greatest potential), its laboratories had a hammerlock on the fundamental technology of disks and heads.

The leadership in storage, as in microprocessors, was seized by other far smaller firms. IBM correctly foresaw that the PC, as an intelligent terminal, would reshape the IT market. It was incorrect in believing that its mainframe dominance would extend naturally into the new markets, by osmosis or any other means. But in 1984, an organisation which had thrown off all challenges was not easily convinced of its ability to make large mistakes. Wherever its executives looked, they saw success.

In social policy, where the company grandly sought 'to cre-ate a political, social and economic environment in which IBM can flourish', IBM was a model even for Marks & Spencer – the most prestigious management in Britain. M & S would refer enquiries to IBM when people asked about executive second-ment to outside organisations, like government. In manufac-turing, Greenock, like other plants round the world, was taking huge strides with flexible automation – and improving inventory turnover, *en route* from 3.7 times to nine.

Wasn't that all part of meeting John Opel's objective, to be the most cost-effective supplier with the highest quality – the absolutely certain way to sustain superiority? In finance, too, the business had transformed its ways fundamentally, and with some pain. Once, the vast rental base had provided enviable stability and enviable margins. The switch to outright purchase had quite traumatic results in terms of financial planning. As the rental base declined, so did the steady income, and the outright purchases were more subject to fluctuation and economic crises.

IBM had become a cyclical business. It was also facing more competition. As software was separated – or 'unbundled' – from hardware, IBM's gigantic software business became a clear target for other companies. That also happened in maintenance, formerly another source of totally reliable bundled profits. All this demanded nothing less than a powerful change in culture. But how was it to be achieved?

Armonk had ordered its affiliates to split up into many smaller businesses. Then, high and clear visibility could ensure that Opel's injunctions about lower costs were being followed. That was simple necessity in a business like personal computers, where relatively low prices left much less room for generous spending on either sales or service. Finance men travelled the organisation to explain what was involved in forming the smaller units: 'Creating babies,' in one IBMer's phrase, 'without the parent eating them alive.'

All over the business, teams were similarly at work to turn Opel's words into reality – for major instance, to get quality up and overheads down. 'Indirects' who didn't sell, manufacture, maintain, or engineer were a prime target. As for quality, the worldwide drive had a target of zero defects which managers felt they had all but reached. Admirably, the quality standard of customer satisfaction was applied internally – each department was subject to quality appraisals by those it served. Suppliers, too, were brought into the net. They either matched IBM's new, more stringent quality criteria, or lost its business.

Small wonder that Peters and Waterman, confronted by all this apparent excellence, placed IBM so high in their pantheon – and in Waterman's case kept it there: IBM rates thirty-six references in his *The Renewal Factor*, all complimentary. That wasn't published until 1987, after IBM had already started to falter. Renewal seemed the right word. IBMers regarded themselves as best at adapting to changing markets in ways that perpetuated that article of IBM faith noted earlier: that the company was *better* than every other company at everything.

But in truth the IBM of the *Excellence* apogee was top-heavy. In the UK 3,000 of the 15,000 employees worked in purely administrative roles. In finance, the monthly 'CONTACT' meeting (standing for CONtrol and ACTion) at which the controller reported the overall company results, highlighting the exceptions, applied a heavy hand. The business planners (the marketing arm) and key line directors reported similarly – and all this took place only eight or nine days after the month-end. The reporting was against the one-year budget, which was an immutable yardstick.

Yet those controls weren't thought to be enough. Internal auditors were sent to patrol the perimeters of the company to ensure that people were doing what they were supposed to do – right up to director level. More than that, Paris directly commanded the finance function and obtained results, which, integrated with those of other European countries, flowed back to Armonk. It wasn't the only, or most important flow, for cash dividends and a 10 per cent royalty on all customer revenue (save that from PCs, which carried a lighter load), went back to America.

Power followed the same route. Eddie Nixon rarely found anything like a directive coming down from on high. Just occasionally, Armonk would say, 'this is what we're going to do', and its will would be done. In reality, though, the whole system worked to eliminate exceptions and to enforce Armonk's will. IBM (UK) was at the receiving end of a long command-and-control trail down which came, not so much direct orders, as directing currents in which all 15,000 British employees were caught.

The break-up of the monolith into smaller business units, necessitated by competition, was necessary for IBM's internal health, too. But the culture change it implied cut across the Armonk culture – the top-heavy, top-down nature of the beast.

As one executive remarked, it's very difficult to get '15,000 people to march to the same tune as the drummer'. If the drummer is separated from the marchers by the breadth of the Atlantic Ocean, the difficulty is multiplied geometrically.

Up there in Armonk, where the drummers drummed their 'excellent' beat, all seemed well: out there in IBM's wide world the rhythms became muffled as they passed down the line. At the centre IBM had managed brilliantly in parcelling out uninterrupted success so that its local companies could believe it was wholly theirs. But in the new age, reality had to match appearance. And the reality was that IBM's huge profits concealed enormous waste. Too many drummers were leading too many marchers away from excellence, while deeply convinced that they were doing precisely the opposite.

III

WHAT THE WATSONS TRULY WROUGHT

7

The High Church
of IBM

What's it like working for IBM? Or rather, at the apogee, what was it like? As John Akers strove in the early Nineties to change IBM into a different, faster, leaner system, the system was pushing back. You couldn't expect so powerful a creation, after so long and successful a life, to do otherwise. The better built the house, the harder it is to knock down.

All organisations breed distinctive cultures, and no two are exactly alike. But IBM was peculiar from early days. Its founding father, Thomas J. Watson Sr, had deliberately created a specific culture that wasn't just a good environment for good business: it was business personified. Buck Rodgers, the former vice president in charge of marketing, chose well when he called his book *The IBM Way*.

In this first exposition by a senior insider, Rodgers stressed that 'The Way' governed all actions at IBM, from job descriptions to closing sales. Like old Tom Watson in the company song, IBM achieved its results and won its glowing success by being 'so big, so square and so true'. Individuals treated with respect treated the customer likewise, and the ultimate expression of respect was excellence – excellence in everything that IBM touched.

A well-placed reviewer begged to doubt this beauteous

vision of The Way. Could IBM really be 'the world's largest Boy Scout troop'? What about the contrary vision of 'a rapacious gargantua that does not care whom it tramples'? The reviewer, Marilyn A. Harris, concluded that, despite the book 'IBM's secret remains secret'. This attracted a sharp volley from Rodgers' co-author, Robert L. Shook. His conclusion was that 'the secret of IBM's success is that there isn't a secret after all'. What really distinguished The IBM Way was 'simplicity. It works for every business'. But management had to be 'smart enough' to learn from 'the world's most profitable and admired company'.

So long as IBM did lead the world in profits and admiration, The Way – whatever it was – had to look wonderful. In the early Nineties, financial losses and bitter criticism, from inside and outside, produced a different environment in which it was natural to draw the opposite conclusion – to stigmatise The Way as an obsolete culture turned irrelevant cult.

But the truth, as with all religions, is that The Way in practice and The Way in preaching were always far apart. For a start, neither IBM nor its ways of doing business were ever simple. Like the Roman Catholic Church, it was a complex, many-layered hierarchy dominated by a central, static organisation. IBM's Vatican was Armonk. The corporate centre was the place where all important decisions were taken; and all IBM careers, like all roads leading to Rome, led to Armonk. To enter the inner circle, the ranks of vice presidents, the careerist had to cultivate the Armonk cardinals. Armonk was the centre of rumour and report. What you knew wasn't as important as who you knew. But without both the what and the who, an IBM career could never progress.

As two of the shrewdest observers tell the tale: 'The idea, if one is not stationed at Armonk, is to find good reasons to visit Armonk. While there, the ambitious visitor should ingratiate himself so that the senior staff at headquarters will welcome more visits. After a while, somebody at Armonk will surely say, "Let's move him up here". To move toward the top at IBM, one has to have daily contact with those who have already arrived' – and who are, of course, all at Armonk.

It followed that the higher men rose in IBM, the more time they spent at Armonk – even if their responsibilities were hundreds, even thousands of miles away. This tended to slow down IBM's responses doubly: first, Armonk had to ratify everything; second, the senior management of any operation might be missing at any time – on the way to Armonk, at the corporate offices, on the way back to base.

There was, of course, ample cover for the travellers. An unspoken rule of IBM was that every manager had an equally able successor waiting in the wings. They wouldn't necessarily take over, because IBM had a capricious attitude towards who went where. The unspoken contract was that IBM traded jobs-for-life employment for the employees' acceptance of each and every move their employer ordered – hence the crack that IBM stood for 'I've Been Moved'.

It followed that IBM had a surplus of managers and that many in this horde were relatively inexperienced in their jobs. Again, this reinforced the centralised power at Armonk. Everything had to be checked and double-checked: the engineering verification process, in which every component and product was rigorously tested and retested, was echoed by the process which submitted every business proposal to examination and re-examination.

The sword of Damocles hung over every manager. At any moment he might be moved from the project on which he was working: or the project itself might be abruptly beheaded. In neither case would the individuals concerned be consulted. IBM was not a democracy, but a theocracy, and the theocrats sat in a body called CMC – the Corporate Management Committee.

Its Pope, the chief executive, had a disproportionately powerful influence on the CMC. New initiatives tended to come by Papal decree, rather than by collective voice. It was Frank Cary, for example, who backed the sensationally radical idea of the

Independent Business Unit or IBU. This was a way of establishing ventures outside the constraints of the corporation, and thus changing the corporation itself – modifying The IBM Way.

Of Cary's seven IBUs, however, only one – the personal computer – had the desired impact, and then not for long. The Way didn't tell what happened when an IBU succeeded. How did it relate to the rest of the corporation? Were its managers allowed to break the corporate rules indefinitely? Would the corporate rules be modified to accommodate the IBU? Or would the IBU have to come into line?

These corporate rules, written and unwritten, were pervasive and powerful. You couldn't, for example, expect to reach the top through technology. IBM made its living by selling high-tech products, but it was the selling, not the technology, that attracted the richest rewards and highest promotions.

The high priests of the CMC took a strictly businesslike attitude towards propositions, leaving scant room for speculative ventures and imposing a swift cut-off for failure, even though it might be only temporary. The rules tended to deter technological leapfrogging (missing out the next stage in the technology to go further ahead) and the recruitment of daring talent. High fliers sought skies where they could fly higher than was possible at IBM. The drain of people interested in new horizons contributed to a good deal of (it was thought) uncharacteristic fumbling in markets with which IBM was unfamiliar. For instance, there was a whole series of flops at the low end, where IBM struggled pitifully with small computers; and the record was equally poor at the opposite pole, the supercomputer market.

But waste of effort didn't cause concern – it was intrinsic to the IBM system. Hundreds of research projects were launched, competed for funds, and vied for Armonk's attention; and hundreds died for every one that finished the course. The competition was supposed to result in the survival of the fittest, and that, too was part of The IBM

Way – for both people and machines.

The CMC would deliberately set two factories at each other's throats, competing for substantially the same 'mission'. The best man, it was assumed, would always win. He might, of course, be better at Armonk politics rather than at devising the best solution for the market. But members understood that part of the IBM church very well. They also well understood the penalties for failure.

Good guys who finished last were probably finished. No written rule laid this down, but over the years the process had become implicit. If you won, you got the chance to go on winning: if you lost (and the 'you' could be collective, applying to the members of a whole group), there was no second chance. Despite that, some IBMers, as individuals, did play dice with their careers. But group norms tended to be more cautious – often too cautious.

The greater the number of groups involved in any project, the slower the progress. This wasn't a question of mere months – the delays could be measured in years. The length of the internal delays is known only to IBM, but the external ones can be measured – eleven years after Digital into mini-computers, four years after the Apple II in PCs, five years after Apollo with an engineering workstation, five years again after Toshiba with a laptop, three years after Sun with an advanced RISC workstation.

Around all these projects, and all others, the political vortex swirled. Those without political instincts could make progress, but only so far. They could win the coveted formal prizes (the Technical/Management Excellence Awards) for merit, getting cash and plaques signed by their divisional president. They could gain regular promotions. Their talents might be recognised by others who had climbed further and faster up the ladder. Who you know worked both ways – it gave senior people the human tools they needed to succeed in their own assignments, and gave those lower down the opportunities to join the most exciting projects around. Some were *ad hoc* groups – task forces, of which the massive effort that produced the 360 range of mainframe computers is the epoch-making example. These temporary groups, however, were generally expected to work within the disciplined structure created and sustained by the high priests.

At the summit the CMC imposed deadlines and issued decrees that could not be appealed. The committee wasn't hidebound, though. It could take heretical decisions and waive orthodox procedures. Nor was it negative. Even its death sentences were not absolute. A particular approach was killed, but a new solution could be proposed and perhaps approved.

Every project had to pass 'checkpoints': meetings at pre-scheduled dates at which go/no-go decisions were made. In this obstacle race, the project backers were running against time, technology and bureaucracy. The term is somewhat unfair if it conjures up forms, manuals and other varieties of red tape. IBM, like all large organisations, had more than enough of these – far more. But that wasn't the worst of it.

The company was full of overlapping jurisdictions – separate departments, each rowing a different course on the same water and thus prone at any time to come into collision. This again happens in all companies, and not only large ones. But in IBM, with its fundamentally homogenous product line, the right policy for entity A might threaten – or seem to threaten – entity B.

In a typical example, the Office Products Division (OPD) objected violently (and, as it happened, futilely) to selling the personal computer through retailers. Why? In part, because it might undercut the sale of the immensely profitable IBM typewriters, which were only available through IBM itself. OPD lost this battle, and eventually the war – as noted, the typewriter business, a decade on, was sold off as a failure.

But in the black-and-white IBM philosophy, for every winner there was at least one loser. To that there was one mighty exception, one which always won: the marketing machine. In the US, the National Accounts Division (NAD) handled the major national and international customers. Those who got to the summit at Armonk mostly came out of this mega-division. It was totally oriented, as they were, towards the large main-frames and large corporate accounts.

The NAD and its equivalents outside the US played a role similar to that of the Italian clergy within the Church of Rome. By and large its executives – who, remember, dominated Armonk – were forces of conservatism, defenders of the status quo. Possibly some of the mainframe's defenders realised that the downsizing trends in computing technology – led by IBM's own PC – were dooming the mainframe to relative and even-tually absolute decline. But that would only intensify their determination to cling to the world's single most profitable business for as long as they could.

There were ways round the marketing block – while the Central Management Committee was largely composed of marketing alumni, it spoke with its own voice. And the chief executive could dominate any divisional or factional interest in IBM if he chose, for his and the CMC's remit was boundless. The CMC even passed judgement on advertising campaigns. The demands on its time were thus very onerous, and that was reflected in its working methods.

Executives arriving for presentations vital to their projects, and possibly to the future of the corporation, had a strict forty-five minutes to flip through their charts and answer a barrage of questions. The decisions would usually be made then and there. The system had the virtue of speed, but nothing else. That's perfectly adequate time for presenting a new product to a dealer audience, say. But the curtailed proceedings inevitably meant that much lobbying went on outside the CMC.

The constant time-consuming visits to Armonk were an essential, unofficial part of the process. If a task force pro-posal passed the first CMC hurdle, though, it became a Product Development Group. This was seldom formally announced: obsessed with secrecy, IBM was supposed never to disclose products until they were ready to market. The rule was honoured as much in the breach as the observance – and the breaches often raised dark suspicions about IBM's motives. Was it really launching a project, or secretly trying to forestall and kill the competition?

Secrecy helped to make the hyperactive grapevine at IBM a mainstay of its people's lives. For business reasons, as well as career prospects, they needed to know who was working on what – and where, for IBM's establishments covered a vast, dispersed geography. As projects developed, naturally, more and more people became privy to the work and dependent on its success – the industrial designers, for example, or the communications people.

All those groups formed sects within the Church, and all had their own articles of faith. When faiths clashed, the Vatican would arbitrate, and the issue climbed, as one side or the other decided to 'non-concur', all the way to the Central Management Committee – and settling non-concurrences involved further delay as the issues awaited their turn. Although the CMC sessions were brisk, the whole process was thus anything but.

Some clashes involved internal business, in which IBM units traded with each other. Making all components in-house, for instance, had been an inviolable rule. That resulted in a complex network of internecine deals. Whether or not this produced the best products, it generated inevitable delays. Every factory had an interest to protect, an entrenched position to defend: Endicott in New York made all printed circuit boards, Burlington all memory chips, Kingston all power supplies. Similar vested interests existed all over the world of IBM.

The vested interests could lobby at various levels below the CMC. Each line of command led to the summit through local, divisional and group levels. And then there were the checkers – the people responsible for seeing (in which they manifestly failed from time to time) that every product leaving IBM was worthy of its name. 'Systems assurance' was the supreme example of this genus: any product had to pass its tough and detailed scrutiny.

Meeting these standards became a motivating factor in itself. Like any great religion, IBM had established a credo whose faith fuelled devotion and total commitment. Even in a committed culture, though, money is basic in managerial motivation. From Thomas Watson's first days, IBM had recognised this force. At the apogee, its compensation programmes were deliberately aimed at giving people on all levels high rewards – but not the highest in big business.

This applied right to the summit. The sums earned by chairman John Akers in 1991 attracted sharp criticism – but only because 'earned' seemed the wrong word, given IBM's awful results. The actual total paid to Akers in straight pay and long-term compensation from 1989 to 1991, $7.2 million, was well down the US corporate lists, over $2 million less than Rod Canion won at the much smaller Compaq.

The disparities became more marked lower down. In the mid-Eighties a superstar like PC launcher Don Estridge, who had created the biggest new business in IBM history, probably earned around a quarter of a million. Maybe a third of that sum was bonus – an exceptional, but hardly mind-boggling amount for a truly exceptional performance. When Steve Jobs asked him to join Apple as chief executive, Estridge could have quadrupled his compensation in the first year. The man who eventually took the Apple job, John Sculley, in 1989–91 pocketed $20.3 million – nearly thrice the take of Akers at the ten times larger IBM. But for a dedicated IBMer like Estridge, the target in his sights – the Central Management Committee – outweighed any questions of immediate reward.

Below CMC level, immediate pay became a matter of literally growing concern over the Eighties. Why should the high-growth, hotly competitive sectors of IBM submit to the same cautiously tailored policies as the rest? The IBM policy was one of stability – steady, steadily rising rewards for men (and some women) who were set on a lifetime career path, and whose compensation would be good, fair and seen to be fair.

The fairness, however, was in comparison to others at IBM. As the company formed more and more relationships with suppliers, retailers and competitors outside IBM, the internal fairness counted less and less. An IBMer might work much of the time with colleagues in far tinier companies who earned much larger rewards. The consequent resentment may have worked its way right to the top.

The exceptional rancour in the dispute with Microsoft over PC operating systems has been widely linked to IBM annoyance over the $6 billion fortune accumulated by founder Bill Gates – a fortune that was initially handed him on a golden plate by IBM. Dozens of Gates' employees, moreover, were millionaires. Very few of IBM's hundreds of thousands of employees, present and past, have reached the same seven digits.

To pursue stable, bureaucratic pay policies in an unstable, entrepreneurial world is to invite trouble. The rules are bound to create anomalies. A key man on the PC project, for instance, in his previous, unremarkable IBM employment could have won a 16 per cent raise in seven months. In contrast, the move to the dynamic success of Boca Raton might generate only a 7 per cent increase in sixteen months. For all that, it's been said that more bonuses were awarded for the PC success than for any other achievement in IBM history – but the bonus could easily be offset by a lower than merited place on the basic pay totem pole. Other benefits, moreover, were tied to the basic, not the augmented amount.

Down the line, leaders might talk to the led about special cash and stock rewards for special achievements, but the bureaucracy stood immovably in the way. Comparisons were most odious in personal computers, where IBM PC's success had brought fortune, fame and fast cars to so many young entrepreneurs outside the company: 'The disparity of how money was distributed in the computer industry created deep dissatisfaction among the "old timers" . . . Several core members of the PC group felt betrayed . . . after working seventy-hour weeks, they received one or two merit increases and a bonus or two in three years,' wrote Chposky and Leonsis.

The inevitable happened: an exodus of talent which, because of IBM's traditional recruitment and remuneration policies, wasn't matched by an inflow of brilliant achievers from outside. The difficulty was formidable and obvious. To reward individuals and individual groups adequately by the standards of the world outside IBM would have shattered the standards within. It was a dilemma that recurred continuously in the post-PC era, and which highlights the crisis that had crept over the old order.

In proportional terms, only a few IBMers found that order intolerable, so intolerable that, like latter-day Martin Luthers, some even quit the church. But the few heretics were enough to destabilise internally what was already being cracked by external forces. The sovereign issue was whether the majority left behind, especially the inner Papal circle, had the imagination and inspiration to lead the Reformation themselves.

8

Total Dominance:
The Salesman Cometh

To discover why IBM's old order cracked, go back to 19 January 1969. In the years between then and 1982, a period of unexampled growth and riches, IBM appeared to have no serious competitors. Only one opponent had the power to interrupt its progress. That was the Federal Government. On that day in January, the Justice Department filed suit against IBM, alleging that it monopolised the digital computer market – as, in terms of market share, it assuredly did.

The Federal anti-trust action struck at the roots, not just of IBM, but of the system of capitalist competition which the Watsons had exploited so brilliantly. Previous monopolies and quasi-monopolies were built on restrictive control of the market – like John D. Rockefeller's hammerlock on the means of transporting oil. But IBM had no stranglehold over either the technology, the productive apparatus, or the channels of distribution.

In the unfolding of the Computer Age, IBM simply combined its power in all three areas to create a profound control over the *customers*. The latter, primarily the big businessmen of America and the world, could have turned safely to the many competitors following in IBM's wake. But in the Fifties and Sixties, the sheer success of IBM in selling to the corporate market bred still more success, still more dominating market power.

The capitalist model gave the prize of market dominance to those who best used the powers of technology, distribution and marketing. As these powers were strengthened and applied, so lesser competitors were increasingly unable to exercise their prime economic function – to provide a viable alternative, profitable both to the customers and to themselves. As Damon Runyon wrote, 'The race isn't always to the swift, nor the victory to the strong. But that's the way to bet it.'

The Justice Department tried to change the odds, to argue that capitalist success could be too extreme, that society, via the Government, could and should intervene to cut the branches of the tallest tree – if its shadow stunted the growth of others. Control Data, as one of the others, had seemed to challenge IBM with its special abilities in larger computers. It, too, had felt the crushing weight of IBM's market power. Hence its private suit, superseded by the Federal filing.

For thirteen years the lawsuit, and the threat of break-up which it embodied, preoccupied the top management of IBM – and for good reason. The suit threatened to destroy, not only the IBM system, but the philosophy behind the structure. IBM offered corporate customers spread across a multitude of industries a platform for safe one-stop shopping. It took the inherently kaleidoscopic technology of electronic data processing and shook it into a pattern that formed one unchanging configuration: IBM.

The turmoil in all markets from 1969 onwards, including oil price shocks and the surge of Japan, did nothing to disturb the dominance of IBM. It ended the Eighties with sales of $63.4 billion, which topped the next five computer and office equipment companies (three Americans and two Japanese) put together. The fifth largest industrial company in the entire world earned profits, at $3.8 billion, which easily exceeded those of all seventeen of the major global contenders in its market – five of which made losses that year.

The anti-trust action had been chuntering away throughout this period. If it aimed at undermining IBM's philosophy and structure, these numbers bear witness to its failure. Yet over the thirteen years of legal confrontation, a very different age took shape. It bore no resemblance to the era in which the Watsons developed their colossus – though anti-monopoly suits marked both periods. The IBM found (in effect) not guilty of restraining trade and maintaining a monopoly in 1982 owes its origins to a very different verdict on the same charges on 13 February 1913.

Thomas J. Watson was among thirty defendants, led by National Cash Register's founder, John H. Patterson, who were tried on criminal charges in Cincinnatti. The verdict was, 'We the jury find the defendants guilty in the manner and form as charged in each of the three counts.' Maximum sentences were passed on Patterson, Watson and his assistant – a year in the Miami County Jail and a $5,000 fine apiece. The sentencing judge said that, 'In your desire for gain you forgot everything else . . .'

What Watson, NCR's outstanding salesman, had done was to run, on Patterson's behalf, a covert company. It had ruthlessly cleaned out everybody else in the used cash register market. The object was to underpin the monopoly of 'The Cash' over new register sales. A few months after the sentences (which were never served), Patterson fired his henchman – and unwittingly launched a company that was to outstrip NCR by far in power and wealth. The sacked Watson was picked up by Charles Ranlett Flink, the man whose Computing-Tabulating-Recording Company held the keys to a new kingdom.

The keys were the patents which Herman Hollerith owned on his electromechanical tabulating machine: the famous punch card system. Under Watson's sales-led drive, this little-regarded tail of C-T-R's began to wag the whole dog – sales doubled and earnings tripled between 1914 and 1917. Watson nurtured his salesmen. They had large sales commissions, quota clubs and exclusive territories. These principles of a sales-led culture, all lessons learnt from NCR, remained the bedrock of IBM right into the Nineties.

But just as important (in some respects more so) was the strategy of financing a rental-only policy by huge profits on sales of the blank cards. Watson's advance was unstoppable. He won total control of the company; he expanded abroad through sales of rights; he adopted the name International Business Machines (in 1924); he collected some stupendous pay packets. In 1934 his 5 per cent share of profits brought in $364,432 – more than any other executive in America. It was a higher salary, even without allowing for inflation, than many CEOs earned in the greedy Eighties.

In 1932, though, the trustbusters struck their first blow at IBM – and seemed to win. With 85.7 per cent of all the tabulating-accounting machines in the US, 86.1 per cent of sorting machines, and 81.6 per cent of key punches, Watson sewed up the market by his monopoly of the supply of three billion blank cards a year. In 1936, the trustbusters forced IBM to mend its ways; but sixteen years later, when the Justice Department returned to the attack, it found little changed.

IBM's hold over punch card equipment was barely scratched, and its cards still accounted for the bulk of sales to IBM users. In 1956, a consent decree forced IBM to offer machines for sale as well as rental, and to cut its share of card sales to half by 1963. It was a Pyrrhic victory for the trustbusters. The market was moving to electronic computers with overwhelming momentum – and the great majority of customers preferred to lease rather than buy.

The profits poured in, underpinning not only IBM's products, but also its tactics. Watson was as determined as NCR's Patterson to exclude competition from his green pastures. But the IBM version was less crude, less obvious. The company's propriety, the code of conduct enforced on all salesmen, and the high corporate standards that IBM publicly professed, were far more conspicuous than its unchanged commercial ethos. That could be summed up as follows: bend when possible, and avoid overly strong-arming the competition, but under no circumstances lose dominance. When push comes to shove, when competition threatens your dominance, take off the gloves and use all available means to knock out the attackers. If that involves potential conflict with the anti-trust laws, remember their complex ambiguity and fight with all your might and main and money.

This policy didn't die with old Tom Watson. His principles survived, even though his personal style had to perish. As his son described the system, 'The company was run essentially by one man, my father. If IBM had had an organisation chart at that time, there would have been a fascinating number of lines – perhaps thirty – running into his office.'

Inevitably that meant a queue of people waiting outside the door, 'sometimes for as long as a week or two . . . He saw the important ones, of course, but when I complained about people wasting time in his anteroom, he said, "Oh Tom, let them wait. They're well paid." ' The old man was equally implacable towards the trustbusters: 'I had the damnedest time getting him convinced that it was better to sign the consent degree [in 1956] than to take the thing to court . . .'

The smooth management machine that replaced one-man rule was young Tom's creation. But under the younger Watson, IBM remained embroiled in litigation of all kinds, quite apart from the Federal anti-trust case. The founding Watson would have been delighted with its outcome. The struggle didn't end, as in 1956, with a hated consent decree, but with total victory for the dominant design.

The dominance theory was expounded explicitly by Tom Watson Jr. 'It was our job to make sure that for the well-placed rivals like GE and RCA, the computer marketplace seemed too risky a bet.' He had an arresting phrase for this they-shall-not-pass mentality: 'Making ourselves tremendously sensitive to toeholds.' That meant stamping on intruding toes with heavy boots – and stamping on any salesman who broke the ultimate commandment. It ran thus: Thou shalt always alert management if an account is in jeopardy. Failure to do so, followed by loss of the account, would see the salesman being 'subjected to discipline'. The record shows how successful the dominance theory was in practice. The two 'well-financed rivals' mentioned by Watson, RCA and GE, both quit the marketplace after combined losses of nearly a billion dollars – a far greater sum in 1993 money.

Several others were compelled to surrender by closure or merger, such as Xerox and Honeywell. At the end of the Eighties, Sperry Univac and Burroughs joined forces to form Unisys, while NCR capitulated to a bid from AT&T in 1991. In Europe, Philips, Bull, Siemens, English Electric and Ferranti were among the large companies which struggled unequally against the champion. Interestingly, much smaller and less 'well-financed' competitors – Control Data Corporation, Cray and Amdahl – stayed in business longer (though shakily in CDC's case). But mainframes, by and large, always brought game, set and match to IBM.

A certain schizophrenia was apparent, though, in the split between the dominance theory and IBM's protestations of fair play – as witnessed by the standard of ethics that Tom Watson Jr circulated in 1961. By his own confession, he was 'desperate about this matter because we had a great business. We had no reason to monopolise, no reason to be predatory in our actions. It would have been stupid'.

His employees were enjoined to put themselves in the shoes of a vulnerable competitor – 'small, precariously financed, without a large support organisation, and without a big reputation in the field' – and to shun any sales action which, wearing those small and painful shoes, they would resent. 'Would you regard the IBM company as taking unfair advantage of you? . . . We simply cannot shoulder people around or give the appearance of doing so.'

Watson and his successors at IBM naturally laid stress on the 1982 withdrawal of the anti-trust suit as final, total vindication. The iron fist had been kept decently clothed in an ethical, velvet glove. If that were so, however, why did IBM settle so expensively with Control Data, whose civil anti-trust suit precipitated the Justice Department action? Why did it pay a 'small fortune' for the index file prepared by CDC's lawyers? To IBM's battered competitors, the answers were all too obvious.

How much of that history survived into the Nineties? IBM's dominance of the mainframe market is an established, incontrovertible fact. But mainframes are a rapidly diminishing part of the total market for computer hardware and software – demand for larger machines is sluggish and they are subject to intense price pressures. Among the first acts of the Gerstner regime (breaking an ancient tradition of dominance) was to reduce the excessive prices of the accompanying software, to make the mainframe package more competitive.

The issue of dominance, fair or foul, no longer matters. The legacy of the mainframe rout remains, however. It confirmed the image, held internally as strongly as externally, of IBM as supreme exemplar of a dominant genus: the high-tech leader which uses unbeatably large investment in its products and processes to compound the impact of equally powerful investment in its marketing.

That image, true or false, has become as irrelevant as IBM's policies in the mainframe market. The dominant design can't cover all the multiplying ramifications of the end-century market. IBM's world is no longer founded on installed bases of expensively acquired office machinery and software. Corner the large corporate market, as IBM did, and you once cornered the industry. But an industry of many markets and many technologies defies the dominance theory.

Or does it? That shrewd observer, William F. Zachmann, writing in *PC Magazine* in 1990, headed his column 'The IBMpire Strikes Back'. He warned readers that it might seem to be a 'bizarre paranoid fantasy': the scenario he painted 'couldn't really happen. Could it?' He wondered what would occur if 'instead of a nice, kind gentle man like John Akers,

some really mean guy, some power-mad evil manipulator –
like me, for instance – took over at IBM. What might I do in
my most sinister campaign to rule the world . . .?'

The demon would aim to establish 'Design of Dominance
(DoD)'. He would loathe and despise the IBM leaders
('Fools!') who, instead of 'ruthlessly acting to stamp out standards (and competition)', had fallen between two stools. That
meant trying to live with open standards (so that they competed on level terms with other PC makers) while also trying
to bring back the proprietary, inimitable systems which had
created IBM's early mainframe success.

The latter was 'a far more sensible effort', which the demon
proposed to reinforce heavily. 'Of course, given the weaknesses
of my predecessors . . . I'll have to pretend, superficially, to follow their sorry, insipid ways for a time. But that will only be a
cover until I can really get the DoD rolling.' The diabolical
plan was to tie up big customers for bigger machines with proprietary software that worked only with IBM PCs.

In addition, 'all sorts of exciting-sounding future enhance-
ments' of IBM's proprietary offerings would be dangled
before buyers' eyes to 'make it seem like anybody who buys
into what any other vendor is offering will be missing some
great things in the future'. That future would include 'fantastic multi-media technologies. Technologies they just won't be
able to live without' . . . and 'probably won't be able to get'
unless they buy IBM ('Heh, heh!').

The software strategy would be complemented on the hardware side. 'All sorts of proprietary' devices would be produced
under 'newly issued IBM patents that give me absolute control
over whether anybody else can build it at all . . .' With all this
devilry in place, this proto-IBM would still have the problem of
ensnaring those customers who weren't captive by habit. So
you make IBM proprietary equipment compatible with 'all
that disgustingly standardised stuff they're using now'.

However reluctantly, buyers would be tempted to upgrade
'by offering initially aggressive price/performance points'.

Then they could be lured into using IBM's proprietary extensions. 'Once they do that, they can't turn back.' As for competitors, 'my standing army of intellectual property attorneys' would ensure that, beset by lawsuits, the rivals would be forced into 'paying protection money in the form of higher royalties and restrictive agreements'. That could be supplemented 'by simply buying all or part of those companies that can either be useful to me or that are potentially serious competitors'.

As for anti-trust problems, the demon would cover himself with Congress and the Administration – 'the usual, uh, support for potential winners in both parties would help here'. Washington and public opinion had to be convinced that 'American competitiveness will be severely damaged by not giving me what I want. I can just wrap myself in the flag and make it look like what's good for IBM is what's good for America.'

All great parody is close to the truth. Zachmann's fantasy was based on real-life announcements and policies from IBM. Events since he wrote have often shown an uncanny similarity to his fantasy. The devil's strategy, moreover, related closely to the complaints made by the trustbusters and IBM's competitors over the decades since Tom Watson seized control of C-T-R. The 'IBMpire' was indeed trying to strike back and to restore in the new world the proprietary dominance that had created its prosperity in the old.

But by mid-1993 the years of ineffective performance had weakened one of the underpinnings of Zachmann's real-life fantasy. 'I've got enough cash to buy most of the industry!' crowed his arch-fiend. At the end of 1991, true, IBM's hoard of cash and cash equivalents was $4 billion, barely changed from the year before. However, its long-term and short-term debt, $27 billion, was equal to a thumping 73 per cent of stockholders' equity. The company was still sound financially – but its own market capitalisation was easily outweighed by the combined figures for its main domestic competitors.

Throw in the heavy weight of the Japanese, and IBM begins to look quite modest. In 1991, IBM accounted for 31 per cent of the sales of the world's fifteen largest computer and office products companies. The figure is impressive, but exaggerated: it doesn't take into account the billions of sales included in conglomerates like Hitachi, Siemens and AT&T (including NCR) – and that's only three.

Even on the narrow definition, the 31 per cent represents a sharp fall from the 39 per cent equivalent share that IBM enjoyed two years previously. No great market leader, no star of such brightness in the corporate firmament, has ever suffered so abrupt a retreat. The old dominant design is dead and buried. It will never dominate again.

9

Innovation Inertia:
The Heel of Achilles

Those contemplating the invincibility and invulnerability of the Watson legacy – including IBM's own people – must have been impressed most of all by two mighty bulwarks: its wealth and its technology. The two are interdependent since nobody else could afford to 'buy' so much technology as IBM.

Its research and development spending in the Nineties, at least $6.6 billion a year, topped the turnover of most of its rivals. But current R&D is only the tip of an iceberg, built by years of expenditure on a similar scale, and made up of an imposing series of powerful patents and pathfinding discoveries. The catalogue far exceeds, in length and breadth, the rosters of any rival in electronics.

Electronics, rather than computers, is IBM's proper habitat. The corporation is among the largest makers of semiconductors, peripherals, modems, software and much else. Its spread of products and technology alike is unmatched. The great numbers, in dollars of spending and masses of patents and products, have fostered a grand illusion. For technology proved to be the Achilles' heel.

The illusion surfaced in the troubles of the Eighties (which it partly explained). Many wise and informed critics praised IBM's endeavours to turn a technology-led company into one more responsive to the market. One Japanese analyst struck the conventional, misled and misleading note late in the decade: 'IBM still has a strong technological drive,' he wrote, 'but they often fail to transfer that technology into competitive products.'

That stood truth neatly on its head. IBM is probably the outstanding example of the market-led species. And, despite its protestations, IBM has often lagged behind the technological pace. Over the Eighties, IBM's time-lags in technology, never a serious marketplace impediment before, barred entry into product sectors where presence was essential; or else doomed IBM to loss of market share.

The old competitors, the 'Seven Dwarfs' of the mainframe era, were prone to the erroneous belief that moving ahead of IBM in technology would win the marketing battle. That didn't work at a time when IBM's product range was perfectly adequate, and its sales and service perfectly reassuring. In the post-mainframe world, however, you either had the technology and will to make timely laptops and palmtops, for example, or you were out of the portable game.

Worse still, getting to Square One wasn't enough. Falling behind in innovation, as computer weights went down and speed and power up, spelt certain defeat in a market where technology truly could tip the balance. Nevertheless, IBM's cupboard surely bulged with the accumulated brilliance of the most accomplished scientists and engineers money could buy, supplied with magnificent equipment, installed in superb laboratories.

No lab is more imposing than La Gaude, occupying a spectacular site on the French Riviera. I went there over twenty years ago and two memories remain from my visit. One was of a printer remorselessly and endlessly grinding out details of specification changes to the 360 range – of no use or interest to the people at La Gaude. What did this tell about the IBM system, and the dominance of procedure over need?

The second memory was of work on voice synthesis –

fascinating and clearly important. Computers before the PC were incommunicado to those (like me) who didn't understand their language. Even in the early Nineties, communication in the IBM world remained stilted and coded. If you could speak to a computer in English and get a reply (the La Gaude machine gave me a commodity price) in the same tongue, the Gordian knot could be sliced through.

Two decades on, IBM had no product using voice synthesis. None of the advances in this technology (considerable and nearing fruition) come from IBM's labs. That shouldn't surprise anybody – there's no positive correlation between what you spend and what you get. Worse, some negative correlation may exist. In 1992, remember, Du Pont's chairman complained that $13 billion of spending had given his company virtually nothing in the way of new products – let alone major breakthroughs.

The deep pools of available finance encourage the pursuit of Big Bangs, the new nylons or polythenes, which are rare by definition. Each programme develops its own momentum, which rolls expensively onwards, sometimes long after the point of no return. Then, the direction of R&D may be badly chosen. The truly outstanding work that created the personal computer was done at Xerox Corporation's Palo Alto Research Center, not at IBM.

Finally, the value of the R&D achievement may not be recognised by management. Xerox never launched any product using PARC's discoveries, let alone a complete PC, until far too late in the day. All the same, how can you spend over $6 billion a year without any benefit? Of course, that's impossible. But is IBM really spending $120 million a week on research and development? Has it ever spent the amounts claimed on this transfusion into the corporate bloodstream?

The definition of R&D depends on who does the defining, and why. If it's a line manager wanting to get expenditure off his operating budget (on which he is judged), the definition can be quite broad. If it's the CEO, boasting of the company's vitality and far-sighted investment in the future, he isn't going to quibble about classification, either. A vast amount of the spend, anyway, doesn't go on stretching the company's frontiers, but on filling in existing territory. In the early Eighties, for instance, the product development laboratory at Hursley (one of eighteen then dotted around the world) was hard at work on colour terminals. The product was an essential add-on to the mainframe and minicomputer business. Its realisation took two years as Phase Zero (the initial proposal) led through Phase One (prototype) to Phase Two (when the 'manufacturability' became all-important and spending grew very substantial), until finally Phase Three (announcement) was achieved.

All over the IBM world similar work is chewing up dollars, pounds, francs and yen and spawning announcements of 'new' products – at impressive frequencies like one a day. But how new is new? Lecturer and consultant Efrem Mallach has paid deserved tribute to IBM's outstanding achievements in basic research: in superconducting, thin film mass storage technology, high density semiconductor memory disks, half-inch magnetic tape recording and optimising compilers. 'Ask IBM about its technology and you will get a long list of milestones plus an armful of literature. It has earned its bragging rights.' On the other side of the ledger, though, is an embarrassingly long list of debits. One is fundamental: 'Since the 1950s, IBM technology has been devoted to producing incremental improvements in the ways things are already being done.'

Take large mass storage devices – superior in capacity and performance, and lower in cost (which needn't mean lower in price) than anybody else's. The technology advances in two-year hops as competitors catch up and IBM again bounds clear. But are faster, less expensive disk drives a conceptual change in the way companies use information?

When it comes to the Big Bang concepts, Mallach lists six: word processing, networking, Unix, virtual memory, data base management, and multiprocessor mainframes. Respectively,

IBM was 'several years later than Wang'; reacting weakly (with Systems Network Architecture) 'to what had been going on in Europe for years'; 'being dragged [into Unix] . . . kicking and screaming'; in virtual memory, following behind a British development proved out by GE and MIT; and again following GE in database management. Finally, in multiprocessor mainframes 'almost every other vendor had one' before IBM.

In this indictment, IBM even has failures equivalent to that of Xerox with the personal computer. Relational database management systems sprang from theoretical work at IBM which 'didn't realise what it had'. In 1987 it was 'still years behind Oracle Corporation and a host of others.' As for the personal computer itself, the industry breakthrough unquestionably came from IBM's incursion – but with technology 'from Intel Corporation, Microsoft Corporation and a host of other suppliers . . . But IBM technology? Not in the PC.'

There's a convincing explanation for IBM's technological conservatism. Those who dominate an industry invariably opt for the status quo. That's simple business economics. Any change threatens to destabilise their hold over markets, and to reduce or terminate the pay-off from their past investments. The incumbent vendor can expect to keep the business and keep it profitable, 'so long as users keep doing things the same way'. But what happens if they don't?

A flood of innovations turned rivulets of change into the rushing tide of IBM's industry. The same tide didn't sweep through IBM's own business. Many accounts of the company fail to grasp this reality. Like King Canute's courtiers, the élite of Armonk sought to resist the flood. Those who believe that IBM was the most efficient, best-managed company in the world until the mid-Eighties must logically accept that its troubles arose because the industry changed, and IBM was slow to react: so it was. But the retarded reaction was a deliberate part of the management process. IBM's economic system was deeply invested in the status quo. The original Thomas Watson Sr, the unscrupulous genius, sentenced to jail for monopolistic practices while working at NCR, perfected a subtler customer-control system at IBM. His thrust was to convince IBM employees, customers and competitors that IBM was best. At IBM, as at NCR, he preferred not to defeat head-on competition, but to eliminate it entirely.

The consequence, for technological policy, was to concentrate on maintaining inviolable proprietary systems (any hardware or software you like, so long as it's IBM); and on keeping a cost advantage – in design, manufacture and maintenance – so great that rivals could never compete, save at IBM's prices. The defect in this strategy only appeared when the technological pace became feverish and forced IBM into expensive, often unsuccessful, games of catch-up.

Take the Systems Network Architecture mentioned above. Despite its late start in 'networking', the technology of linking computers together, IBM exploited its fabulous base of installed machines to the usual overwhelming effect. In 1992, according to Business Research Group, over three-fifths of America's largest companies were primary users of SNA. With more than 50,000 data networks based on the architecture (to quote IBM figures), US business depended on this technology – but in 1992 it had aged.

The problem that dogged SNA bedevilled the whole of IBM: the mainframe mentality. SNA was invented to handle mainframes and the unintelligent terminals through which the users addressed the all-powerful machine. But the future (and increasingly the present) of information technology lies in linking new kinds of terminals – personal computers. These highly intelligent beings are joined together in local area networks (LANs) that may not connect to a mainframe at all.

IBM's delay in entering the PC market was later followed by a lag in competing in LANs; and that was compounded in turn by another delay – in joining the market for systems that linked local area networks. Once again, the small fish were nibbling away at IBM's feet – obscure companies like Cisco Systems, Wellfleet and Cabletron Systems. Once again, IBM's reaction was not to introduce a product but to announce one.

In 1993, new Advanced Peer-to-Peer Networking software would 'make mainframes work as equals with other network devices' – even PCs, making it far easier for PCs to get at mainframe data. A first-rate, new network processor would 'connect different brands of local area networks'. Meanwhile, back at the labs . . . the scientists were working on Planet, aiming at switching 300,000 pages of information a second, against a mere 2,000 for the fastest route on the market in 1992.

With such speeds, IBM would be able to manage the fast-coming high-quality video and graphics that networks will use. But here's the snag. SNA is too slow to exploit Planet's proposed speeds. Speed is crucial in two senses. First, without a faster architecture the whole project collapses; second, without getting the necessary products out fast enough, IBM could fail even if the project is technologically successful.

An almost unthinkably long leap forward is in train. Data that in 1957 moved at 750 bits per second, in 1974 at 9,600 bits, in 1985 at 4 million bits and in 1990 at 100 million bits will, in the new century, be up to gigabit speeds. That's 10 *billion* bits per second, a speed that will be able to cope with three-dimensional moving images.

The people working on 'high performance computing and communications at IBM's multi-media unit' in Hawthorne, NY, told *Business Week* how much they wanted to 'make sure that technologies that we understand better than anybody else get used in the marketplace'. Out there in the market, however, the customers had heard that one before. The remark of one user resonates: 'Are they really going to be able to deliver a usable product?' A Litton man, this customer had no doubt that the peer-to-peer announcement was 'a freeze tactic to get you to not make a decision'. His attitude is understandable given IBM's history. Indeed, 'freeze tactics' were the foundation of the Control Data anti-trust suit that, leading on to the Federal case, dominated IBM's history for a decade and more.

By announcing new products (like supercomputers) which never saw the light of commercial day, IBM inevitably encouraged customers to hold back from rivals whose offerings already existed. The Watson strategy, after all, had convinced the clients that IBM was always best – and, anyway, most were locked into costly IBM systems. But what had worked brilliantly in the Sixties and Seventies no longer applied in the Eighties, and still less the Nineties. IBM has lost its proprietary grip on the market; nor can it any longer trust big users like Litton to wait for Godot. Articles about IBM's technology in the Eighties and Nineties habitually ended like the *Business Week* piece: 'The trick is persuading customers to wait while the wheel spins.'

In markets where IBM was absent, though, patience was readily exhausted. Reporters might ask for years, 'if IBM is such a good company, why can't it build a decent laptop?' Customers wouldn't waste even a minute on the question or its answer: they would be too busy buying, and using, Toshibas and Compaqs, etc.

Without any question, the top management of IBM simply missed the potential of laptops, a mistake even less easy to explain than the original lag in PCs. After all, a laptop is simply a smaller, lighter, more convenient PC. The mistake showed extraordinary myopia – and arrogance – for a market-leader. As with the original PCs, a crash programme was mandatory to crash the market. Once again, IBM had to short-circuit its established ways of doing business – a process that casts light on IBM's defects as much as its virtues.

As the *Wall Street Journal* reported, 'to get the product right IBM had to shake up its organisation and take some risks'. That meant, for the most part, managing in the intelligent, time-compressing ways (see items 3 to 8 below) that were commonplace in Japan – and in alert Western firms:

1 Relying overwhelmingly on proven technology.

2   Designing and assembling the machines, save for some of the chips, from components supplied by other firms.

3   Abandoning the traditional insistence that every detail of the specification be worked out and agreed before production began.

4   Bringing in some manufacturing and marketing people at the start of development.

5   Speeding up negotiations with outside suppliers.

6   Using a very small team – a mere nineteen people in Boca Raton, Florida, worked on the laptop.

7   Refusing to allow changes to specification once set.

8   Listening to customers when designing the product.

Despite component setbacks that delayed the product announcement from October 1990 to late March 1991, the laptop took only fourteen months to develop, compared to a typical IBM gestation period of two to three years. But was this a one-off? Or had IBM permanently changed its ways? After all, the original PC development, on the same Florida site, had only taken a year, had also broken IBM shibboleths (including the non-use of outside suppliers), and had also been created by a tiny team: the 'Dirty Dozen' creators of the PC had passed into IBM mythology.

But the PC episode remained a profound exception to rigid product development rules. According to the *Journal*, these involved groups of 190 people – ten times the size of the laptop venturers. In consequence, 'too many people made too many decisions too many times.' IBM had perfected a system that was geared to eliminating risk in developing existing products or their variants. The product manager put in charge of a 'mission' would spend the first year on developing the innovation – and this developer-in-chief would come from a marketing, not a technological background. His project would have to pass six-monthly 'phase reviews' by presenting a market forecast at three different prices, a cost estimate (for three different plants in the US, UK and Asia) and three assumed quantity levels. Participants were encouraged to 'non-concur', to object. Not only did ironing out disagreements take many meetings and much time, but non-concurrence contributed to a high mortality rate.

Only one out of three or four products survived to face the ultimate go/no-go decision, ideally a year after the start. At this point slaughter was rare, and the manufacturing people were at last added to the team. In theory, a product was announced to the market a year later. In practice, all manner of slippages were possible – including later alterations to products, causing lengthy last-minute delays. With its products introduced simultaneously across the world, IBM didn't dare to take risks – certainly none as hairy as the hard disk decision on the laptop. If this high-capacity 2½ inch drive had failed the whole system would have required redesign – and it was the last component to work.

The question remained whether IBM could mobilise its inventive power continuously, not merely in crash programmes. 'In terms of raw ability to innovate, IBM can keep up with anyone', said Andy Heller, a disenchanted IBM research fellow, and a key figure in developing its workstation. 'Fellows' like Heller were a creation of Thomas Watson Sr. Their 'primary task', as described by Robert Sobel, 'was the consideration of new ideas'. He noted that, 'Their concepts needn't have been practical or even realistic, but IBM hoped they might serve to stimulate thought . . . spark imaginative forays . . . and in general keep the company aware of new possibilities in all fields touching upon its business'.

That 'blue sky' approach no doubt sprang from the elder Watson's early struggles to pull ahead of his rival in the technical proficiency of punch card machines. Even the best salesmen, he realised, couldn't sell inferior merchandise – not for long, anyway. On top of this central perception, in his later years, as a 'captain of industry', Watson took real pride in associating with scientific advance and advanced scientists.

The pride paid off with the catch-up in computers, and the apotheosis came with the 360 series – the 'third generation' computers. The 360s completed the IBM legend. To this day they represent the largest single investment ever made in electronic data processing – costing more than twice as much as the Manhattan Project which created the A-bomb. The 360s also marked the last time IBM seized technological leadership or, in any positive sense, gambled with the company's future.

For IBM, the product line and its smashing success set in motion a chain of unforeseen events that were eventually to have a more profound effect on the company's fortunes than the 360 computers. The effects on innovation itself were long-lasting. Sobel writes that, as 'the directions of innovation' paradoxically became 'commonplace' outsiders might have thought that 'a variety of corporate sclerosis of the imagination' had set in. He goes on, 'Some who recognised this early attributed it to the letdown after the 360 introduction, an understandable pause after so major an effort.' As in other industries entering their maturity, after 'the initial rash of invention and originality . . . the companies started to suffer from signs of gigantism, and a stiff formalism began to envelop the organisation'. This accurately describes what happened to IBM, but the analysis of the computer industry completely missed the truth.

Far from becoming mature and technologically sedate, it was heading for a new explosion of entrepreneurial pioneering that made the earlier history of the computer look almost pedestrian. As late as 1981, when Sobel published his book, *IBM: Colossus in Transition*, the staggering extent of that revolution wasn't apparent – certainly not to IBM.

The 'gigantism' and 'formalism' that developed in the wake

of the 360 inhibited IBM's reactions in laboratories and executive suites alike. Even within the 360 itself, the seeds of conservatism were sown. Instead of going bald-headed for the new integrated circuitry, IBM understandably (given the horrendous financial risks of the project) stuck at so-called hybrid circuits - against the vehement opposition of the brilliant designer, Gene Amdahl, who later departed to become IBM's first consistently successful mainframe competitor.

The hybrids were a technological dead-end, the first of many pulled punches which were to lead to endless defeats by the all-out sluggers of the new technology. More and more, IBM came to fit Mallach's description, 'doing the same old things a little bit better, a little bit faster and a little less expensively'. In an era when the 'big pay-off calls for systems that deal with information in new and innovative ways,' he concluded, 'the technology isn't likely to come from IBM.'

The fault thus lay, not with the maturity and relative stagnation of the industry, but with IBM's. It liked, for public relations purposes, to present 'the very picture of a colossus in a chronic state of siege,' wrote Sobel, when its competition was truly 'so limited in power and resources' that the 'enemy was fictitious, a mirror image of IBM itself'. Sobel meant this to be comforting ('there is only one IBM'). It was no comfort. For IBM had become its own worst enemy.

IV

SILICON VALLEY STEALS THE SHOW

10

The Boom
of the Breakaways

The most famous man to emerge from IBM, next to the first Tom Watson, never climbed above salesman. H. Ross Perot, the future Presidential gadfly and billionaire, became much richer than the Watsons by seeing and seizing a business opportunity which IBM let pass. Perot was superbly successful at selling IBM computers. He observed, however, that the customers, ostensibly sold solutions, actually purchased problems.

In the mainframe era, making best use of your expensive new computer, or even making an effective return on the investment, plagued users. Perot's idea was to open a new stream of income by developing workable systems that could run on the IBM computers. When the company showed no interest in his concept, Perot left and started up Electronic Data Systems. He could easily afford the move, thanks to another failure of the corporation.

Once, Thomas Watson Jr had made his bones by meeting his entire selling quota for the year on its very first day. Admittedly, he had Wall Street for his territory, where being his father's son was helped mightily. And admittedly, the record was achieved 'when US Steel Products, an account that had been thrown into my territory to make me look good, came across with a huge order'. But nobody stopped Watson from carrying on with the good work.

Not so with Ross Perot. Without any special favours, he hit his annual quota in the year's first month, and promptly ran into a road block. The bureaucracy had decreed that nobody could earn more than the chairman – then Tom Watson Jr. With his stunning performance in the Dallas territory, Perot had reached the ceiling on his earnings for the year. He had every incentive to quit – and none whatsoever to stay.

In his new career, Perot showed more nous than the elder Tom Watson in another matter – equity ownership. The great founder never held more than 5 per cent of the IBM equity (which would have been worth $2.5 billion, even in IBM's already reduced circumstances of mid-1992). Perot, however, clung to four-fifths of EDS. Many other individuals in the industry that the Watsons lorded over for decades made more millions than the founding family. IBM dominated the highways. But the fast-breeding byways of computing continued to hold out the prospect of equally fast capital gains.

As the century draws to its close, that same lure – the vision of capitalism richly triumphant – is still one of the strongest cards in America's technological hand. Allied with a restless search for achievement, the lure has generated an unprecedented and uniquely productive migration of people between companies. What, for example, do the following firms have in common, apart from some whizzing and wonderful names? Tangram, Digital Equipment, GRiD Systems Corporation, Adobe Systems, Cauzin Systems, Apple, Metaphor Computer Systems, 3-Com Corporation, Acorn Computer, Data Point Corporation and Microsoft.

All are evidently in the information technology game. But that's not the significant connection. These companies are the 1988 business residences, according to a superb book called *Fumbling the Future*, of men who created the personal computer inside the Xerox Corporation. Most of this incomparable team left after their employer thumbed down their wonderful invention – maybe the most wonderful of a won-drous century.

In several cases, these technological aces co-founded their new companies. These creations had unnumbered contem-poraries of similar origin: breakaways led by brilliant people seeking to exploit their brilliance under their own control. As Irwin Federman, semiconductor boss turned venture capital-ist, expressed the phenomenon, 'Silicon Valley is a technology crucible. Every engineer in the valley has at the back of his mind that if he comes up with an interesting product, he can start a company.'

Federman was quoted in the *Financial Times* in an article, by Geoffrey Owen and Louise Kehoe, which observed that 'the hyper-competitive atmosphere of Silicon Valley, with its *adap-table giants* [my italics], cheeky spin-offs and ambitious start-ups, is an American asset which no other country has yet been able to match'.

The 'adaptable giants' are companies like Hewlett-Packard, which has shown a rare capacity for renewal and recovery, and Apple Corp, whose versatility enabled it to survive potentially fatal technological isolation. It was Steve Jobs of Apple who saw the astounding results of the personal computer work done for Xerox at the Palo Alto Research Centre, picked up the ball that Xerox fumbled, and ran with it – producing the Macintosh computer and inadvertently setting the stage for Windows, the best-selling Microsoft program.

By absolutely no coincidence, three of the Xerox emigrés ended up with Apple. They include perhaps the most original genius of the bunch, Alan Kay – the man who once uttered an immortal line: 'The only way to predict the future is to invent it.' Another distinguished trio of inventors of the future moved to Digital Equipment: Butler Lampson, Bob Taylor and Chuck Thacker – recognised by the industry as the great pioneers of 'distributed processing', in which linked computers are located throughout the organisation.

Nobody on the list, though, joined IBM. The insularity of

the industry leader seems to have extended to its recruitment of top technologists and managers. Others have poached liberally from the giant. Compaq was founded by three breakaways from Texas Instruments, but crucial roles in its success were played by IBM refugees. Even more conspicuous was the breakaway of Gene Amdahl, whose large mainframes, given Fujitsu's major stake in Amdahl's success, could be described as Japan's Trojan horses.

The IBM of the early Nineties tried to cover every technological bet, like a roulette player covering every number. This boosted the breakaway movement doubly, if not trebly. The giant's cutbacks in personnel encouraged thousands of able IBMers to invest their financial pay-offs in start-ups, or to join former spin-offs. At the same time, many lesser firms were backed by IBM funds. The largesse extended not only to software houses, whose *quid pro quo* was to write programs for IBM's OS/2 operating system, but hardware developers as well.

The most conspicuous example, the brilliant designer Steve Chen, received $100 million to help develop the world-beating supercomputer that had always eluded IBM's internal researchers. Chen was a breakaway from Cray Research, whose founder, Seymour Cray, was a breakaway from Control Data Corporation. IBM's choice of Chen ultimately proved unfortunate. His funds were cut off in the last, tortured, financially stretched days of the Akers regime.

Chen had been an important exception to the rule. The steady outflow of intellectual blood from IBM should have been counteracted by a recruitment campaign. It couldn't, of course, have matched Xerox's serendipitous assembly of Alan Kay and other talents whose work underpinned all future PC development. Xerox was starting a new lab in a research field where neither it nor any other company had a presence. IBM had an enormous scientific and technological establishment, which was mostly geared to its own mainframe-driven needs, rather than invention of brave new worlds.

The nature of the stunning solutions devised at the Palo Alto Research Center meant that when the PC moment came, after a four-year time-lag, IBM could make a machine without any recourse to its own labs. Engineers could design and assemble a world-class product from commercially available components. But PARC also generated two powerful threats to IBM. First, the Macintosh concept – the mouse-driven computer with the graphical user interface (GUI), which Apple's Steve Jobs picked up from PARC – eventually undermined IBM's 'industry standard'. The easy-to-use Windows, a product complete with GUI, extended and consolidated Microsoft's leadership of the software business.

Second, the experts in distributed processing who went to Digital from PARC helped to rupture IBM's business-user quasi-monopoly. The VAX line of computers, with their ability to intercommunicate fully and freely, cracked a problem with which IBM was still wrestling in the early Nineties. It's a much-repeated lesson of technology, ignored at dire peril. The highest pitch of technology doesn't necessarily make the largest sales, but unless the market leader holds the commanding heights of technology, its leadership is in danger.

The brightest hope for the US industry as a whole, therefore, lies in the belief that worldwide electronic leadership is safely based at home; that 'Silicon Valley' is a unique resource, a fount of technology and enterprise, with a 'rich infrastructure of electronics engineers, subcontractors, venture capitalists, public relations advisers, headhunters and lawyers'. It is a place where you can generate new ventures at the lifting of a receiver – 'I could start a semiconductor company on the telephone from my home,' as Wilf Corrigan told the *FT*.

The latter, chairman of semiconductor company LSI Logic, is another epitome of the breakaway boom. Both he and Andrew Grove, chairman of microprocessor kings Intel, were once employed by Fairchild Camera. The eponymous Fairchild, Sherman M., was by coincidence the inheritor of a large line of IBM stock. A playboy investor, he financed the breakaway of Robert Noyce and his colleagues from Shockley Laboratories (founded in turn by William Shockley, who invented the transistor at Bell Laboratories).

Fairchild reaped monster profits from the Noyce group, which broke away to form Intel after the managerial gyrations of the parent proved unbearable. The new start-up changed the world, not just Silicon Valley, with the invention of the microprocessor. But Intel's own impetus has been maintained by more than its own inventiveness; that of the competition is a continual threat, spur and goad.

Advanced Micro Devices, led by another breakaway from Fairchild, Jerry Sanders, has landed in court tangles with Intel thanks to his company's successful efforts to clone the larger company's chips. Sanders himself has suffered from the breakaway phenomenon – some of his best designers walked out in the mid-1980s. Their company, Cypress Semiconductor, has become yet another force in the Valley. The deserted Sanders thought in 1992 that Cypress would 'never become an important global competitor'. That may or may not be true – the potency of large scale has commonly been exaggerated, and the long-term viability of start-ups underestimated, throughout the industry's history. But even if the competition stays local, it can be more than an irritant – as Intel found to its cost when Chips and Technologies, a total newcomer, stole a march.

PCs use several semiconductors in addition to the microprocessor which is Intel's speciality. The small company simply packaged the other devices in 'chip sets', taking away a substantial chunk of Intel's non-microprocessor sales. 'In retrospect it was a simple thing to do,' Intel's Grove admitted. 'They thought of it, we didn't.' In a field of burgeoning, vital technologies and ideas, monopoly of thought can never be achieved.

The newcomers keep on coming – and coming on strong. While still battling with AMD over the latter's attack on the 386 market, Intel was challenged by the far smaller Cyrix on territory occupied by the more powerful 486 microprocessor. To quote *PC Magazine*, 'When Cyrix announced its 486SLC chip,

Intel immediately filed a lawsuit in its familiar sue-now-ask-questions-later manner, allegedly before seeing the chip, which Cyrix claims consists of an entirely original design.' The original feature to which Intel most objected was the price of the Cyrix chip. Designed for the fast-growing notebook market, it undercut the Intel rival by half. Mere announcement of the Cyrix assault dropped Intel's share price by 15 per cent in a day: the microprocessor champion 'in late May, moved to cut the price of the genuine article to a price equal to or below that of the Cyrix chip'.

That's the raw stuff of the competitive, dog-eat-dog free market. From that strenuous dialectic, according to capitalist theory, technological and economic advance most readily flows. If that theory holds, so does American supremacy in the Olympic Games of technology. But doubt has been cast on the theory, or at least the practice, from the Valley itself. There the problems now loom as large as the opportunities, to judge by a 1992 report on the region.

'Silicon Valley: An Economy at Risk' blared the title of the document, produced by the Center for Economic Competitiveness at the SRI International consultancy. A self-styled 'wake-up call', the report was intended to arouse the Valley's businessmen to the dangers that were eroding their competitive prowess. For once, this wasn't a matter of the fearsome Japanese – the Valley's wounds were self-inflicted.

The Valley has been subject to recurrent bouts of self-doubt ever since its initial explorers turned their new-found lands into established world powers. Led by Hewlett-Packard, which developed from the rented garage where Bill Hewlett and Dave Packard set up shop in 1938, the top companies of the Valley have become global makers and sellers of highly complex product lines – HP makes everything from Reduced Instruction Set Computing chips to the electronic instruments with which the partners started.

Beneath the leaders, a host of middle-sized companies has international presence. Most are breakaways, just as Apple,

119

now a veteran leader, was an early-stage breakaway from HP. Steve Jobs was only a summer employee, but his co-founder, Stephen Wozniak, had worked for HP. His employer's lack of interest in the enthusiasms of Wozniak's 'Homebrew Computing Club' made the young engineer susceptible to Jobs' notion that they should make and market their own little computer, which became the Apple I.

HP itself was actually a closet computer company. As Hewlett explained, 'HP researchers came up with the idea of a desktop calculator. It really was a computer, but we didn't want to call it a computer, because every customer company had a computer guru and all they wanted was IBM.' The same inhibition may well have governed HP's further development. Although computers were providing the larger share of its $14.5 billion revenues by the early Nineties, the growth had been won well away from IBM's data-processing heartland.

Most of the Valley's growth had been achieved the same way – either steering clear of IBM, or operating round what were at first its fringes (personal computers, scientific hardware, etc), or becoming an indispensable supplier to the colossus. As IBM expanded into nearly every market (whether successfully or not), sought out new suppliers, and stumbled in its own growth, the Valley's breakaways, old and new, were bound to feel the effects.

Louise Kehoe reported the 'warning signs' noted by SRI. The economic omens included 'slower employment growth, a decline in venture capital financing, slowing growth in pre-competitive research and development spending and a shortage of skilled workers'. As she pointed out, however, 'several of the problems' assigned to Silicon Valley 'are common to all high technology regions in the US'. She saw no need (although the report did) for joint private and public initiatives to turn the Valley into an 'American Technopolis': 'The Valley has its problems, but it has spawned more new ventures and more important new technologies than any other place on earth. It ain't broke and it doesn't need fixing.'

The Valley, anyway, is short-hand for an American Technopolis that already exists – in the report's words, 'a dynamic community that supports technology enterprises and retains value-added manufacturing, employment and wealth'. That description still applies pre-eminently to the US. It matters little where the members of the Technopolis settle, whether they are start-ups by kids fresh from school (like Microsoft) or breakaways from breakaways (like Next, where Steve Jobs has spent frustrating years trying to create a new Apple).

So long as a cluster of like-minded firms gets together within easy reach of a powerful academic campus, the Technopolis can expand and flourish. When one PC firm was considering where to locate a new plant in Europe, an American consultant wisely suggested that his clients should follow this same prescription. They instead chose to expand at the existing site, which was close neither to other high-tech business nor academics. Their choice was much the cheaper option, but similar decisions by indigenous European firms explain why Europe's Technopolis has failed to compete with 'the Valley'.

America's Technopolis has proved endlessly extendable. Take the story of James B. Moon, a man who, on one account, had every reason 'to be loyal to Silicon Valley': 'He grew up there, studied there, and joined Intel Corp. Then in 1979, Intel moved his operation to Oregon . . . During the 1980s . . . Moon watched dozens of technology companies spring up and succeed in the Northwest. In 1986, he started his own company to make portable patient monitors. That company, Protocol Systems Inc, nearly doubled its sales last year to $23 million, and went public in March.'

Moon and his public company are only a tiny part of what *Business Week* billed as 'High-Tech Heaven' in the Pacific Northwest. In mid-1992 the three states of the region housed 3,200 high-tech operations, of which 2,100 were in electronic hardware and software. Bill Gates' Seattle-based Microsoft, while by far the biggest, is only one of 1,500 software companies whose main concentration is in the eastern suburban 'technology corridor'.

In Portland, 'Silicon Forest' provides suburban homes for hardware ranging from tiny semiconductors to the hugely powerful supercomputers which use 'massively parallel processing'. Intel's supercomputers are made there, as are those of Sequent Computer Systems – an Intel spin-off, note. Breakaways are a way of life in the Northwest as in the West: at least twenty-two are said to have spun away from Tektronix alone.

But the Northwest and the West by no means monopolise the Technopolis. North Carolina has the 'Research Triangle'; San Diego, California, and Austin, Texas, are other centres; and Route 128 near Boston shouldn't be written off following the harsh difficulties experienced by its leaders, Digital Equipment and Wang. The Route 128 pioneers have suffered because the early breakthroughs, in minicomputers and word processing, have been overtaken by newer technologies. Newer ones still are on their way. Where they will settle is never certain. But the high-tech heavens of America are not ringed by unbreachable walls. Some twenty-five Japanese electronics companies are thought to have invested more than $750 million in the Northwest alone. The invaders include the biggest names in printers, disk drives, fibre-optic telecom systems, ceramic capacitators, silicon wafers and other chip-related products.

Behind Epson, NEC, Fujistsu, Kyocera and Shin-Estu, massive plants were being lined up in mid-1992 by Fujitsu, Matsushita and Toshiba. As the Nineties develop, the boom of the American breakaways has lost none of its impetus, nationally and internationally. But as the new companies which America is still spawning spread outwards, IBM's rivals are moving in, and some Americans are moving out. Wilf Corrigan's LSI Logic has shifted almost all its production out of the Valley – and the US. The Global Technopolis is developing fast. America's valleys will remain its heartland – but they won't be all-American territory in any sense of the phrase.

11

Intel: The Front Seat in Technology

'IBM takes a back seat to no one in technology, and that technology lead is growing, not shrinking.' That proud boast by Jack D. Kuehler, then the giant's technology czar, contrasts oddly with a key IBM decision – to purchase a 12 per cent interest in Intel for $250 million in 1982, precisely because of its lead in a technology vital to the development of IBM and the whole computer industry.

Of all the companies that created the electronics revolution, Intel can claim the pivotal role. It brought together scientists and engineers without whose achievements the revolution couldn't have happened – but so did Xerox at its Palo Alto Research Center. The difference was that Intel kept its team together and developed their creations into lastingly, superbly successful commercial products.

In 1991, Intel had $4.8 billion of sales and $819 million of profits: double Microsoft on the first count, it was 40 per cent higher on the second. Yet the software company was the talked about and talked-up hero. The world's largest maker of microprocessors, the core products of the revolution, plays second fiddle – but only in the publicity. In an amazing decade, IBM's best investment achieved a 20.6 per cent annual rise in total return to its shareholders. That was founded on a 34.4 per

123

cent gain in earnings per share, the eighth fastest growth in the *Fortune* 500.

Moreover, this is one major sector of the revolution where US supremacy is unchallenged. Intel's challengers are strictly home-grown: Advanced Micro Devices, Texas Instruments, MIPS Computer Systems, Cypress, Cyrix, Sun Microsystems, Motorola, Hewlett-Packard – and IBM. The giant has shown a disconcerting habit of biting the hands that it has fed. IBM hasn't turned on Intel with the same ferocity brought to bear on Microsoft, but it has teamed up with Apple Corp and Motorola to develop a new, competitive microprocessor.

The significance is that Apple, using Motorola chips, is the only sizeable standout in a PC world dominated by Intel; and that IBM is an unquestioned leader in the RISC technology (reduced instruction set computing) that constitutes one of several strong challenges to Intel's pre-eminence. The challenge starts from so far behind, though, as to be out of sight. Intel's products are the heart of 100 million IBM and IBM-compatible computers all over the world. In 1991, five years after RISC chips first arrived, Intel beat them all by a mighty margin: 20.4 million to 308,000.

'We have won the RISC battle,' boasted Intel CEO Andrew S. Grove. For all that, the competition from all sides is real and rugged. Intel faces energetic cloners (though cloning an advanced microprocessor is among the most intellectually taxing tasks in industry), plus leapfrogging innovators. Indeed, the many-sided, meaningful competition in this sector – very different from the situation in IBM-occupied territory like mainframes – is a potent factor in America's continued and colossal superiority.

It stems back to the moment when the late Robert Norton Noyce filed for an historic patent on 30 July 1959. The patent covered an integrated circuit that used the 'planar' process. By spreading a flat plane of oxide over silicon, wireless connections could be made between two transistors and other components on the chip. Noyce was working at the time as general manager for Fairchild Semiconductor, which he left in 1968 to establish Intel.

With Gordon Moore (who had also worked at Shockley Laboratories, founded by the inventor of the transistor), Noyce got $30,000 of venture capital from the far-sighted financier Arthur Rock. The partners started making memory chips in Santa Clara. The DRAM or dynamic random-access memory, Intel's first smash-hit invention, is one of the areas where Japanese competitors have since seized the lead. But the 1971 invention of the microprocessor by Ted Hoff took Intel into regions where no one had trod before.

Paradoxically, given the failure of the Japanese to follow, the invention was spurred by a customer from Japan. Called Busacom, this firm made complex scientific calculators. Ted Hoff was given the task (one of his first jobs at Intel) of designing a set of a dozen integrated circuit chips for a Busacom calculator. His inspired response was to wonder why such work had to be constantly repeated: 'Why design twelve special purpose ICs for the Japanese calculator this time, another set for a missile guidance system and yet more for a music synthesiser? Why not put all the circuitry on a single integrated circuit and then, like a normal computer, program it to do whatever you want?'

Hoff's insight was that integrated circuits are proto-computers which, if made programmable, will work like computers – hence the 'computer on a chip' sobriquet for what became known as a microprocessor. Even though the Japanese customer had no interest in Hoff's idea, Noyce did. He saw that this masterstroke of genius would revolutionise the industry.

For a long time, though, Intel's customers couldn't see the power or value of the concept. In 1966, when I started the magazine *Management Today*, I rejoiced in the satirical contributions of author Ivor Williams, who had concealed the identity of his bumbling corporate employer behind a mythical name, Minipute, and a mythical product – the expendable computer. Now Hoff was making myth into reality: 'It's like a light bulb. When it burns out you unplug it and throw it in the garbage and plug in a new one.'

Until the personal computer was born, Hoff's invention couldn't come into its full glory, but without the microprocessor the PC couldn't be given life. What one book calls 'the hobbyists, the hackers and the nerds – highly technical people at the margins of society' were to break the vicious circle, seeing and seizing the opportunity. Both IBM and DEC considered the prospects, but let them pass by: 'They could not imagine why anyone would need or want a small computer.' Nor, to be fair, could some of the pioneers. The earliest product was an act of desperation, not calculation – except in the sense that the progenitor was a small calculator company. Ed Roberts, the owner of M-I-T-S, or MITS, was in business between a massage parlour and laundromat in Albuquerque, New Mexico. MITS was withering on the vine commercially when he gave the world a small $500 computer based on Intel's 8080 microprocessor.

Unveiled on the cover of *Popular Electronics* in January 1975, the primitive personal computer, the Altair, attracted five enquiries in the first day and 25–30 a day within a week. It was the tiny beginning which led to Intel's 100 million IBM-compatible sales and to the revolution which shook the mammoth IBM itself to its foundations. In the process, Intel's management and financial resources were often stretched – hence the acceptance of an IBM stake. As a commentator noted at the time, the original deal 'basically solves a financing problem at a price somewhat above the market'.

Intel needed further injections of help as it struggled with immense and mounting development and capital costs. A piece-by-piece increase in IBM's stake to 20 per cent in 1983–84 seemed to cement the relationship. But in early 1986 the giant dismayed Intel supporters by using the stock as security for its own convertible debt issue. The result was to reduce the shareholding to 13 per cent, and it took a later 1986 announcement, of a technology exchange agreement between the two companies, to confirm that the relationship was still solid.

Intel had lost money for five consecutive quarters leading up to the swap. Even so, it had used the IBM connection astutely. IBM business never rose above 20 per cent of Intel's sales and was only 15 per cent in 1986. The fact that Intel could also supply the IBM clones without let or hindrance gave it the best of both worlds. In terms of cumulative sales, Intel took 80 per cent of the world's fastest-growing electronics market.

Even in 1991, its market share was estimated at two-thirds, dwarfing everybody from Motorola (13 per cent) downwards. By 1993, it had overtaken the Japanese giants, by then overdependent on memory chips, to regain the lead as the largest supplier of semiconductors. Symbolically, America was back on top. But while Intel's domination in microprocessors is reminiscent of IBM at its peak, the *modus operandi* of the chip-maker differs markedly. Intel's position rests genuinely on technological supremacy, and in 1992, as Grove himself admitted, that was 'under attack'.

Against existing competition like that of Digital's superfast Alpha chip, let alone the potential onslaught from the IBM-Apple-Motorola combination, Intel had few weapons other than its product prowess – and its lawyers. Taking the cloners to court was one additional weapon, unprecedented price-cutting another, and (also unprecedented) TV advertising a third. But all the tactics depended on having something to advertise – on repeating breakthroughs like the 386 and 486.

The 386 development also marked a watershed in IBM's love-hate relationship with the personal computer. The management at Armonk knew all about the greater powers of the 386, yet they held back plans for incorporating the chip into IBM machines. The motive for this delay – fateful, in hindsight – is by no means confined to IBM. All market leaders are reluctant to cannibalise their own best-sellers by introducing new products with superior characteristics. But on this occasion, IBM opened a gap through which Compaq moved at speed.

The mistake wasn't repeated with the next wonder, the 486. Compaq argues that, while IBM announced first, it was beaten into production by the Texan upstart. Still, the lesson is that the microprocessor – not the brand-name on the computer – drives the market. The success or failure of Intel and the chips it fathers over the Nineties are thus vital to the battle among its customers. Among these, IBM is still by far the largest.

The spawning in the decade promises to be prolific, if Grove's plans come to fruition. The previous pattern consisted of 'one or two new-generation chips annually and a whole new microprocessor family every three or four years'. Against that, reported *Business Week*, Intel planned a profusion of variants (thirty for the 486 in 1992 alone), and new families every two years. And 1993 saw the birth of the Pentium family – 'a *veritable one-chip mainframe*'.

My italics make the point. Intel's research and development encroaches at many points on the former preserves of IBM. Intel's superchip features three million transistors and the ability to process 100 million instructions per second. It has double the capability of the 486. Like the top RISC chips, the Pentium emulates the power of what, only a few years ago, would have been an IBM mainframe product. And that's only the present. The future offers the prospect – rather, the certainty – of giant leaps forward.

The three million transistors of 1992, an enormous advance itself, should be twenty million at the public unveiling of the next family in 1995. That family is scheduled to have two and a half times the speed of the Pentium while proceeding *en route* for a hundred million transistor chip by the year 2000. By then two BIPS (two billion instructions per second) should be achieved too. These designs are not just components, but genuine computers, and when strung together even supercomputers, capable of massive feats. In this field, the appropriately named 'massively parallel computing' is expected to own the future.

Winning a third of the $270 million market for this strongly emerging technology, Intel had sold 375 supercomputer systems by the spring of 1992. Its Pentium chip is aimed at computers which span the entire IBM range. And at the bottom of that range, Intel is in direct competition as supplier of complete PCs to Digital, Unisys and other IBM rivals. In areas like interactive digital video and flash memory (storing data on semiconductors rather than magnetic disks), Intel's R&D teams are again treading on IBM ground, if not on IBM toes.

In contrast to IBM, however, Intel has an excellent record of turning innovation into products and profits. Not that the chip-making game leaves any alternative – to any company, that is, except the old IBM. The latter's impressive chip operation at East Fishkill, until very recent times, was dedicated solely to supplying its parent. While this protected the business from the fluctuations which Intel had to suffer, it also removed the urgency of staying at the cutting edge.

Intel's strategy was the inverse of its shareholder's. IBM sought to achieve the longest possible runs of basically unchanged designs. Far from cannibalising its own sales by introducing improved products, IBM sought to keep old and new as far apart as possible. Thus, its small System Three computers were incompatible with the 360 and 370 mainframes – just one example of misplaced strategy. The consequent welter of incompatible machines gave IBM a persistent and blinding headache from the mid-Eighties onwards.

In contrast to the history of the 370 mainframes, still the basis of IBM's flagship products in 1992, nineteen years after their first appearance, Intel had created four new families of microprocessor in thirteen years. Accelerating the creative process meant climbing progressively higher mountains, both technically and financially. The 486's development cost over $250 million and 450 work-years, but before it was announced, in 1989, the team was already sketching in the design of the Pentium.

As that proceeded towards the market, work on the next miracle was already in hand. Such overlaps are the essence of the development programmes that the Japanese have made into powerful competitive weapons in many industries: develop the new so far and so long before the old reaches its peak that competition is left at the starting gate. To quote *Business Week*, Intel is setting 'a blistering pace that Grove thinks will keep cloners in a perpetual catch-up mode'.

Intel's hopes of achieving perpetual supremacy rest overwhelmingly on highly advanced technology that the customer can't buy – that of design and manufacture. Once Intel was thought to lag behind IBM in the design department – IBM's computer-aided engineering tools (CAE) were part of the five-year technology agreement signed in 1986. But today Intel's proprietary design tools are a primary weapon in the competitive war.

It's not above taking help from others, however. A start-up named Quickturn Systems has a new technique for 'hardware emulation'. This not only makes debugging faster and more reliable, but enables PC makers and software developers to see the new product at work many months before public announcement. One highly beneficial result for Intel's latest wonder, apparently, was Compaq's consequent decision to drop its plan to build a new computer round a non-Intel RISC chip.

In addition, the emulation technique, which could shorten the development cycle by six critical months, fits well with Intel's conversion from an unworthy arrogance towards its customers. Now Intel is a collaborative ally engaged in 'concurrent engineering'. In this guru-approved process, supplier and customer work closely together from early in the project. Before the Pentium got under way, Intel people visited all major customers and key software producers. The result was a list of 147 specific features. The outcome is typical of well-executed customer research. What the customers wanted proved to differ markedly from Intel's expectations. Once again, this management practice is one which the gurus warmly advocate – make the customer a partner, listen to what he says in all fields. By spring 1992 the Pentium customers were already in a position to start engineering their computers. On the software side, the writers had 'compilers', new software tools to help them make a similarly fast start on their programs.

As *Business Week* pointed out, 'The lack of compilers is one reason that software has lagged at least a generation behind Intel's silicon. Today, six years after the 386's birth, only a smattering of programs takes full advantage of its power.' The article concerned, by Robert C. Hof, brilliantly sets out the ways in which Intel is leading the computer industry into the next phase of development – Intel, note, not IBM. In a long text, the world's largest computer company, and Intel's biggest customer, didn't appear at all.

The name did crop up in one table – that of RISC chips. Among four named suppliers, IBM had the fastest chip, but a mere 11 per cent of the 1991 desktop market. Back in 1986, when the technology swap with Intel was made, IBM had caused ripples by using an earlier RISC product, rather than an Intel chip, in a high-end workstation. The speculation was that IBM might be hoping to boot out Intel altogether. So it might, still. But in 1992, the boot was on the other foot.

The company that IBM's 12 per cent purchase valued at $2 billion in 1982 was worth $13 billion in the market a decade later. Despite heavy spending on R&D ($800 million in 1992) and capital investment ($1.2 billion), Intel had more year-end cash in its hoard ($2.3 billion) than IBM. Its sales per employee, at $197,000, were higher than IBM's $188,000. Its R&D spend, as a percentage of revenue, was far higher: 16.7 per cent against 10.2 per cent. And Intel was highly profitable, while IBM was deep in loss.

In consequence, with only 7 per cent of IBM's sales, in mid-1992 Intel was valued in the stock market at one-third of the giant's capitalisation. All these financial numbers, moreover, were not mere froth, but reflected the profound change in the industry, the technology and the relative and real strengths of the two partners since 1982. Intel, faced with far more severe head-on competition than IBM, had fought its way forward – and in doing so, paradoxically, had intensified the pressure on IBM.

The chairman of its executive committee, John Opel, could, of course, have congratulated himself on the above performance. After all, his original $250 million investment, a flea-bite commitment at the time, looks inspired compared to the value of a similar stake ten years on: $1.56 billion. The original aims, of preserving Intel's independent strength and protecting IBM's supplies of microprocessors, had been met. The relationship had been in many ways exemplary.

Announcing the deal, Opel said emphatically that 'This is an investment and we will not participate in the day-to-day operations of Intel.' IBM merely appointed a director to look after its interests, and where either side judged that these interests were in conflict with others, the IBM nominee would step aside, taking no part in resolving the issue. IBM would continue to buy semiconductors from other suppliers, and Intel could sell to other customers.

Even though IBM had failed to exploit the commercial relationship to the full (notably by the belated use of the 386 chip that opened the barn door to Compaq), that was no fault of the partner. But how many of IBM's businesses matched the fivefold rise in Intel's turnover over the decade to 1992, or achieved the same level of profitability (17.1 per cent on sales in 1991)? How many of them achieved the same market results and technological advance in face of genuinely rough competition?

IBM can point to some superstars, led by the AS-400 mid-range computer, which muscled very successfully (though belatedly) into Digital territory. For most of its operations in the front line of the electronics revolution, however, the answer is certainly dusty. But then, none of IBM's businesses had Intel's freedom. Far from playing no part in their day-to-day operations, top management, under both Opel and John Akers, intervened and interfered constantly.

Freedom to buy and sell outside IBM at will was unknown to IBM's businesses for most of its history. The insistence that IBM companies sell to internal customers only on competitive merit arrived as late as the Nineties. It's unfair, naturally, to compare a start-up whose employees have always owned a large share of their company with the captive divisions of a vast multinational. But the unfairness makes a fair and telling point.

In the type of business in which Intel – and IBM – are engaged, captive divisions of huge organisations are inappropriate lifeforms. Speed, intensity and innovation are inexorable necessities. Intel needed to take capital from IBM, but IBM needed to take organisational lessons from Intel. The necessity was plain long before the traumatic losses of 1991 turned Akers' thoughts in that direction. The gulf in cultures is illustrated neatly by 'Open Door'. IBM has long prided itself on this programme, which allows employees to take issues up the organisation – right to the top, if need be.

Very few IBMers use this doorway. In 1992 the general manager of a 15,000-strong business had received five Open Doors in the past year: that's ·033 per cent. Doubtless, fear of repercussions for the IBMer's career slams shut the open door. The door-openers, moreover, get no guarantees. Intel's comparable programme also allows employees higher access to any executive on any issue. The key phrase, though, is AR – 'action required'. The executive approached mustn't merely answer, but *act*. There you have the central, essential difference in a single word.

12

The Non-Eating
of Apple

'Welcome IBM. Welcome to the most exciting and important marketplace since the computer revolution began thirty-five years ago. We look forward to responsible competition in the massive effort to distribute this American technology to the world.'

When Apple Corporation took expensive advertising space to welcome IBM into its industry, the gesture seemed typically bouncy and maverick – a wild, unbusinesslike expression of high spirits. To some, the impudence seemed to tempt fortune, for this was the IBM of 1981, the giant (thirty times Apple's size even three years later) that never mis-stepped, but whose gigantic feet, placed with ponderous care, had crushed upstarts far more shrewdly directed than Apple.

All the stories about Steve Jobs, the amazingly young joint founder, celebrated his impulsiveness. He had impatiently named his company after the half-eaten apple in his hand. A man like that was light years away from the IBM mould. But his mentality thrived on the new age of galloping, indiscriminate technological advance. In the same way that Jobs seized on his apple, so he grabbed at the vision unveiled by the men at the Palo Alto Research Center.

They had used Xerox's billions to invent the future. 'Why

don't you market this?' an astounded Jobs asked. 'You could sweep the world.' 'This' was the mouse-driven personal computer with a 'graphical user interface', or GUI. Technically complex, a monument to man's fantastic ingenuity, the Alto – PARC's prototype machine – achieved remarkable simplicity in use. The GUI meant simply that the user saw on the screen a pictorial guide to the work on the computer. The mouse, the now familiar desktop device that operates a little pointer on the screen, was another inspired breakthrough.

Together the inventions bypassed the keyboard. Users no longer had to master coded instructions. The computer took its orders, and 'spoke' back visually, in plain English. Jobs had seen the future and recognised it. But even he can't have imagined that this visit to the Xerox labs would ensure Apple's own future – more, would save it from what, at one point, seemed certain doom.

In one sense, Jobs had been right to welcome IBM. Its entry widened the market far beyond its existing frontiers, far beyond IBM's own expectations. As the ad foresaw, IBM had given the PC the most valuable imprimatur in computing. From being a sideshow, personal computing became a main event. The drawback, however, rapidly appeared as IBM's sales exploded. The new PCs, using the Microsoft operating system MS–DOS, swiftly established an 'industry standard' where none had operated before.

Apple and the other makers, mavericks all, each had their own systems, none of which could share hardware or software with the others. It was as if every make of car ran on a different fuel. The situation was a replay of the original mainframe computer story. There, too, all the systems and all the software were proprietary, the exclusive property of each manufacturer. Once a customer had invested in a system, he was massively inhibited from changing. That seemed an excellent idea commercially, but it played into the hands of the strongest supplier – IBM.

The war between the leader and the vendors of 'plug-compatible' equipment, peripherals which could be connected with IBM machines, was the main arena of competition as IBM's rivals fought to break through the proprietary wall. In personal computing, though, all competitors started from scratch. Nobody had an inherent customer base to match the strength that IBM had inherited from punch cards when it entered digital computing. It wasn't even clear where the customer base lay. Was it in the home? Education? Small business?

After IBM's entry, the question was answered emphatically: the base was the same as for mainframes – the business user – though the market worked very differently. The differences seemed irrelevant as IBM's PC sales soared away. As in mainframes, the industry standard carried the day. But there was a crucial distinction. This was an open standard, the first in the history of computers – even of business machines.

Anybody could gain access to MS–DOS, and anybody could write programs to run on the system. Anybody, that is, except the other existing PC suppliers – including Apple. One by one, Tandy and the rest saw the writing on the wall. To be a serious contender in the mass market brought to life by IBM, you had to be 'compatible' with its operating system. But this time, there was no war: for better or (in its case) for worse, IBM couldn't defend its proprietary position – because there wasn't one.

For Apple, though, the new standard was a disaster. Thousands of programs had been written, and millions sold, for the Apple II, which was neither compatible nor capable of fighting the IBM PC for the corporate market. It was a market of which Steve Jobs knew little, and nobody else at Apple knew much more. Moreover, Jobs was well down the road in developing the new, equally incompatible approach to computing which he had discovered at PARC – first, with the abortive Lisa, then the Macintosh (with typically extravagant Jobsian insouciance, Lisa and Mac were developed separately).

These computers weren't just incompatible with MS–DOS. They represented an entirely new concept, an architecture that was to revolutionise fields into which computing hadn't penetrated – above all, graphics. WYSIWG were the magic initials: what you see is what you get. Printers and designers would one day be able to create on their screens, in glorious colour, the pages and images on which they were working – and to manipulate their work in any way they wished.

But as the first phase of the IBM-led explosion ended, that future seemed anything but assured. The Macintosh, despite its infinite charms, was a slow starter; the Apple II's market had slumped; and the accounts showed the company's first ever loss in the third quarter of 1986. With the shares slumping, too, to a mere $14, it seemed as if Apple might well be eaten.

Revolutions often devour their own children, and Steve Jobs certainly seemed a good candidate for the role of Danton or Trotsky. Disorganised, haphazard and inspirational, Jobs had allowed not only overhead departments but whole factories to mushroom as the product line broadened. Worse still, his preoccupation with the Macintosh – an operation he personally headed – was weakening the performance of the company as a whole.

When the company's annual meeting took place in January 1985, Macintosh employees listened to Jobs speaking about Apple and its future; symbolically enough, they occupied front row seats. Like journalists at the Oscar ceremony, Apple II people had to watch the event on closed circuit television. As it happened, Jobs was dead right about the future and the Mac, but the AGM was another sign of the mismanagement which Jobs, to be fair, had sought to cure.

He had first offered the presidency to Don Estridge, the father of the IBM PC. Had Estridge accepted, he would quite possibly have become one of America's best-known CEO's – and he and his wife would very probably still be alive. The couple died, along with 135 others, when a TriStar jet crashed while trying to land at Dallas Fort Worth on an August day in 1985. Estridge was flying to and fro to complete his transfer from running IBM's PC operation in Florida.

His transfer to Armonk marked the turning point in Apple's struggle against IBM. The charismatic energy that Estridge had brought to launching the PC was lost to Boca anyway. But that energy had long since been dissipated by the internal politics of IBM – by then Estridge was spending 80 per cent of his time away from the office: nearly all his week was passed at the centre of power in Armonk. At the time of Estridge's death, IBM's troubles with two new PC products had prevented it from pressing home the attack on Apple. IBM had failed utterly to penetrate the domestic market with the first product, the PC Jr. With the second, the AT, the delays and setbacks allowed Apple to seize the high-performance ground with the Macintosh Plus. This was the first desktop with a million bytes of random access memory, half as powerful again as its top IBM and IBM-compatible rivals.

Apple was now under new management. Having failed to net Estridge, Jobs had gone outside the industry to hire a man whose credentials lay in neither management nor computing, but in marketing. The man from Pepsico, John Sculley, proved himself the right choice by a paradoxical action: he ousted the man who had chosen him. While Jobs needed somebody to tidy up his messy company, he had no intention of relaxing his grip on power. The rows became incessant – and instead of letting go, Jobs left.

The two men who personified the PC breakthrough – Jobs and Estridge – were thus both gone within twelve months. IBM never recovered the élan and the drive (or the market share) that Estridge had achieved; but Apple without Jobs grew stronger as Sculley moved on from clean-up guy to business creator. The clean-up was essential to reduce Apple's bloated base – half its factories had to be closed, and a fifth of its employees left the company.

The product-oriented marketing of the past also disappeared as marketer Sculley instead built the business round its three markets. Of the three – education, domestic and corporate – the latter was by far the most valuable prize and the most difficult for Apple to seize. The buyers were intrinsically hostile. The management information systems people who place the fat corporate orders hadn't liked the arrogant way in which Jobs promoted the technological wonders of his computers. The wonders, though real, were limited. True, the desktop presentation on the Mac's screen was thoroughly business-like. Users opened and closed files, put them into folders, threw unwanted papers into the 'trash' or 'wastebasket'. Every piece of software obeyed the same rules, so that moving from one program to another was much simpler than in the IBM-compatible world.

Against that, the original Mac was underpowered, couldn't be expanded and was uncommunicative – you couldn't connect it with other computers. Apple started to tackle these problems with the launch of the Mac Plus in January 1986. For all that, and for all Sculley's marketing skills, Apple might never have got past the hostile guardians of the corporate gate. But the technological wonders of which Jobs boasted opened the back door – the Mac's eminent suitability for desktop publishing of all kinds delivered the market into Apple's lap as demand boomed for software like Aldus Pagemaker.

Coupled with the formatting and printing powers of the laser-printer (developed by Apple well before it appeared in the IBM world), the new software did for the Mac what Visicalc had done for the Apple II. Visicalc, the first of the spreadsheet programs, had enabled small businesses to lay out their financial statistics and manipulate them – to see what happened if sales fell, inventories rose, or margins came under pressure. Now all users of graphics, from great corporations to small design companies, could achieve commercial printing quality – without using commercial printers.

The advance of the Mac in power and versatility was accompanied by major developments in the quantity and quality of Mac software. Sculley had given himself two years to prove that the Mac was a serious alternative to IBM. As it happened, Apple didn't succeed in seriously cracking the big business market – despite the appearance of further eminently usable machines which matched the competition at most points. Yet the threatened company not only survived: it flourished.

In 1985, the industry's flat year, sales were $1.9 billion and profits a mere $120 million. The next year sales barely budged, but profits were up 150 per cent. By 1991, as the industry hit another, and far more serious recession, Apple's turnover was $6.3 billion and its profits $310 million – and this despite heavy price cuts across the range, plus the impact of a new low-priced line. In thus recognising the sea-change in the business, Apple was a full year ahead of both IBM and Compaq: Sculley had created a more sensitive, responsive corporation without losing the innovative abilities of the original Jobs creation.

But you can't attribute Apple's survival wholly to Sculley or anybody else at the Cupertino company. The fall in IBM's share of the personal computer market, down from 63 per cent in 1984 to 38 per cent three years later, has several explanations. Apple and Compaq are certainly among the causes. So is the multiplication of low-cost clones. Apple's achievement was to preserve an important corner of the market to which IBM simply couldn't gain access. The very factor that put Apple at risk, its lack of immediate compatibility with IBM, became a Unique Selling Proposition.

The Mac was the only different computer – different and, in its ease of use, distinctively better. For those who didn't need compatibility, or did need the Mac's superior graphic abilities, the Apple products were the first choice. This niche market wasn't endangered until the advanced versions of Microsoft's Windows software arrived, imitating the Apple configuration, in the early Nineties. Before then, however, IBM had damaged its own cause by a series of heavy blows that would have shattered any company.

The trio of failed 1986 products were self-inflicted wounds: an engineering workstation; a 12 lb convertible laptop/desktop computer; and a lower-cost high performance computer.

None met the requirements of the marketplace, in concept, positioning or price; none met the requirements of defect-free manufacture. How could this catalogue of commercial crimes occur in a company that in 1986 was deep into John Opel's quality crusade and supposed to be steeped in marketing intelligence?

In the case of the workstation, IBM was once again reverting to type – trying to establish a proprietary standard to counter the rivals (Apollo, Sun and Digital Equipment) who had raced away in this segment. 'Workstation' is really a fancy word for a powerful personal computer that comes with all the paraphernalia required to suit the exigent needs of technicians of all kinds. IBM's effort was very expensive, but relatively poor on some performance comparisons, and deeply unwanted by the marketplace.

That was also true of the convertible. Just as IBM had failed with its first portable computer, coming in overweight and underperforming, so it completely missed the laptop target. The card was trumped within weeks by a Toshiba product, the T3100, which beat the IBM offering on every criterion. The convertible feature of IBM's machine, enabling the laptop to be used on the desk, was negated by its high cost, more than double that of comparable desktops.

As for the lower-cost, high-performance machine, you had to take off the casing lid, and keep it off, to use the circuit cards which had been designed for the larger PC AT. This terrible threesome can't be blamed for more than part of IBM's sharp loss of market share. But the fiascos were certainly symbolic of the long-run crisis which made IBM strangely ineffective at pressing home its attack, not just on Apple, but on the gathering hordes on every flank.

The threefold fiascos of 1986 were not, after all, isolated events. They came after the portable failure, the flop of the Junior venture into home computing, and the incompetence which so long delayed the AT. The mistake preceded the excruciating delay in re-entering the portable market, the failure of the first OS/2 operating system for the PS/2 computers and a host of relatively minor mishaps.

IBM had become accident prone. The dream of being to PCs what the company had once been to mainframe computers – the omnipotent supplier, calling the tune to which the market danced – couldn't be realised. IBM lacked the sureness of touch and swiftness of reaction that Apple developed to grow within its niche. For example, Sculley's people laid as addled an egg as any of IBM's when the first Mac portable was unveiled: like IBM's offering, it was too heavy and too expensive. Within two years of its flop, however, Apple launched the Powerbook, much lighter, brilliantly designed, better priced. At once, it became a best-seller. The time-lag between IBM's portable flop and the appearance of its laptop in early 1992 wasn't measured in a couple of years – but eight of them. The IBMers who, back in the glory days, had ignored Apple and scorned the Mac now sang a different song. Apple plainly had something IBM didn't – but which could perhaps be begged and borrowed.

First, IBM looked for the needed magic in Steve Jobs, forming an alliance with Next, the advanced technology firm the Apple founder had launched after being ousted from his foundation. When that $50 million fling failed, IBM turned at last to an alliance with the master company and John Sculley – trading IBM's access to the corporate market for the ingenuity and imagination which Apple was thought to enjoy. Far from being eaten or beaten, Apple, on one criterion, was joining forces on equal terms. Its share of the PC market has been running neck and neck with IBM's. If matters rest there (which they won't – Apple was again running into serious problems in mid-1993) it would be a fairytale ending to the fairytale story of Apple . . . a story that runs something like this:

Once upon a time there was a handsome young prince, richer than all the other princes, richer than many of the kings and emperors. His symbol was an Apple – not golden, but multi-coloured, with all the hues of the rainbow. Handsome and charismatic, Prince Steve cared nothing for splendid garments and courtly ways. He rode to battle wearing blue jeans, and won all his wars with panache and enthusiasm,

He came to the environs of a great fortress, greater than any other known to man: Fortress IBM. The barons within observed the Prince's progress and his impetuosity and decided to teach the young upstart a lesson. They chose some of their younger knights and sent them forth to battle. And lo, a miracle occurred – the young knights swept past the Prince's army and onto the plains beyond in a ride of conquest such as the world had never seen.

The young knights, and the barons inside the Fortress, no longer had any interest in the Prince. He and his army, they reasoned, could be left to starve to death – for all the lands around them had been seized. But Prince Steve had other, better ideas. He found a champion, Sir John, and they formed a doughty combination, like Roland and Oliver – until Sir John turned and smote Prince Steve and sent him into exile. And the barons of the Fortress sought out the Prince and bribed him with much gold – but little good it did them, for the power of the Prince's realm remained, and so did Sir John.

The barons of the Fortress deserted Prince Stephen and left him to his lonely cause. And they made peace with Sir John, the better to fight the infidel from the East. But nobody believed that they would live happily ever after.

V

IBM'S ARMOUR:
THE FATEFUL CRACKS

13

Ken Olsen:
The Maverick in Minis

Long before niche marketing became a cliché, Ken Olsen, a computer engineer, never famous for his marketing skills, had created its most spectacular example. Long before it became permissible even to question IBM's competence, Olsen not only queried its technological supremacy, he also dismissed the Watson culture as regimented, insular – and above all inefficient.

Olsen knew whereof he spoke. As a graduate researcher at MIT when it gave IBM the crucial contract to develop its SAGE early warning computer, Olsen acted as liaison at IBM's Poughkeepsie plant. That added an insider's view to an outsider's perspective. 'It was like going to a Communist state,' he once said. 'They knew nothing about the rest of the world, and the rest of the world knew nothing about what went on inside.' Just like the Communist state, too, the monolithic façade covered up awful production inefficiencies.

His MIT supervisor recalled Olsen's reaction: 'I can beat these guys at their own game.' His genius, however, lay in *not* playing IBM's game, or at least not playing on the same pitch. The multinationals who challenged IBM all made the mistake of mounting frontal assaults on the market created by large corporate and institutional customers – like MIT. But IBM

147

showed scant interest in another market, in which scientist spoke unto scientist, and engineer unto engineer.

The market saw several small companies edge into this niche: among their leaders, the two which settled for multinational takeover (by Honeywell and Xerox respectively) disappeared without trace, victims of the same large company disease that Olsen detected at IBM. Olsen's independence of mind, which became celebrated, kept him independent – and created the second corporate phenomenon of the computer age.

Like the phenomenal IBM, Olsen's Digital Equipment, founded in 1957, grew at a tremendous pace. By 1986 sales were pushing towards $8 billion. Number Two in the world computer industry (a fact which the general public didn't grasp), Olsen's business had taken a clear lead over all other challengers to IBM's dominance, and largely because Digital (unlike these far greater firms) had avoided the dominant domain.

As an engineer, Olsen could see that many labs would benefit from electronic data processing. But they didn't need (and often couldn't afford) large, costly mainframes. Digital's machines provided computing on the cheap, produced on the cheap. The start-up capital was only $70,000: Olsen put some lawn furniture and a rolltop desk into an abandoned textile mill in Massachusetts, and kept his designs just as simple, cheap and rugged.

His founding partner and former MIT assistant, Harlan Anderson, recalled that simple and cheap ideas poured out of Olsen by the thousand – like using plastic bottle caps for Digital's first pulse transformer instead of costly, tailored insulators. Where IBM tolerated excess costs (because they were translated by standard mark-ups into excess profits), Olsen loathed them.

This was only one of many acute differences. IBM, under the younger Watson, developed a smooth, large management structure in which it rejoiced. Digital's early years were practically free-form. In one description, 'the company consisted largely of bands of engineers who would form fluidly round projects.' In 1964, faced with mounting evidence of confusion and overlapping, Olsen found a solution that was again poles apart from the IBM system – what later became known as the 'product champion'.

Full responsibility for a single product line went to a single manager. Reporting direct to the operating committee headed by Olsen, the champion would obtain his manufacturing and sales force support from centralised organisations. But for development, marketing and producing bottom-line results, he was on his own. Held together by Olsen's hands-on proprietorial style, the system, if you judge by results, deserves his own description: 'a miracle'.

For nineteen years, revenue and profits grew by 30 per cent annually as engineers proved that they could be entrepreneurs. New markets and new products fed off each other – and off the strange fact that no minicomputer competition appeared from IBM until 1975. Even then, Digital kept a hold on the scientific and engineering market worthy of IBM's grip on businessmen (whose applications produced IBM's own excellent minicomputer sales, with the AS 400 – selling 200,000 copies in four years – rapidly winning reputation and market share).

After surviving some notorious product snafus, Olsen struck pay-dirt with the PDP series. The PDP became the workhorse of the scientific and engineering communities. After three years of brilliantly dodging IBM's competition, the thirty semi-autonomous operations that composed Digital were generating sales of $1.4 billion and earning a 10 per cent net margin. What IBM won in its vastly larger world by economies of scale, marketing and quasi-monopoly, Olsen had achieved by technology.

At this crucial juncture, he didn't just double his technological bets – he raised the ante enormously. The VAX (Virtual Address Extension) range cost billions to develop. But it promised to achieve what IBM had never delivered: the VAX machines, covering all needs from the desktop to lower mainframe levels, would be able to communicate with each other, using identical software throughout the range.

The sweeping ambitions of the concept are hard to grasp at this distance, in a time when networking is commonplace. Apart from its conceptual leap, the VAX strategy went far beyond Digital's technological scope. It had never made large disk-storage units, never made microprocessors, never produced the advanced type of software needed to run networks - and never sold to the corporate customers who were IBM's fiefdom.

Once again, Olsen re-thought the company in a messy process that was deeply painful. In *Fortune*'s words, Olsen worked his will 'by teasing, goading and teaching employees, by sermonising – and by remorselessly pillorying those who stood in his way'. The turnover among executives was awful in size and nature: 'Not one was fired, but some left wounded, with heart problems, ulcers, or wrecked nerves.'

After five years of blood, sweat and other people's tears, the product manager organisation was formally disbanded in favour of a centralised marketing organisation similar in function to IBM's. The new Digital was committed to the company's first direct, frontal assault on IBM's heartland. Yet Digital looked unfit for the unequal contest. Earnings had plunged because of an accounting mix-up, and Olsen also failed embarrassingly in the personal computer market.

All error was forgiven when the VAX took off – a brilliant success both technically and commercially, VAX produced the first significant bite into IBM's share of the office market. The new range won orders worth $2 billion in 1986 alone. To some, as total sales soared to $7.6 billion, it seemed as if the future might lie, not with IBM, but with Olsen – that he was the new Thomas Watson Sr.

There were obvious differences. While Watson, a super-sales-man, created a sales-driven company in his own image, Olsen, an engineer down to the laces on his thick shoes, ran a tech-nology-led business. The Watson culture evolved into the ultimate empire of the Organisation Man, neatly suited and tied. Olsen's style (like its creator) remained rumpled, home-spun, eccentric and unpredictable. Both styles, though, were essentially autocratic – and both leaders made life unnecessarily uncomfortable for their subordinates.

Where Watson made them wait for days outside his office, Olsen kept them for days in committees. Decisions were supposed to emerge by consensus as the issue under review was worn down (like some of the committee members) to elemental simplicity. That suited Olsen's prime management theory: 'A good manager never has to make any decisions at all' – because, if the groundwork is done properly, the decision makes itself.

That was the excuse for dragging out the switch from decentralised product managers to a centralised sales and marketing organisation. Olsen could have commanded the change. Instead, he undermined the previous system (his own creation) by actions and interventions which made the old way untenable and the new way inevitable.

Olsen paid salesmen on straight salaries (in case commissions tempted them to oversell customers); he worked occasionally as an engineer himself; he spewed out ideas and business 'parables'; he seemed to have found a better, if inimitable, way to run a computer company. Yet the Digital brand of management was no more foolproof than IBM's. The recession of the early Nineties was disastrous for both companies – and the root cause was the same.

If IBM's mainframes were an endangered species, so were Digital's minis. By 1992, top-of-the-range, PC-based workstations rivalled mainframes in power and capacity – minis were being challenged for power, and thrashed for cost, by micros. The early Nineties produced a series of grim announcements, reminiscent in nature as in causes of the rundown of IBM. In mid-1992 Olsen announced that 3,700 more US employees would depart. That brought the total decline from the end-1989 peak of 126,000 to near 10 per cent; nor would it end the shrinkage.

Even more startling than the numbers were the names heading the exit list: vice presidents in charge of marketing; finance; strategic relations; operations staff; image, voice and video products: US sales; corporate relations; and Far East manufacturing. A whole layer of senior management, covering a wide swathe of Digital's activities, had been cut out – or cut off.

Headless chickens are not the best oriented of beings, and neither are headless corporations. But Digital did have a head – the increasingly autocratic Ken Olsen. In the early years, Olsen's autocratic leanings had been tempered by the sage General Doriot, the venture capitalist who originally held 77 per cent of the company. In his own late eighties, when Olsen was sixty, Doriot still acted as mentor, advising Olsen on the delicate issues – like choosing a successor.

Five years later, with Doriot dead, Olsen still had no heir, apparent or otherwise. This was one simple decision that refused to make itself – or wasn't allowed to. Consciously or subconsciously, Olsen had seen one potential successor after another off the premises. Against that background, with the troubles of the Nineties piling up, accusations of 'founder's disease' were unavoidable and understandable.

During the great VAX reshuffle, earlier critics thought Olsen had perhaps succumbed to this dread disease, in which the creator, having hung on too long, pulls his own house down around his ears by insensitive arrogance. The VAX triumph seemed to clear Olsen of the charge: consistent clashes with his long-time lieutenants were their fault, not his; they were unable to adapt to external change, to become true entrepreneurs, not proto-bureaucrats.

In 1992, though, Olsen had reached the normal age of retirement. The company's business – which had merely wobbled in 1983 – was degenerating fast. Return on equity, 12 per cent in 1985, evaporated under the strain: the company lost $617.4 million in 1991 - and its return on equity was a *negative* 8 per cent. Over a decade its investors had received a return of only 2.5 per cent per annum compound.

Even IBM, the arch-enemy, had done far better by share-holders with a still inadequate 8.7 per cent. Both were comfortably led by Hewlett-Packard, the best managed of all the electronics giants. But outside comments that concentrate only on a company's financial numbers invariably miss half the truth.

The blunting of Digital's edge is better illuminated by the saga of a spectacularly brilliant recruit, David Cutler, a legendary software designer. Publicity for Digital's invasion of IBM territory concentrated on the VAX computers, but the onslaught could not have succeeded without Cutler's VMS software – produced under the aegis of computer designer Gordon Bell.

When Bell joined Digital's many distinguished exiles in the early Eighties, Cutler, dismayed by the Olsen brand of office politics, took his Digital team away from Massachusetts to a haven in Redmond, Washington State. The team's work for Digital on designing hardware and software round RISC (reduced instruction set computing) chips was well-timed and well-directed. No RISC chip has received more praise than Digital's Alpha.

But by then Cutler and his team had quit. The impelling event was Olsen's decision to build workstations round a different RISC chip. Since the disgruntled Cutler group already lived in the Northwest, Seattle's most famous computer tycoon, Bill Gates of Microsoft, was perfectly placed to add them to his strength. The hundred programmers at Redmond constituted a formidable new armoury for Microsoft's challenge to IBM.

As described by an Apple man, Cutler sounds like perfect Digital material, a classic software type without formal computer-science training: 'He's an iconoclast and he has rough edges, but he hardly ever makes mistakes.' That could once have been said of Olsen himself. But Digital's mistakes as its market fundamentally changed proved that the magic touch had fled. Undeniable errors multiplied. The loss of key people like Cutler was plainly among them. That departure of seven vice presidents at one swoop in May 1992, though, was different, designed to strengthen the two-year struggle to get back to reasonable profitability. As noted, the situation was markedly similar to IBM's: the two came to resemble each other far more in adversity than ever in their times of maximum success.

Digital still made brave noises about minis and IBM about mainframes. But for a growing, eventually dominant number of commercial uses, both product lines represented expensive solutions to needs that microprocessor-based machines could satisfy as well – and far more cheaply. Significantly, a Digital rival like Prime had given up on hardware, spinning off the residual mini business into a separate company: IBM's old enemy, Control Data, had done likewise with its residual mainframe interests.

Both these managements now saw their future only in computer services. For IBM and Digital, with their much heavier investment in selling hardware, that course was impossible. Both opted for improvement to their traditional business, which would be achieved by better organisation – or reorganisation. Like Akers at IBM, Olsen ordained upheaval to reorient the company and turn losses ($294 million on $3.25 billion of operating revenues in a single quarter of 1992) into profits.

Just as the British operation at IBM was something of a guinea pig for new ideas on running IBM, so Digital UK led the way towards a new order. The object was to get closer to the customer, and, in organisation terms, to put asunder what had previously been joined together. By abolishing its geographical structure, with different managements responsible for different countries, Digital sought to concentrate on industrial sectors – five in all.

The UK model was extended to Europe. Across the European frontiers, sector managements (looking after financial services, say, or telecommunications) now worked through dedicated units. They were supposed to act like entrepreneurs as they concentrated on specific industries and customers. One entire layer of management (for which read managers) was removed from the Digital scene: only three layers were left to cope – and the European model was to be adopted for the US.

This fourth great revolution in Digital's style – from loose creativity to product-based entrepreneurship to centralised marketing to customer-based profit centres – had good reason to spring from Europe, rather than the US. Europe had become the company's largest market, accounting for over half of revenues. Almost unnoticed, the European tail had been wagging dogs, not only at Digital, but Apple and Compaq – and IBM.

IBM World Trade had risen to outdo the parent long before. The separate identity outside the US probably stimulated the organisation's overall growth, but the non-US business hadn't won independence for any strong commercial and managerial reasons. It was simply that the senior Watson wanted to give his younger son, Dick, a job of equal stature to Tom Jr's – much to the latter's resentment. The sweeping successes of World Trade didn't reduce the jealousies, but intensified them; and World Trade's loss of independence, linked to the epochal emergence of the 360 range, spelt the end of Dick's career at IBM.

In another parallel between IBM and Digital, the latter's European shake-up at Digital was accompanied by historic change at the top. Pier Carlo Falotti, the man credited with Digital's impressive build-up in Europe, departed for his own reasons. 'It would be wrong to portray him as throwing his rattle out of the crib,' said a colleague. Falotti might have had reason to throw, for an American, Robert Palmer, had been named to replace another departure – the most significant possible.

At sixty-five, Olsen had finally bowed to the years, the weight of the problems faced by his creation, and the pressure of unhappy executives (including Palmer). The age of the mini was passing: its greatest figure passed, too, retiring in the October of 1992. His successor was neither a Digital nor a mini veteran. His background, before joining Olsen in 1985, was in semiconductors – he had helped to found Mostek, later sold to the conglomerate United Technologies.

While his Digital vice presidency was in the corpocratic function of manufacturing and logistics, Palmer is thus no corpocrat. His career blends two strands that now dominate the industry – the rise of the microprocessor to universal supremacy in hardware, and the necessity to inject entrepreneurial blood into bureaucratic veins. Whether Digital's medicine will work, given the difficulty of its strategic situation, is another matter. But the dosage is the most promising available.

First, inject new leadership from outside the company and outside its traditional business. Second, abolish a tier of top management. Third, push through wholesale reorganisation. Fourth, make a highly symbolic personal break with a glorious but increasingly irrelevant past.

The question for Digital was whether an attempt to achieve entrepreneurial reorganisation could win the day that the great Ken Olsen was at last deserting. Everything depended on the new range of computers, designed around the Alpha chip and covering the gamut of business needs. Digital's companion in adversity, IBM, was still condemned to struggle with an unwieldy product portfolio. But otherwise, new CEO Lou Gerstner's regime could hope to apply the four-fold formula.

Gerstner and his management imports provided the outside infusion, and the symbolic break with the past – they also had the opportunity and the power to break the Armonk mandarins and remake the system. What they required as well was the same ultimate attribute that had given Olsen, the maverick in minis, his greatness: ruthless tenacity.

14

Telecommunications:
The Rolm Catastrophe

On 7 May 1992, IBM made one of its increasingly common admissions of defeat. This was no big deal in itself – merely the disposal of a half-share to its equal partner in a marketing and service company. It handled the telecommunications equipment made by Rolm Systems in California. But thereby hung a much larger story.

The partner who swallowed IBM's half-share was Siemens, the king of European electronics. Once, IBM had owned all of Rolm. This was its first ever corporate purchase, acquired in 1984 as part of a grand design and broad vision. As technologies converged, computers and communications would form an indivisible whole. Private branch telephone exchanges (which Rolm made) would offer IBM the desired entry into this new and wonderful world.

As it was, the telecommunications market, dominated by monopolistic giants like AT&T and the national corporations of Europe and Japan, was incomparably vast. It dwarfed even the computer industry ruled by IBM. To add piquancy to its strategy, a move into telecommunications would be a counter-attack. AT&T had been trying, with ill success, to find a place in computing. It wasn't finally achieved until

1992 with the purchase of NCR (*alma mater*, in another piquant twist, of old Tom Watson).

To ensure its position in this new, interconnected world, IBM paid $1.3 billion for Rolm, then at the crest of an outstanding climb. Unfortunately, the path from crests leads downwards. The Rolm shareholders got out while the going, from their point of view, was good – even superlative. Their entrepreneurial leader, co-founder M. Kenneth Oshman, stayed with his new employer for precisely fourteen months.

The experience was reminiscent of Xerox Corporation's disastrous buy of a computer firm, Scientific Data Systems. Like Xerox, IBM became the anxious owner of a money-losing pup. Another billion was wasted in absorbing losses and development costs before IBM washed its hands of the mess in late 1988. Selling the manufacturing side to Siemens, it kept only the half-stake, confined to the marketing arm, that disappeared four years later.

The net loss was $1.35 billion in money and a fortune more in intangible terms. Not only had IBM lost its potential place as a major player in telecommunications, but the episode had shown its vaunted management powers, in their first real test outside the walls of the corporation, to be ineffective. The many IBM managers drafted into Rolm floundered in this unfamiliar territory. Having bought in badly, IBM couldn't manage its way out.

In a way, this wasn't surprising. Over this same period IBM was simultaneously mismanaging its way out of a business which it had always owned – typewriters and printers. The company was not helped by lack of experience in acquisitions: one of its most justifiable prides was that all its mighty growth had been organic. But Rolm's market became harshly competitive, and without the ability to manage the marketplace, IBM was no managerial superpower.

The 1992 sale (on undisclosed terms) fitted in with a new strategy which recognised that reality. From now on, IBM would concentrate on its areas of expertise. If it needed related technologies, they would be obtained by strategic alliances, rather than strategic takeovers. This climb-down totally denied the vision held inside and even outside IBM when the original Rolm deal was struck. 'Soon IBM will become the first – and likely the only – worldwide telephone company,' wrote the well-informed Richard Thomas DeLamarter. He recognised that some might find this reading difficult to believe. 'IBM the global phone company? Preposterous idea. Impossible.' Not only was AT&T the 'undisputed world leader' (and moving to build its international strength), but national telecommunications companies had monopolies or quasi-monopolies in every country. 'Besides, IBM makes its money processing data, not selling telephones or moving calls between them.'

For all that, DeLamarter was convinced that 'IBM the telephone company seems much more than just likely – it seems inevitable'. The observations on which he built this remarkable, and remarkably wrong, thesis are an interesting guide to IBM's own strategic thinking of the mid-Eighties, and to the upheavals which undermined the strategy. First, DeLamarter saw how IBM's enormous business rested on a tiny base in terms of customer numbers – 'a relatively few large corporations'.

As their communications networks proliferated, they would eventually find it 'economically compelling to combine all networks into one'. Pure telecommunications companies would be unable to bridge national boundaries, but in a digital age IBM – the supreme digital supplier – 'would become a one-stop shop for all sorts of telecommunications gear and services'. The primary service would be communication itself, not only through dedicated networks built for its multinational customers, but through 'switching': that is, telephone exchanges.

Rolm's private branch exchanges (PBX) were only a start – 'in late 1985 IBM dropped broad hints that it would soon enter the telephone central switch market as part of an effort to double its sales of telecommunications gear in Europe'. Investments in the long-distance carrier, MCI, and interests in US-wide radio links (with Motorola and the Public Broadcasting System), seemed to hint at the same conclusion: IBM was set on building an 'international telecommunications network' that would 'greatly expand' its corporate power.

A former trustbuster, DeLamarter scarcely welcomed the thought of customers being secured and dragooned into the IBM net. It would be able to exclude competitive products from a system built on IBM standards – standards, moreover, that could be changed at will to disadvantage the competition. Two French critics saw the threat to national communications companies in near-apocalyptic terms: IBM is 'going beyond data processing . . . IBM is entrenched . . . with such reserves of power that it cannot be seriously threatened'.

Compared to this 'dominant' force, the world's telephone monopolies, even AT&T, were puny, depending on over-priced services and outdated technology. Leapfrogging the latter, and undercutting the former, IBM occupied the 'high ground', overlooking a battlefield on which the monopolies were being fragmented by irresistible technological, economic and political pressures. In DeLamarter's view, IBM was bound to 'prevail, for it held significant advantages'.

The latter ranged from its transnational spread to the 'sweeteners' it could offer to national governments (like the $2 billion distributed round 50,000 European suppliers in 1984 and 'co-operative arrangements with local schools'). Above all, though, IBM would be able to offer its large corporate customers unique equipment and services. That would win their lucrative business and leave the national telephone networks (the PTTs) 'to tend to low-profit residential and small business customers'.

Against this fantasy, DeLamarter scrupulously recorded some contrary facts. First, IBM's past telecommunications products had been disconcerting flops, including one 'deliberately perverse' offering that simply ignored what customers wanted. Rolm had only been purchased, at a grossly excessive price, because IBM had 'failed several times to build a marketable PBX product'. Above and beyond these defects lay the persistent weakness that, like cholesterol deposits, had been steadily clogging IBM's commercial arteries over the years: incompatibility.

The 'great difficulties in getting its unreasonably diverse set of incompatible computer families to communicate effectively with each other' were still bedevilling IBM in 1993. DeLamarter believed that IBM could overcome any product weaknesses by opening its architecture to outsiders. Hadn't the PC spectacularly overtaken Apple by the same means? In 1986 few foresaw that the open architecture of the PC would work in the opposite direction – opening the door not to later sales of IBM equipment, but to an army of rivals.

Working from his intimate knowledge of the company's competitive processes, DeLamarter did foresee, amusingly enough, how IBM would try to move from open systems back to proprietary quasi-monopoly: 'Once its customers are wedded to the IBM computer system that others have enhanced, and once IBM has designed its own add-on capabilities, it can begin to close the system's architecture to outsiders. A subsequent variation of the original system may be designed to preserve customers' software investment even as it closes the door to others trying to attach products.'

The passage almost precisely maps the way in which IBM hoped to use the OS/2 operating system to recreate its lost early dominance of the PC market. DeLamarter had read IBM's psychology right, but misread its capabilities. In that he was by no means alone. A year after the Rolm deal, for example, *Business Week* reported on 'How IBM is Getting the Most Out of Rolm'.

'Respect for the phone switchboard maker's more casual culture has paid off.' Three and a half years later, the same magazine reported the sale of Rolm, which 'will put an end to one of the most embarrassing chapters in Big Blue's history'.

Respect for Rolm's culture, far from paying off, had delayed and muffled IBM's reaction to its acquisition's poor performance. Both former and current insiders thought that IBM should have seized hold as soon as the problems emerged.

Instead, 'IBM people kept saying: "No, no, no!" They wanted to try their hand at more entrepreneurial methods,' said a former Rolm insider. At the very beginning, when there were understandable doubts about this West–East marriage between Santa Clara and Armonk, two IBM dignitaries had travelled west to reassure their about-to-be employees – choosing an impromptu beer bash in the company's outdoor amphitheatre to stress the point.

The ambassadors even broke a time-honoured IBM rule against drinking on the job, accepting two cans of Miller beer from Oshman. They reassured Rolm people about their operating independence and their informal ways. One of the IBM pair said graphically that, 'We're not here to drain your pool.' His name was John F. Akers, president and future chairman of the company: he was showing early on the flair for the telling phrase that highlighted his darkly troubled reign.

The Rolm calamity which Akers set in motion is fascinating, not only for itself, but for the pattern of events – one repeated often in IBM's long fall from grace. The circumstances varied, but the step-by-step rake's progress was much the same.

One, *top management at Armonk makes a grand strategic decision.* This was the one which so impressed DeLamarter. As telecommunications and computing converged, IBM would emerge as the leading supplier of both. The *Washington Post* spelt out the grand strategy in down-to-earth English: 'Today, an IBM customer could begin processing data on an IBM personal computer, send it to an IBM mainframe computer that sends it an IBM/Rolm telecommunications switch, which relays it to a Satellite Business Systems/IBM satellite, which then beams it to another IBM customer a continent away. IBM is becoming a vertically integrated information technologies and service company.'

Two, *the strategy is shown to be inoperable because of weak or missing links all along the line.* The SBS satellite business was a market failure: IBM exchanged its holding for 16 per cent of MCI, the long-distance operator: then this investment, too, was abandoned. In the Rolm case, the weak link was IBM's disastrous inability to crack the PBX market by developing its own technology (similar failures in technologies new to IBM are a recurrent theme).

In such cases, IBM doesn't change the strategy – it looks for tactical escapes. The spectacular success of the PC operation had shown the tactical way out of such dilemmas – buy the technology from independent, outside partners. That was the original justification for buying into Rolm, intended to be a strategic alliance, not an acquisition.

Three, *the tactical solution doesn't work.* IBM's 15 per cent stake in Rolm (later raised to 17.7 per cent) emulated the deal which gave it 12 per cent of Intel (a buy which differed in that it wasn't part of a grand strategy). The idea was to develop joint products, and to sell Rolm exchanges to large IBM customers. But in practice any marketing and technological initiatives foundered on IBM's secrecy and who-does-what disputes.

Four, *IBM decides on a radical, risky break-out to bust the problem.* It took over Rolm completely. The risks are self-evident in hindsight, and enormous. IBM knew nothing about managing acquisitions and little about Rolm's market. Not only were the cultures incompatible, so were the reward systems. A clash of corporate cultures was inevitable. The greatest risk was throwing out the baby with the bathwater: getting control over Rolm, but losing the entrepreneurial characteristics that made it worth controlling.

Five, *stages one to four achieve almost universal adulation,* encouraged by IBM publicity and public statements. The *Washington Post* thought the Rolm deal a 'vital link' in IBM's corporate strategy; *Business Week*, as noted, believed IBM 'to be managing the buyout of Rolm Corp as deftly as it dominates the computer industry'. Earlier the magazine had paid tribute to the advanced PBX that showed 'why IBM bought into Rolm'.

In fact, like the strategic wisdom of IBM's decision, the virtues of this machine were a mirage. As *Business Week* later reported, the new marvel 'was based on a eight-year old central processor that ran so hot it required special air-conditioning and more space than rival machines'. That puts into proper perspective *Fortune*'s hopeful comment that 'when Big Blue moves beyond its basic data-processing businesses . . . its risks are hedged with other people's money and expertise'.

Six, despite the general outside view that IBM knows exactly what it's doing, why and how, *insiders discover grave weaknesses in the new, risky tactical programme.* The choice of Intel was inspired, that of Rolm ruinous. As one obituary noted, 'The bigger company should have known what was amiss. As early as 1982 Rolm was under stress.' Gross margins were sinking, technology was lagging (even a Rolm man described its basic product as an 'ageing workhorse'), and financing was running low.

Seven, *the personal commitment of very senior IBMers has a profound influence on events.* President John Akers was accompanied to the Rolm beer bust by vice chairman Paul J. Rizzo. The next IBM president, Jack D. Kuehler, was the man first approached by Rolm's Oshman for financing – and the man who took the proposition to Armonk. There, executives apparently ignored a 1983 internal study showing Rolm to be in decline.

The company's chairman, John R. Opel, vice chairman Rizzo and chief financial officer Allen J. Krowe were among those who signed off on the Rolm purchase. If they got the message about Rolm's condition, they can't have taken it seriously. Characteristically, according to an ex-IBMer, 'People who understood the market best weren't asked for their views' by the top men. The latter are exceedingly and sometimes dangerously reluctant to admit to mistakes at any point – even, as the Rolm story was to show, when the damage has been publicly revealed.

Eight, *conflicts arise between IBM's culture and its policy objectives.* The culture wins. Akers & Co foresaw the danger of personnel departures if Rolm's freer and easier ways were disturbed. The threat materialised at once. One key man left the day IBM arrived, because he 'didn't want to work for the post office'.

The IBM bureaucracy undermined the good intentions by methods like insisting on reviewing Rolm's prices – a review that caused infuriating four-week delays in a fast-moving market. In the autumn of 1985, Rolm was further ordered to hire only IBMers from then on. Within a year, the experience of working not just with IBM, but within, had caused wide disaffection. Led by Oshman himself, the exodus of top people became total.

Nine, after unnecessary procrastination, *IBM finally takes the necessary action – too late.* In October 1986, Krowe had to take charge of manufacturing. Rolm's costs were hopelessly inflated by Oshman's policy of setting up three separate, separately managed, competitive production lines. In March 1987, the 6,000-strong Rolm sales force was merged into IBM's, and more defections occurred. In December 1987, Rolm became an IBM division.

Ten, *the policy begins to self-destruct.* By August 1988, no longer even a division, Rolm Systems was 'immersed in IBM culture', reported *Computer World.* The promise that Rolm would maintain its entrepreneurial spirit was as much a thing of the past as its twelve-week sabbaticals and lavish sales commissions. The interviewer found several veteran employees who 'said the Rolm culture, which had fostered independence, has been replaced by bureaucracy'.

Neither interviewer nor interviewed were aware that Ellen M. Hancock, the most senior woman in IBM, and Rolm's ultimate boss as head of communications products, had ordered a review that became a death warrant. Rolm was going to lose big money for the fourth successive year (maybe $300 million), and would continue to do so; the latest PBX product was suffering serious delays; and four years after his fatal sips of beer at Santa Clara, Akers, now CEO, was advised that Rolm didn't offer a winning equation'.

Finally, comes total failure – and near-total denial. At the press conference that handed Rolm over to Siemens, Akers even denied that it was a takeover. Siemens was 'not taking over anything. We're forming an important partnership.' As for accusations that IBM 'superimposed its culture on Rolm', Akers didn't think so: 'In some respects, Rolm superimposed their culture on us – in a very positive way.'

Quite what that meant is wonderfully unclear. According to a reporter who was there, 'Mr Akers and other IBMers' weren't in a communicative mood. They 'fended off questions', as well they might. During their reign Rolm had shrunk from 8,000 employees to 3,000, lost nearly all its senior managers within the first year or so, and utterly failed to deliver any of IBM's objectives. *Electronics Weekly* quoted the former marketing vice president, Richard Moley, to devastating effect: 'To succeed in the PBX market . . . "You've got to be mean and lean, very scrappy and quick to react." But IBM replaced Rolm-bred managers with IBMers and gradually imposed the company's "uniform process" of management . . . "With the entrepreneurial nature of Rolm, you managed by exception" . . . IBM's uniform approach "wasn't a great process for the PBX business".'

In fairness, Rolm's great days as a West Coast growth star were behind it when IBM bought in. That makes the decision to buy the business no better, but also meant that many disciplines introduced by IBM were badly needed. The buyer's interference was on balance harmful, both in managing and developing the business: but external changes after the purchase would have severely challenged any management, including Oshman's. The PBX market, according to one insider, had simply become 'a horrible place to be'.

That wasn't the worst aspect of the buy. Go back down the eleven-point cycle to the very first one – the grand strategy by which Armonk and its fans set such great store. It was proved disastrously wrong by events. The premise on which IBM based the acquisition was invalidated. Computing and telecommunications did not converge in the anticipated way. IBM didn't need exchange switching capabilities to enable its customers to talk to their computers.

Instead, computers were linked primarily by local area networks. As for the challenge being mounted by AT&T in IBM's heartland, the phone company only succeeded in losing enormous sums of money in computers without getting much further than first base. IBM needn't have worried and needn't have bothered – and all the thousands of words spilt about 'IBM's move into telecommunications' and 'a vertically integrated information technologies and service company' need not have been written.

But the real tragedy of Rolm, apart from the personal disasters of the thousands whose jobs were destroyed, lies in the eleven-point life-and-death cycle. Its last stage, the final denial of final failure, meant that IBM never learnt the lessons of Rolm. This humiliation wasn't a one-off incident, but a systemic failure. Because nothing was done to change the system, catastrophes far more serious than Rolm – after all, what was a billion dollars to IBM? – were bound to follow.

15

The Junking
of Junior

If there's a turning point in the saga of IBM, a moment when the seeds of decay within every success visibly started to sprout, it was the launch of PC Jr – or 'Peanut'. That's how it was christened by frustrated media men, hungry to know exactly what IBM was planning. The project didn't disappoint them: Jr was designed to fling wide the casements to a magic world – taking IBM not only into every office, but potentially into every home.

The ambitions for the PC had been wildly understated, but those for Jr were almost grandiloquent. It wasn't the only major project which Don Estridge and the Entry Systems Division at Boca Raton had on their suddenly golden plates. The Corporate Management Committee at Armonk, flushed with its Florida child's success, had approved no fewer than three ventures. These were a more powerful version of the existing PC, a still more advanced personal computer (which would incorporate Intel's latest 286 chip) – and Jr.

Add to that the burden of sustaining and exploiting the PC's breakthrough and you have a workload heavy enough to crack most managements. If the new projects had been set wholly free, like the original PC, the task would have been easier. That had been possible within the totality of IBM because of Estridge's direct line to the top. It wasn't possible within Boca Raton. Estridge carried the can, and the project managers reported to him through IBM's conventional checkpoint system.

For Jr, the manager was engineer Bill Sydnes, a key member of the original PC team. Like that group, the Jr people were up against a terribly tight schedule. Sydnes was put in command in the spring of 1982 and charged with announcing his baby in July the next year. Like the Dirty Dozen again, Sydnes started from a blank sheet of paper: no staff, no product plan, nothing. Unlike them, however, he faced some powerful constraints.

What was Jr's relationship to its PC father? The more capable the machine, the more easily upgraded to work like the PC, the more it would 'cannibalise' PC sales. Then, where would a 'home' computer be sold? Selling it through the specialist computer outlets that carried the PC would restrict sales. That was likely even if the dealers didn't (as they certainly would) steer buyers towards the costlier and more profitable senior PCs.

On both these central issues, hindsight proves Sydnes right. IBM opposition to the first PC was ultimately founded on fear that the microprocessor would cannibalise sales of larger computers. This fear was probably never articulated – nor, probably, was the riposte that, if IBM didn't cannibalise itself, others would. In the end, years down the line, IBM found itself following a Sydnes strategy – selling fully-fledged PCs via electrical stores and discounters, and introducing fully compatible, low-priced machines at the bottom of its range.

That was in the Nineties. In the early Eighties, nobody in power at IBM would countenance such radical departures – and that included Estridge. He and his original team had been free to pursue their own strategy: the potentially vexed issue of marketing through non-IBM outlets had only been raised at the last moment. But the Jr group's legs were cut from beneath them by diktat. The machine couldn't be sold through mass merchandisers: nor could Junior be compatible with the PC. The strategy made no sense to Sydnes, who resigned before his baby went into production – to encounter a horrendous set of defects.

The ultimate tragedy is that the PC Jr was unnecessary. The vision of an IBM computer on every desk didn't require a low-priced entry model. There truly was a market for a computer that the executive could take home, but that was almost by definition a genuinely portable market – and one which IBM unaccountably missed, leaving it for Compaq and Toshiba. As for the computer in every home, that market was misread.

There *was* an untapped domestic demand – for a really cheap word processor. The British entrepreneur Alan Sugar proved that with a spectacular success priced at £399. As the one-time overlord of electronic typewriters, IBM might have spotted that gap. But its typewriters were *office* products, and the connection was never made. Anyway, Sugar's original market died as computer prices fell. Why buy a dedicated word processor when the same money bought a genuine computer with a word processing program – and much else besides?

The Jr task was as formidable as the original PC project, yet it was entrusted to a notably less competent team with a much less enabling mandate. Moreover, the reliance on outside vendors had been taken a deal too far. The entire machine was built by Teledyne at the conglomerate's Tennessee plant – and the vendor botched the job. The Teledyne problems couldn't be swept under the carpet. IBM's corporate executives, including the new president, John F. Akers, immediately knew all about a disaster that set the launch back by many months.

Bad projects, as every manager knows, feed on their badness. Murphy's Law (whatever can go wrong, will) goes into overtime. The more money was thrown at Jr, the more it demanded. Workers in the disaster area now believe it would have been better to scrap the original project and start again. But too much publicity pressure had built up. IBM's standard safeguard (never announce a product until it's good and ready) had in effect been blown away.

Still, the machine came out. On 1 November 1983, the Jr and its specifications – impressive enough at the time – were unveiled before a generally enthusiastic press. But Murphy's Law couldn't be denied. The worst thing that could happen to Jr (apart from not working at all) was to have a single feature so conspicuously bad that critics and customers alike would seize on the defect. And Jr did: the infamous rubber keyboard.

That feature was bad enough in itself. But Murphy and his law intervened yet again. Emergency action, of the kind that the original PC team brought off in crisis, might have saved the situation. But indecision prevailed. Jr was stuck with the awful keyboard as the first 1,700 models were rushed to the dealers. The rush was unnecessary, it turned out, because nobody bothered to demonstrate the product before Christmas. Why? It wouldn't be available until the New Year.

In 1984, the Jr duly missed its ludicrous target of 1.2 million units. At $699, the product was too expensive for the home market. Sydnes had been very wrong about many things, but right in his marketing perception. A lower-priced mass-merchandised product compatible with the PC was a feasible runner: a costly, incompatible computer sold through the same outlets as the PC stood no chance.

If the Jr collapse had been the sole failure of the new Entry Systems Division, that would have been serious and ominous enough. But IBM's efforts to recoup only compounded the failure. An improved product with a decent keyboard appeared on 21 July 1984. Massive direct mail campaigns were then directed at twelve million households and eight million professionals and business people. The TV and press blitz achieved the ultimate in overkill. The marketers sought to reach virtually the entire universe of potential Jr purchasers at least thirty times apiece in the last quarter of 1984.

With authorised prices, including a colour monitor, cut to $799, the Jr had been given every chance. But sales slumped after Christmas, and on 19 March 1985 the product was axed. Tested for the first time against the truly mass market, IBM had failed lamentably and in embarrassingly public view. The blow to the pride, prestige and profits of the entire corporation was less grave, on a longer view, than the damage done to Estridge's whole operation.

As noted, Jr was débâcle enough for any lifetime. But the new division, in that make-or-break year of 1984, was broken by three further disasters. The least important was the rapid flop of the first portable attempt. The first of the really deadly decisions was to end all development and thus eventually all marketing of the original PCs based on the 8086 chip. What IBM carelessly abandoned, other makers greedily exploited.

Second, the new line, the PC/AT, built around the 286 microprocessor, was a great leap forward. But Estridge's ill luck with market forecasts persisted. Underestimation of demand was compounded by a grotesque failure of supply – the hard disks were defective in the worst way: they would suddenly wipe out all their contents. The AT had been eighteen months behind schedule, anyway – now it was clumsily withdrawn with IBM insisting, against all the evidence, that no problem existed. Since there was no alternative supplier for the disks, potential customers had to wait nine more months before supplies were resumed.

In introducing the original PC, Estridge's unit had done everything right – if you include in that definition (as you should) rapidly correcting each and every mistake as soon as it appeared. From that magic moment on, the unit seemed to have done too many things wrong – critical errors had been allowed to run riot. Who or what was to blame? The buck, at its simplest, stops at Don Estridge's door. It's one of the oldest truisms in management. The man who is supremely the right choice for launching a new enterprise is the wrong man to lead the business into maturity. Estridge had taken Boca Raton in two years to $4 billion of sales. It was equivalent in size to the seventy-fourth largest industrial corporation, bigger than all IBM's mainframe rivals and not far behind Digital Equipment.

The style that had created the PC, the engine of this unprecedented growth, was charismatic, loose-limbed, improvisational, lean, concentrated. Estridge had licence to act freely to meet his one-year deadline, and expertly exploited his freedom. In doing so, he not only broke IBM rules – he also created an organisation inside IBM that bore little resemblance to its host.

Dan Wilkie, who took over manufacturing early in the Dirty Dozen days, defined the differences: 'Don would give us an assignment, or our assignments would require us to take some action, and so we would just go and do it. We didn't have to wade through the layers of the corporation's bureaucracy. We knew what counted and we could see the results . . . Before I went to work on the team, I helped deliver a printer. The printer was in development for seven years! I kept telling myself, "It's coming . . . it's coming". But the printer was hopelessly mired in design changes and bureaucracy.'

What Wilkie called these 'layers and layers at IBM' arose 'because every job at IBM is so vertical, so specialised. No individual, or any group, has a clear, visible identity – not even an opportunity to see . . . "the whole pie" of a product, including the research and development, the marketing expenses, the direct cost, everything.' At Boca Raton, seeing the whole pie for the first time, Wilkie 'made more decisions in my first thirty days with that group than I made during my first fourteen years with IBM'.

Read with the hindsight of the unavailing efforts to change IBM in the Eighties and Nineties, that's an uncanny precursor of the new ideal sought vainly by John Akers, the chief executive who took over at the turn in Boca Raton's fortunes. The following words of Estridge's, taken from an IBM house magazine, have the Akers ring, too. 'Our management style is geared to eliminating overhead, unnecessary meetings and discussion; to operating with lower cost, fewer people and shorter development cycles.'

Unfortunately much of that related to the past, not the present. Far from operating with 'lower cost, fewer people and shorter development cycles', his division was adding cost, people and time in exponential increases. According to Sydnes, 'Estridge was allowing the organisation to grow far past the point of profitability . . . there was no earthly reason to have thousands of people working on the IBM personal computer. . . . My God! Look at Apple; they had more than half our revenues with about a third of the people we were carrying on our payroll.'

The man who started and then resigned from the Jr project is not an impartial witness. He deeply resented the way Estridge overrode him on policy, and couldn't forgive his boss for allowing him to apply for a job elsewhere in IBM – and then forbidding the move. But his indictment rings true. Some of these new people, in Sydnes' account, were middle managers of the standard IBM pattern, wished on Estridge by 'corporate management' – and that also rings true.

It's not enough to blame the string of errors on Estridge alone. A large contribution to the calamities came from Armonk, which wasn't inclined to let so successful an Independent Business Unit stay independent. Its rebirth on 1 August 1983 as the Entry Systems Division (president, Don Estridge) could have been construed as the ultimate accolade. It was in some respects the kiss of death. ESD's payroll immediately expanded from 4,000 to 10,000 as plants in Austin, Texas, Greenock, Scotland, and Wanganatta, Australia came under Estridge's span of control.

The division kept the marketing responsibilities that, for other products, lay with the IBM sales organisation. That apart, it was no longer a maverick. The eagle had landed. Nor did Estridge resist the clipping of its wings – he had the strongest of personal reasons to accept, even encourage, the integration of the PC business into the rest of IBM. As he often said, 'All roads must eventually lead to Armonk.' Only a few months after his new division was formed, Estridge was named a vice president of the corporation.

If the original group has been 'us' against 'them', where did Estridge stand now? A long way from Boca Raton, according to Wilkie: 'The company came in and set up multiple levels of managers, multiple disciplines, new policies and procedures, and reviews upon reviews . . . This protocol and discipline started to cause problems because Don was spending almost 80 per cent of his time in Armonk, with just unbelievable travelling back and forth to report to all the people he now had to deal with in IBM.'

Among these people were the critics of the failures at Boca Raton. In the internecine fighting with other powers – such as the Communications Products Division, which had its own ideas about the PC's future – Estridge held his own for a while. But in January 1985, the writing appeared on Boca Raton's wall. The PC people at last lost control of their own retail sales. The mightiest powers in IBM were massed for this victory – the National Accounts Division and the National Marketing Division, jointly forming the Informations Systems Group.

There were sound reasons for the change. The NAD and NMD were in sales conflict with retailers offering Boca Raton's products to the same corporate customers. A large, vigorous 'gray market' in PCs had developed, fed by the retailers from their excess orders. Pricing and advertising, however, were left with Estridge's division, which only confused the issue: who was responsible for profit? More important, how much profit was there?

The initial profitability of the PC, which shot up as the numbers made and sold exceeded the budgets, had been deeply eroded by the rise in overheads and the colossal, wasted expenditures on the lost cause of Jr. Also, the drive and sheer zing had moved out of Boca Raton as the bureaucrats moved in. For the residue of the Dirty Dozen and those who had joined them, it was a demotivating experience, well described by Chposky and Leonsis in *Blue Magic*: 'They had been superb at what they did best, and now they had to ask to be able to do it. Instead, they were told to work on presentations, or status reports, or presentations that were like reports. Or reports on how presentations can be more like reports.'

To outsiders it seemed that Estridge had been kicked upstairs to pay the price for the series of failures in his command. Insiders insisted that nothing had diminished Estridge's heroic stature, and that his new staff role – as vice president of manufacturing worldwide – was a further step towards the IBM summit. The truth probably lay somewhere in-between. Estridge had to be removed, not simply because of the fiascos, but because (with the latter partly in mind) the whole PC operation was to be regularised.

All trace of autonomy was to be eradicated. That meant installing a new boss who would accept this brief. Ironically, the mantle fell on Bill Lowe, the consummate IBM politician. His original insistence that IBM couldn't make a PC on its own had led to the true independence of the Independent Business Unit, and his choice of Estridge had guaranteed that an iconoclastic, radical style would prevail.

Now, the organisation that had so brilliantly combined product development and manufacturing with marketing and sales reverted to the IBM norm. Marketing and sales were lost. Shortly, Lowe moved with a couple of hundred staff to New Jersey. The new location, within easy reach of Armonk, was more than symbolic – the step was probably planned before Estridge was removed. Yet there's no evidence of intent to punish the hero of Boca Raton, or to take revenge for the endless publicity – flattering to him, but by implication critical of the traditional IBM. The entire high-flying operation had simply fallen to earth.

By a desperately tragic coincidence, that literally happened to the Estridges when their airliner crashed at Dallas on 2 August 1985. The dead man had given IBM two enormous blessings. One was the PC business, which at last cracked the small machine market for IBM, and won the leading place in the new world beyond mainframes. That leadership was considerably misused, partially lost and to some extent squandered. But Estridge also fathered an innovation that could have proved of even greater importance.

The Dirty Dozen showed that IBM had an organisational vitality that fully matched its technological potential. The overlords at Armonk were absolutely right, however. The magical rise of the PC operation was incompatible with the systems and procedures that governed IBM. Where Armonk went wrong was in deciding that, if something had to give, it was the Independent Business Unit.

Early in 1984, John F. Akers, then company president, talked to security analysts at a significant location. Speaking in Boca Raton, home of the PC, he said, 'We must keep an eye on planning its integration into the full IBM product line and carefully manage its role in our total business.' He returned to the integration theme in April 1985. By then he was chairman – and the integration, not only of the PC, but of those who made it, was his confirmed strategy.

The Akers of those days was a centraliser. He didn't come round to advocating decentralisation and devolution of power until the alternative policy had sunk IBM into years of underperformance. Then, too slowly, Akers arrived at a philosophy of decentralisation that went well beyond any predecessor's. He still stopped short of anything that would rob Armonk of decisive power. In the end, that brought the PC operation down to IBM's management standards – rather than raising the latter to the levels that Estridge had shown to be feasible.

The PC's success had seduced everybody, including the top men at Armonk. They fell for a new strategy in which the machine would serve as the gateway to a new world. IBM's corporate customers, a definition extended to cover companies of all sizes, would satisfy their computing needs through many desktop computers. They would be linked through an ascending hierarchy to mainframes, which would thus remain the cornerstone of IBM.

The PC management had to be reabsorbed to serve a strategy that proved untenable. Customers were less eager to become dependent on IBM than IBM was to ensure their dependence. Second, at vital junctures IBM couldn't or didn't deliver the hardware and software needed to make the strategy work. To the extent that this resulted from the PC division's loss of independence, initiative and able people, the scattered heroes of Boca Raton had the last and most hollow laugh.

VI

THE WINNING WAR OF THE CLONES

16

The Conquests
of Compaq

Technical wizardry and mysterious words and symbols abound in computing. But behind the science and the esoteric language lie personal stories of pure romance. Three Texans of no great achievement sit at a café table and sketch out their ambitious business ideas. Their leader approaches a New York financier. He spots the flaws in the plan, advises on suitable changes, and advances the $10 million capital required – a record for high-tech venture investment.

In their first full year, the partners sell a world record of $111 million of products – three times their absurdly high initial thoughts. The next year, they all but treble their sales, another record. One year on, their little company isn't little any more – it's a member of the *Fortune* 500, with half a billion dollars worth of sales. Two years later, that's doubled. From start-up to billionaire has also taken the least time on record. Reaching the double billion needs only twelve months more.

The business romance of Compaq, of its founders (Rod Canion, Bill Murto and Jim Harris) and of its venture capital backer (Ben Rosen of Savin Rosen) couldn't have been written without IBM. At all points, the company needed the giant's involuntary co-operation to prosper and grow. The trio were the first entrepreneurs to take full advantage of IBM's fundamental but fateful decision to create an open 'industry standard'.

Theirs was America's first computer to duplicate or 'clone' the IBM PC. Compaq's clones remained the best-sellers world-wide throughout the tumultuous years which saw cloners burgeon in every country. The burgeoning helped take an amazing four-fifths out of IBM's market share. Yet Canion & Co's company was never perceived as an imitator – their second stroke of genius was to promote Compaq as a new and innovative force, a brand-name rival to IBM.

For all practical purposes, Compaq's first computer was identical with an IBM PC. Its buyers had access to the full battery of programs written for the market leader. Canion's team was very quick off the mark. The IBM PC was only five months old when Compaq was founded, and the first Compaq product reached the market in less than a year. It differed from its model, however, in one key respect. The Compaq had a Unique Selling Proposition. It was portable.

The attractions of a portable were obvious to everybody, including IBM. After all, the prime view of the PC lay in the 'P': it was *personal*. Users had all the programs they needed under their personal control. They were no longer tied to departmental or mainframe computing. They were on their own, liberated. But freedom was partly illusory if you could only use the computer in the office.

A duplicate computer at home provided a solution, but an expensive and inflexible one. A travelling computer, though, allowed owners to take their office with them. An entrepreneur named Adam Osborne had shown the way in April 1981, a few months before IBM announced the PC. Inevitably, his portable was incompatible with IBM (whose MS–DOS operating system had not then been unveiled). But it sold phenomenally.

Peaking at 10,000 units a month, the first portable took Osborne's sales to $100 million in two years. In 1983, however, the company failed, partly because of a foolishly premature announcement of an improved machine. To many observers, Osborne seemed the first, not of the few, but the many. IBM's advent was expected to destroy most of the PC pioneers, from Apple downwards, who had pioneered the market. That, however, wasn't IBM's intention, if you believe Dan Wilkie, one of the Boca Raton pioneers.

According to Wilkie, 'we didn't think about [Apple] too much at all . . . Apple was just another competitor . . . to be honest, the absolutely worst thing that IBM would ever want would be for Apple to crumble.' The thought was that 'everybody would say IBM was responsible, and we'd look like the bad guys'. Of course, more than public relations was involved. IBM felt confident in its ability, as with the PC itself, to enter the market when and where it liked and to cream off the best part of any sector pioneered by others.

As with mainframes, IBM needed marketplace dominance rather than true monopoly. But repeating the mainframe stranglehold depended on proving a vital point – that IBM could, whenever it wished, transcend the competition. IBM waited comfortably until February 1984 before entering the portable market. That gave Compaq a year's free run, during which Canion & Co waited with some anxiety for IBM to move.

They needn't have worried. The champion at first competed ineptly – the machine unveiled that February was heavier than the Compaq rival (itself no lightweight) and inferior in performance. In a typical piece of strategic thought (or thoughtlessness), IBM wanted to keep the portable as far away as possible from its own non-portable machines. Within sixteen months, the resulting half-measure, like most half-measures, failed.

In April 1986, IBM tried again. The PC Convertible was genuinely light in its laptop mode (12 lbs) and was supposed to convert to desktop use. But the over-pricing, coupled with technical failures in design and supply, doomed it to another rapid demise. From then on, to general and continuing surprise, IBM didn't compete in the portable market at all. The company had quit supercomputers in apparent disgust at its own failures; so, apparently, it left portables to others until the early Nineties.

In a sector of outstanding technological advance, with weight falling precipitately as performance rose steeply, other companies ran away with the market. It was a dangerous strategic lapse. You didn't need to buy both a Compaq and an IBM – the upstart's machines would do all the computing you wanted, and for a lower price. This was another favour from IBM. It held its price umbrella just high enough for Compaq to earn large margins – much larger than IBM's – while charging less for its computers.

They were sold, moreover, through the outlets that IBM had kindly pioneered – wherever IBM had appointed a dealer, there Compaq wanted to be. The difference (which created both the vital higher margins and considerable dealer loyalty) was that Compaq, unlike IBM, didn't run its own expensive direct sales force. But Canion was by no means content to bypass IBM via the portable market. Instead, Compaq pulled off one of business history's rarest feats – a frontal assault on a market leader by a far smaller competitor.

Just as many feared that Osborne's demise would be a forerunner of many failures, so the pessimists believed that Compaq had signed its own death warrant by turning to the desktop. Its Deskpro entry was unveiled in the summer of 1984. At that point, Compaq's portables had only been on the market for eighteen months. But the entrepreneurs now knew their market well. They cleverly targeted the Deskpro at the top of the IBM line, the PC AT, with its Intel 286 microprocessor.

Compaq accentuated the differences – not only did it use the 286 for a portable, but its desktop version improved on the AT in performance (by a quarter) and undercut its price (by a tenth). Up to then, Compaq had allowed IBM to set the pace (and the standard) while following with equal or improved versions. But in 1985, IBM left the barn door wide open. Yet

184

again, it dangerously delayed the inevitable response to technological opportunity.

The progress of personal computing is necessarily dominated by advances in the technology of the microprocessor. Each new microprocessor family has produced spectacular advances in speed and power for the computers built around the chips. IBM could certainly have created a computer using the new 80386 microprocessor from Intel – a company, after all, in which IBM held a significant stake. But the leader chose not to proceed for the time being, no doubt because it wished to milk further profits from the 286.

Seeing the open door, Compaq barged right in. It launched the 386 family in April 1986, seven months before IBM was forced to follow suit. At a single stroke, the Texan upstart laid claim to technological leadership, stole the lead in what proved to be the fastest-growing sector of the market, and reversed its previous relationship with IBM. Follower and leader were now the other way round. Not that it was very easy to tell the difference, according to those shrewd observers Ted Leonsis and James Chposky: 'On the inside Compaq is a button-downed [sic] clone of IBM. Its corporate culture is more reminiscent of the blue suit atmosphere of IBM than the blue jean environment of Apple.'

The cultural cloning wasn't that surprising, given the number of key personnel who came to Compaq from the IBM personal computer operation. While the founders were refugees from Texas Instruments, they showed a healthy regard for the men who had created the PC saga at Boca Raton.

Jim D'Arezzo, the advertising and promotion supremo for the PC, mastermind of the Charlie Chaplin ads, fulfilled the same function for Compaq – spending the biggest budgets ever allotted to a start-up. The man who brought D'Arezzo to Boca Raton, Sparky Sparks, also moved to Houston. As vice president of sales and service, he played a central role in implementing the fundamental decision that Compaq would not compete with its dealers. They and they alone would have the exclusive right to sell Compaq machines.

The D'Arezzo-Sparks combination was crucial to Compaq's astonishing first three years. What sustained the surge thereafter was a continuous flow of new products and an early strategic realisation. To stay in the race with IBM, Compaq needed a world and specifically a European presence. In October 1983, Compaq opened for business in Munich. The venture was led by a German, Eckhard Pfeiffer, who was to play a pivotal role in the corporation's history in both Europe and the US.

By the summer of 1990, the Compaq romance had become far more than a get-rich-quick saga. Powered by the insistence on technological leadership, Compaq had developed, like the IBM myth, into a management exemplar of the highest order. It was praised for 'consensus, continuity and common sense' by the bi-monthly bible of American business, the *Harvard Business Review*. In its introduction to an interview with Canion, the *HBR* wrote:

> While the company's product-introduction strategy depends on speed-to-market, Compaq believes absolutely in a slow, methodical decision-making process. In an industry that is driven by innovation, Compaq defines innovation as staying within the boundaries of accepted industry standards . . . In a company that has achieved such remarkable financial results, cost ranks relatively low on the list of manufacturing priorities.

A few months later, as the company lavished millions on its first sports championship, a tennis tournament in Munich, the above thesis still seemed perfectly tenable. Rosen (who is non-executive) and Canion led an executive team whose other key members, Jim Swaveley (in charge of North American operations) and Pfeiffer, articulated the Compaq credo as eloquently as Canion had in the *HBR* interview.

There was the same emphasis on caution. From the start 'we began to look for things that would bring Compaq down' (Canion). There was the supreme confidence – in 1990, 'we couldn't have executed better' (Rosen). An 'almost impeccable record of new product development' (Canion) was a cause of tremendous pride. Over-achievement had become a way of expected life. European growth was 'much beyond what we thought we could have achieved' (Pfeiffer).

Any accusations of falling behind were brushed away. Had IBM (and everybody else) beaten Compaq with the first computers using the 486 chip? When full supplies from Intel began 'Compaq had 75 per cent of the market. It started when we began to ship', and IBM was a 'year late' (Canion). A long lag in the smaller, lighter portables known as laptops was justified in much the same way, in an interview which Canion gave to the *European*:

In 1984 . . . he wanted the company to produce a laptop, largely because he liked having one to work on. The results of his market researchers showed that the demand for a Compaq laptop would be modest. So Mr Canion postponed that project until the conditions were right. And the Compaq laptop that was finally produced is now enjoying great success.

That wasn't until October 1988, over two years after the introduction of Toshiba's best-selling T3100. To IBM-watchers, that quote on Canion has a familiar ring of procrastination combined with justification by hindsight. As Compaq grew, the resemblances to IBM spotted by Leonsis and Chposky were increasing. Although Digital's personal style differed from Compaq's, a similar lookalike process had affected its behaviour in minicomputers. In management, great success almost inevitably breeds invincible attachment to the philosophy and strategies that wrought the magic.

Asked in December 1990 about whether past Compaq

strategy still held good for the present and future, Swaveley – featured a few months back as corporate hero by a business magazine – reported that top management had examined the strategy, weighed it and found it good, at least for another five or ten years. Within a matter of weeks, Swaveley was out. Within months Compaq's famed strategy was shattered by the very same phenomenon that had created its initial success.

This was the PC's ease of imitation. The microprocessor and the operating system could be bought freely on the open market; all other components were also available off the shelf; and no vital patents protected IBM, Compaq or anybody else. The barn door was still open. Other mimics poured in. The top-end emphasis, high margins and investment in branding that had made Compaq rich, under the still higher price umbrella held aloft by IBM, now worked to its disadvantage.

Nobody has counted how many firms in North America, Europe and the Far East joined the charge of the clones. Radio Shack, whose Tandy brand had joined Apple in the initial surge of personal computing, was an early convert. This mass-market retailer had only stumbled into computers after the death of founder Charles Tandy. His successor, a lawyer, saw that the business needed a new product line – and the only candidate was this strange device knocked up by a hobbyist in the company's employ.

Under future CEO John V. Roach, computers became the drive that powered Radio Shack to 1991 sales of $4.7 billion. The ease with which an electrical goods retailer became a major force in PCs (with 7.5 per cent of the 1986 market) was echoed by a British trader in down-market audio. Alan Sugar of Amstrad was for a time among Europe's richest men as his machines, first word processors built round obsolete components, and then fully compatible and competitive clones, surged into a highly price-conscious market.

While price was the basic weapon of the clones, and the fundamental weakness of Compaq and IBM, it didn't complete the mimics' armoury. Some majored on special features.

Others followed Compaq by seeking out new distribution strategies – notably Michael Dell, the most youthful of all the winners: he found that these high-tech tools could be sold by the low-tech method that made Sears Roebuck and L.L. Bean rich: mail order. By 1992, Dell had squeezed into the *Fortune* 500 with $546 million of sales, $27.2 million of profit and a market value of $861 million.

IBM, Compaq and Dell were equal in one respect: all three had manufacturing plants in the US. AST Research, on the other hand, kept its manufacturing lines in lower-cost Asia and specialised in selling through so-called 'value-added retailers', who sold its machines complete with purpose-directed software. Gateway 2000, a pure assembler, with no manufacturing capability, imitated Dell by selling via mail order. Packard Bell (still privately owned after 1992's forced cancellation of a public offer) also depended on sub-contractors.

These were merely some of the taller trees in a forest which wasn't likely to be cut down. Thomas C. Yuen, who co-founded AST Research, observed that 'The significant players are not going to have a total failure, like bankruptcy. We also won't see anyone give up major market share. We have come to the conclusion that no one is willing to concede.'

Whether or not he was right about the future, Yuen had correctly described the past. Total failures in the clone era had been very few and far between, despite setbacks and losses. Players like Radio Shack, despite a market share that had slipped in half a dozen years from 7.5 per cent to 4.5 per cent, could stay in the game – even though, with only a quarter of revenues coming from PCs, it could afford to take other directions.

For many of the multitude, that wasn't possible. Their profusion can be demonstrated from a single article in *PC World*. In August 1992, it listed no less than twenty-eight brands, from Aries and Atomstyle via Ness and Osicom to T'ko and Wren. They were bound together by one factor: a chip called the 40MHz 386DX. It wasn't made by Intel. However, it delivered

30 per cent more speed than the Intel rival, which was 15 per cent more expensive.

The comparisons are reminiscent of the advantages over IBM which gave Compaq its head start. Chip-makers, too, had become adept at jumping on market-leading bandwagons. Nor was cloning confined to PCs or the heart of the PC, the micro-processor – not by any means. Any successful component or machine was imitated as fast as possible by the hordes of eager and successful competitors. Advanced Micro Devices, maker of the 386DX, claimed to have secured 60 per cent of a market which only recently had belonged wholly to Intel.

In such conditions, with prices tumbling all round, the search for competitive advantage had to take new turns. All the five tried and tested routes had lost their certainty: branding, speed to market, technological superiority, marketing strategies, price-cutting. That left untried and untested modes as the only resort. The IBM-compatible race would go to the company that could combine all five routes with the adaptable resilience that came to the rescue of Apple in its darkest hours.

The challenge to Compaq was thus in some respects identical to that facing IBM – to free itself of the traditions of the past (even so young a past) and fight in the world's fiercest product wars with new methods honed to meet new necessities. Here the smaller company had the advantage of its smaller size, and IBM the corresponding diseconomies of scale. It could not afford to fumble the challenge of the lesser clones: but, as usual, IBM left its response desperately late.

17

Bill Gates:
The Super-Nerd
from Seattle

A colleague in the software business once described Bill Gates, the founder and chief executive of Microsoft, as 'the best businessman and salesman in the micro-computer industry. His image as a nerd and visionary hacker is baloney'. By the early Nineties, the non-nerd image had not only triumphed, but expanded to the tune of $6 billion – that being the paper value of Gates' personal holding.

His fortune naturally made Gates a hero manager. In any overriding boom, the beneficiaries are liable to appear as managerial supermen. The natural belief is that, however a star company like Microsoft goes about its business, that way must be supremely right. You can hardly argue with a performance that, lifting sales and earnings by over 50 per cent per annum to $2.7 billion and $700 million respectively in 1991, elevated Microsoft's market value to more than that of General Motors.

It's a terrific tale, too: that of the schoolboy computer freak, William H. Gates III, who, among other precocious activities, hacks his way into a University of Washington computer – and gets caught. At sixteen, with a friend, he makes a micro-processor. Then he writes a traffic control program, Traf-O-Data, for his first business, which fails. While still officially at high school, he joins the conglomerate TRW with his pal to develop software, and after a brief flirtation with law and Harvard, he quits to write a BASIC language for the Intel 8088 chip.

That was the beginning of Microsoft, the pathway to the IBM connection (the 8088 was the chip chosen for the PC), and the start of the legend. It includes, as a vital component, the Gates family's connection with John Opel, the IBM chairman, through his work for a powerful charity, the United Way. Mary Gates, Bill's mother, sat on the same board. When John Akers succeeded Opel at IBM, he also took the United Way seat – again with beneficial results for Mary's son.

No mistake is more infuriating than your own. The original contract for the PC's operating system, which left Gates free to sell to IBM's competitors, was the fount of grievous ills – the assault of the clones, the dwindling of IBM's market share, and its inability to achieve a proprietary position in PCs. It's easy to understand the later efforts of IBM executives to escape from a relationship with Gates which benefited the young man so much more than the old company.

Every piece of publicity for Gates and Microsoft, every million and billion added to Gates' net worth, only rubbed salt in the wounds. Personally, though, the IBMers who came into contact with Gates couldn't help being impressed by the man. Like the four PC men who first visited Microsoft, they found Gates serious, likeable and brilliant at his work. Gates was able to blend serious purpose with a management style whose breezy informality lies at the opposite pole from the corporate habits of his IBM customers.

The Gates style grew in fame as it powered this middling company (sales of $2.7 billion were 4 per cent of IBM's in 1991) to a market valuation which eventually matched that of the colossus. IBM coming down met Microsoft coming up. The public assumption, that the management style must be as magical as the numbers, has only enhanced the legend. The style is intensely personal in two senses – Gates still owns a third of the company and utterly dominates all aspects of its activity, and he sensibly runs a people company with intense emphasis on people and their relationships.

That being so, the driving force is recruitment. In the average week of 1992 Microsoft hired seventy of the brightest people it could find from campuses and competitors. Its numbers doubled in two years to June 1991. The people emphasis is applied effectively, to judge by the best indicator – i.e. how many stay with Microsoft. Retention has been unusually high, with labour turnover running at only 6 per cent of the workforce.

Ethos and capital gains are the retentive cement, rather than high incomes. Over 100 Microsoft employees have become millionaires thanks to stock options – and a million dollars is a mighty attractive carrot. The ethos is not that of the stick, but of rah-rah consumer marketing, long hours (sixty to eighty-hour weeks), youth (Gates himself wasn't out of his thirties by 1990), heavy emphasis on 'thinking', and an extreme of informality.

According to one executive, training is minimal: 'The training we do is on-the-job. Throw them in, and good luck.' In return, recruits stay relatively free from rules and bureaucracy. The main controls include formal inquisitions, in which Gates sharply accentuates the negative to aim at positive results. He's a good grand inquisitor. An outside lawyer, indeed, was awed by Gates' ability (which would have greatly assisted the legal career he almost had) to come up with a rapid-fire fusillade of cogent questions.

Applying control through face-to-face inquisition can't stand alone in a company of 10,000 people, growing fast. The organisation is held together by electronic mail, which Gates uses more intensively than anybody else ('flame mail' is Microsoft-speak for electronic mail that's 'caustic or emotional'). The key organisational principle is small groups. They are never larger than 200, and each is divided into manageable sub-groups to maintain individuality and accountability.

Even 10,000 employees, though, must mean well over 100

groups. Obviously, they only hold together because of high growth (which always covers up hosts of errors) and homogeneity. On the bedrock of the operating system monopoly for IBM-compatible PCs, conferred by that original contract, Microsoft sells only software. And only one of its products, Windows (which mimics the easy-to-use features of the Apple Mac), is another blockbuster. Its success makes IBM managers especially envious.

Could those managers, competing across the board in highly differentiated markets, have taken any management lessons from the software upstart? Microsoft's emphasis goes on individuality and originality, obtained by stress on youth, recruitment, technical challenge and initiative. That can never be easily repeated in a large corporation. Apart from anything else, a company like IBM has thousands of executives and engineers who are by no means young. In many cases, their individuality and originality were left behind with their youth.

At Microsoft, communication and results are far more important than lines of command and bureaucracy, and override them: at IBM, it's often the other way round. At IBM monetary reward is used systematically in an often self-defeating attempt to achieve corporate ends. At Microsoft, reward flows irregularly (and much more heavily) from personal achievement. At IBM, the ethos of 'the way we do things around here' is strong: at Microsoft, it gives way to 'the spirit in which we do them'.

At its apogee, IBM could claim for its employees (as it still does, with less justice) powerful personal identification with the organisation's leadership, with the individual's work, and with clearly defined missions. In the far smaller Microsoft, that identification has the greater reality. The Gates-driven eccentricity, with its in-house jargon and high-jinks junkets, is a natural way for this young company to behave – but it's deeply unnatural for IBM.

The management forces at work in Microsoft, however, are plainly going to affect all organisations, including IBM, as the next century unfolds. New century management needs all these features:

1 Defined, homogenous missions that are known to and shared by all employees.

2 Vigorous recruitment policies aimed at providing a steady flow of the brightest and best talent available.

3 Rapid deployment of talent into mission tasks that will stretch and develop people's abilities.

4 Provision of electronic communications, preferably full networking of PCs, that are freely available to all.

5 Deliberate opening of loopholes and bypasses so that individuals are not confined within the system.

6 Loose methods of payment that relate reward to results rather than hierarchy.

7 Personalising management – encouraging ownership of business groups by long-term leaders, so that they become 'Mr Windows' (or 'Mr IBM PC'), or whatever.

8 Keeping such groups to a controllable size.

9 Becoming 'product-led' – in the sense of concentrating efforts on improving and innovating products and services that will increase customer satisfaction.

10 Finding informal ways of ensuring that everybody, including top management, knows what's going on – above all, what's new.

In the early Nineties, IBM is striving to become as powerful and ubiquitous in software as in hardware. Those ten necessities loom larger and larger. In terms of the contest with Microsoft, the cultural war is obviously an unequal battle. Doing what comes naturally is ideally suited to the new world that Bill Gates has done much to shape. But unless IBM can turn the unnatural, in terms of its entrenched culture, into its own second nature, the grave problems must persist.

The battle is on to seize the high ground in a market which has not only relentlessly expanded, but changed profoundly. It's a struggle in which traditional hardware has been sidelined. The winners will be the suppliers of the winning marvels of solid state technology, the microprocessors, the computers on a chip. The hectic and ferocious competition in the chip jungle is paralleled by the battle in software.

Before the end of the century new generations of chips will emerge that will have more computing power, packed in a tiny space, than current top-of-the-range IBM mainframes. You could say that Intel, in producing these amazing devices, 'Takes Aim at the Heart of IBM'. But the *New York Times* story thus titled refers, not to Intel or any other hardware company, but to Microsoft.

'Once best friends, now quarrelling enemies,' explains the story, 'Microsoft . . . and IBM . . . are edging towards a much wider war. The battle is the heart of [IBM's] market: the data processing centres of Corporate America.' In mid-1992, after a $400 million investment, Microsoft introduced outside software developers to Windows NT. This 'new technology' software would be able to operate, not only the spreadsheets that fuelled the growth of the business PC, but also payroll, accounting, inventory and other business computer applications.

The threat to IBM is clear. These operations, run on mainframes and minis, have been its bread and butter from the start of the computer business - and have also provided plenty of jam. IBM's inventory control programs have been the industry's biggest selling software product, earning untold billions over the years. In 1991, software was IBM's only product line, apart from the mainframe and mini processor businesses, to reach eleven-digit sales – $10.5 billion.

Moreover, software continued its remorseless advance in that woeful year, in which processors dropped 9 per cent, personal systems 12 per cent and storage peripherals 36 per cent. The gain in software was small (5 per cent). But that raised sales a quarter above 1989 levels at a time when the hardware lines were all in retreat. The *Times* pointed out that 'as computer hardware has fallen in price and become more of a commodity, operating systems have taken centre stage in the industry wars'.

Gates rubbed in the reality with a cold prediction. In his view, whoever comes out winner in the competition to supply the new generation of operating system (thirty-two-bit, compared to the sixteen-bit with which the IBM PC and Microsoft's DOS system conquered the world) will control the industry. It sounds a ludicrously large boast. How can a mere program, capable of being reproduced more easily than a book, take over from the gigantic design, production and marketing apparatus that created IBM's dominance?

The answer, as expressed by Gates, is that his new technology 'represents the end of the dichotomy between what's a PC and what's a workstation or a mainframe.' To put it another way, the astronomical rise in power and capacity of the microprocessor has eroded, in some cases to vanishing point, the chief advantages of the mainframe (speed, capacity and the ability to handle many tasks at once). At the same time, the microprocessor has accentuated the mainframe's disadvantage – vastly greater cost per unit of processing power.

In fact, this stunning advance isn't entirely to Microsoft's benefit, because hardly anybody has a desktop machine that can use the new software. The first draft of this book was written on a personal computer with one megabyte of memory and 20 megabytes on its hard disk. To use Windows NT, eight times the memory and five times the disk capacity are essential. The owners of most existing PCs won't be rushing to replace perfectly satisfactory set-ups to take advantage of powers that they don't require.

To succeed commercially, Windows NT must therefore use the top of the desktop market as a springboard to leap upwards into IBM's heartland. The new software has been designed to work with the multi-chip computers that look certain to take over the top-end market, and also to cope with many varieties of hardware. The NT system also has a defensive role: NT is essential to protect Microsoft's existing monopoly of the IBM-compatible market against attack from IBM itself.

IBM's new generation software (the latest version of OS/2) was first onto the market. Until NT was ready, Microsoft could at best mount a holding action. In doing so, Gates may have learnt from his enemy. Some suspect that NT, in the best (or worst) IBM style, was 'pre-announced' before it was ready, to check buyers who might otherwise have chosen the new version of OS/2. That was only one example of the tactics that have seen Microsoft stigmatised as a recreation in software of the IBM quasi-monopoly – with all its bad habits.

'Big Green' has replaced Big Blue as the object of 'fear and loathing' as software has moved onto stage centre. In March 1993, *Business Week* listed some of the accusations made against Gates. In addition to pre-announcement, they include use of inside knowledge to beat rivals to application programs for Windows (where it has 60 per cent of the market); having PC makers pay for MS–DOS even if they don't install it, thus shutting out other operating systems; predatory pricing to undermine rivals such as Novell, the leader in software for networks.

Novell, with nearly a billion dollars in sales, is the only competitor of significant size. Just as IBM in its heyday towered over the Seven Dwarfs, so does Microsoft outreach the next seven companies. With Novell, sales are about even – without it, Microsoft is heading for a two-to-one lead. In profits, the gap is far larger – more than double with Novell, tenfold without it. In yet another parallel with its hardware foe, Microsoft is so strong that the 'FUD' factor operates in its favour.

'Fear, Uncertainty and Doubt' used to stop customers from buying non-IBM hardware. Now, it takes a brave buyer to choose an alternative operating system if he fears that the supplier may withdraw from the market, or that the product won't be compatible with Windows. And Microsoft, says its critics, doesn't mind giving the FUD factor a helpful nudge. It's not surprising to hear a veteran of the failed anti-trust suit against IBM say that 'It sure sounds familiar. Microsoft is using its power in ways that are just like IBM's.'

In this most intense of arenas, the first enemy is yourself. IBM suffered well-told agonies in getting glitches out of its advanced version of OS/2, after the commercial flop of the first version. Even if Microsoft keeps its teething troubles under reasonable control, its enemies are many: IBM alone; IBM in concert with Apple; Sun Microsystems; Unix in partnership with Novell Corp; and the highly praised Unix version produced by Steve Jobs, the Apple founder at Next Inc.

Like the advanced OS/2, the Next software was already in the field as Microsoft moved over the NT start line. It was far too early to declare winners: all the same, IBM dare not be complacent. A pie chart in the *Times* showed that over $18 billion of IBM's $64 billion revenue was 'expected to face increased competition because of NT'. Much more IBM business would be on even rockier foundations because of its traditional strategy. That relied on securing the customer base with large processors and then adding other hardware and software sales to the semi-captives.

Thus, NT is the first shot in a whole new war. A hundred or so 'evangelists' were gathered together by Gates to go on the road and preach the gospel of the crusade against IBM. Their mission was to convert independent developers to rewrite for NT programs written for IBM and Unix workstations. Like the conversion of pagan tribes to Christianity, it promised to be a long and uphill task, but the prize could hardly be bigger.

If Microsoft wins, its power will be enormously enhanced.

That power is already great enough to raise questions on both sides of the Atlantic – not only among competitors and the media, but with regulators like the Federal Trade Commission. In 1992 Microsoft's *increase* in sales was greater than Novell's total volume: it supplies 81 per cent of the IBM-compatible operating systems, has 73 per cent of the Windows spreadsheet market and 53 per cent of that for word processing. And Microsoft is no less aggressive against smaller software suppliers than against IBM.

The hope of a counter-balance against Big Green, however, lies with these lesser firms. Microsoft's operating system beyond Windows NT is codenamed Cairo and is in drawing-board competition with Pink, the Apple–IBM system being developed by the Taligent consortium. Its CEO is Joe Guglielmi, who used to work for IBM. As he told *Business Week,* 'There are thousands of Bill Gateses out there who will find pieces of the market and win them.'

Microsoft's market will change, and such changes, as they did with IBM, are liable to work against a dominant design. Meanwhile, the confrontation between Microsoft and IBM isn't only a war between two technologies. It's a battle between two styles of management and between two coasts. The West Coast growth businesses like Microsoft are managed as a bunch in a freer and easier style even than their high-tech counterparts on the East Coast.

The distinctive West Coast style, what's more, has proved the more successful in most of the East-West conflicts to date. The sensible assumption is that high-tech companies, with their insatiable demands for originality and innovation, have to lead the way in establishing new organisational norms if they are to meet those demands. In its retaliation against the Super-Nerd from Seattle, IBM has relied little on managerial innovation and much more on mustering the heavy weapons of technology. To win today's wars, you need to attack on both fronts.

18

Software:
The Trouble with OS/2

On 24 March 1993, Louis Gerstner left an airport near Rancho Mirage, California, flying in an RJR Nabisco private jet for the last time. He was heading for an IBM in deep trouble, from mainframes to personal computers. The difficulties in PCs were especially irritating. IBM's hardware was now a techno-logical match for anybody's. In software, a new operating system, all its own work, was comparable with anything in the industry, and sales were brisk. Yet in 1992, world market share slumped to 10.9 per cent.

Part of the problem was straight price competition. In the year before the removal of John Akers, Compaq had followed Apple in changing strategies. Both had slashed prices and introduced cheaper models at the bottom end. Faced with the challenge, IBM appeared to hesitate. One observer found it 'a surprising development' that 'IBM is the most prominent vic-tim of the PC price wars so far'. But that often happens to the market leader, especially one who is charging $1,647 against a brand-name rival's $928.

IBM had cut prices by up to 30 per cent, but chose to delay its major reaction until new models appeared in the autumn. The surprise, however, wasn't caused by IBM's tardiness – that had become a habit – but by the resistance of the clones. Many of the hundreds of 'third tier' companies had been expected to suffer most from the new price aggression. Not only Compaq, but Dell, the mail order leaders, were applying the pressure.

If you hold *half* the market, as the clones did, your share doesn't collapse overnight. In 1991, IBM led with 14.4 per cent of the nine million-plus PC units sold in the US. Apple was breathing down its neck with 14 per cent. But nobody else, not even Compaq, reached 5 per cent. 'Other' makers (including major brands with minute shares like Digital and Intel) had 53.6 per cent, or nearly four times those of the leader. Put another way, IBM had only 16.7 per cent of the IBM-compatible market.

Over the decade, its executives had somehow mislaid 83.3 per cent of potential sales to other users of the MS–DOS system that Bill Gates had created to IBM's order. The PC progenitors were probably right – they had to create an open product to stimulate the software writers. That was inseparable from the genesis of the project. They didn't, true, have to free Gates and Microsoft to make their fortune by selling MS–DOS to all-comers. That error was also crucial in laying the market wide open to cloning.

In so doing, IBM unquestionably created a strikingly vigorous and usually profitable industry. This was an inevitable unfolding, given the power and potential of the technology. How long would it have taken if IBM had followed a different strategy? Plainly the growth of the business, without an industry standard, must have been seriously retarded. But IBM is not an altruistic organisation. The mistakes, and the price paid for them, were unintended.

Wise outsiders, with inside knowledge, believe that, on some accounting principles, IBM has never made a penny profit from its PCs – one of the most 'successful' products ever created. And that is not the IBM way. On the other hand, others have generated huge riches from industry standard products – not only multi-billionaire Bill Gates of Microsoft, but the entrepreneurs and shareholders in Compaq and Dell (headed by that other relative juvenile, Michael Dell), and uncounted others.

The runners-up form a league whose membership is vast, but largely anonymous. Nobody knows what fortunes the Asian clone-makers have squirrelled away. IBM doesn't, for sure. It is acutely aware, though, that every dollar of sales by compatible manufacturers has come out of its own potential market. The PC reversed the traditional situation. In mainframes IBM had skilfully used a dominant market share to maximise earnings – coining profits while everybody else lost money. In PCs, sometimes, it was almost the other way round.

Strategic thinking naturally hinged on reverting to the old IBM norm. But how? Why would purchasers who had bought non-IBM products revert to IBM? Customers who have enjoyed an open selection won't voluntarily retreat into Hobson's Choice. Yet the prize of sounding that retreat was irresistibly attractive. And there was a strategy which could conceivably work. Bring out a new generation line of PCs, link it with a proprietary operating system – one that could not be cloned – and the mainframe hegemony could be recreated.

The PS/2 personal computers would ride into the market with their very own software, OS/2. PS stood for Personal System and OS for Operating System. Over six years to end-1991, IBM probably spent the best part of $2.5 billion on OS/2 and its applications. At that point around $350 million a year was still being sunk into the software, while no more than $100 million of revenue had accrued.

To make matters worse, the OS/2 and PS/2 linkage probably contributed to the halving of IBM's market share in the six years. That setback had cost an annual $8 billion of sales income. Nor was the damage confined to IBM. Market research suggested that $1 billion had been expended by software developers on OS/2 products – also for a nil return. The financial numbers are large enough, but don't give the full dimensions of IBM's effort and failure.

Altogether, no less than 1,700 people were working on OS/2 at three sites on two continents. The strategy only made compelling sense if the project was exclusively IBM's. Yet at the beginning, Microsoft, the supplier of the original operating system, was deeply involved in the new drive to replace MS–DOS. This can't have been the intention of the OS/2 strategists. IBM's ambitions would best be served by eliminating the independent – they wanted Gates out, not in.

IBM was seeking to set a new proprietary standard of its own. It was inconsistent to perpetuate a relationship with a software supplier which sold its programs to all and sundry – and as many programs as possible. The connection seemed doomed. As a shrewd businessman, Gates couldn't miss or dismiss this danger – he moved fast, vigorously and personally to avert the threat. In June 1986, over lunch, John Akers, the relatively new chief executive, granted Gates a reprieve.

Did the same family connection that helped Gates on his IBM way work again? Did his mother, finding herself on the board of the United Way charity with a second IBM boss, again use her influence wisely and well? Whatever Akers' reasons, the decision shouldn't have been his to make. He should never have intervened – unless, that is, there was unresolved 'non-concurrence' down the line. In those circumstance, the CEO was compelled to resolve the issue.

Either way, the management was bad, and so were the results. The first version of OS/2 was a disaster. The combination of Microsoft and IBM made the development process more cumbersome and expensive. The product was also criticised for its complexity, excessive power and overly radical nature. OS/2 was an advance in which the public – nursing a large hardware and software investment threatened with obsolescence – didn't want to join.

Another route was available, if IBM had started from the assumption that the Microsoft partnership would and should continue. The Gates company had produced Windows, a genuinely clever piece of software. It mimicked the key features which, despite incompatability with the IBM world, had made the Apple Macintosh so popular. Like the Mac, Windows gave access to applications through graphic icons and pull-down menus. It provided a degree of user-friendliness for the millions of DOS users who had coped so heroically with hostility.

Early versions of Windows, while selling respectably enough, had failed to make the commercial breakthrough that Microsoft desired. IBM could certainly have pursued the Windows alternative; but that would have been self-defeating. For while the product was proprietary, the proprietor wasn't John Akers – it was Bill Gates. The joint development of OS/2 was a compromise that couldn't ultimately satisfy either side. The private lunch led inexorably to a public showdown – this time, over dinner.

In November 1989, the partners agreed on an announcement, to be made to thirty dinner guests, software executives who were in Las Vegas for the Comdex trade exhibition. The diners would be told that Windows was looking after the lower end of the PS/2 spectrum, keeping MS–DOS in business. OS/2 would handle the higher end – where companies needed its greater power and could afford to change from MS–DOS. No sooner had the accord been announced, however, than the ambiguities became painfully obvious.

Was IBM making a tactical retreat from OS/2, or was Microsoft giving up on the long-term future of Windows? The software executives were understandably confused. Their confusion wasn't cleared up by a press conference two days later. At that gathering IBM appeared to back away from Windows. It provoked a predictably hostile reaction from Microsoft. Phoney peace had turned to war. Within six months, Windows 3.0 was launched on an avid market. Eighteen months on, the product had become the greatest seller in PC history.

Sales passed seven million units at a time when, on the most optimistic count, sales of OS/2 were well short of seven figures. In embarrassing contrast, in 1993 Windows was selling a million copies a month. In the war with its own supplier, IBM had come off a poor second best. Worse still, the pursuit of a new industry standard seemed to have succeeded. But the standard wasn't IBM's. By 1992, it was commonplace for rival PC makers to advertise their products 'complete with Windows 3·0'.

The Microsoft triumph was both galling and damaging to IBM. The OS/2 project, and the split with Microsoft (now a bitter and deep divide), only made sense if the IBM product could win the hearts and minds of the marketplace. It would have helped if OS/2 had reached the market when planned. The target date of end-1990 was so important that Akers, appearing before audiences of customers, software developers and industry analysts, publicly pledged to meet the deadline.

He was said to have made the deadline an 'or else' matter. Certainly something galvanised the IBMers into frenzied effort. Lee Reiswig, a key figure in the OS/2 saga, adopted the name 'the blue Ninja' for himself, and used it for internal electronic mail, to dramatise the intensity of the assault on Microsoft. The incongruity of a middle-aged IBMer dressing up his persona in the clothes of a child's fantasy figure is self-evident – and significant.

IBM was attempting to fill a role outside its own character and history: to become a software developer scrapping on equal terms with a rival (as Lotus, say, had battled with and destroyed Visicalc in spreadsheets); depending for its success on a perceived and real technological advantage; and entering far behind in a contest where the brand-name advantages of IBM counted for little or nothing. For IBM lacked reputation in the software business.

The Comdex fiasco wasn't unique. At the end of 1990, IBM had finally given up on OfficeVision – its grandiose attempt to link all types of machine together in interrelated networks. Possibly this flop contributed to the determination to proceed with OS/2 after Microsoft's defection from the project. IBM executives saw this as an act of dastardly betrayal, but they, of course, had themselves been dead set on dropping Microsoft.

To restore its credibility, IBM had to hit its OS/2 targets. Yet the software imitated its hardware partner, the PS/2, in its delays. Despite Akers' promises, IBM missed the most obvious and important of the targets – the deadline. The delay into 1992 was humiliating. All the same, on arrival the improved software was immediately hailed in the technical press. It won on some key comparisons with Windows, whose own more advanced version, the NT, was up to a year away.

But in the crucial primary market, that of the developers, IBM was starting far behind the game. Promised applications were lagging six to one behind those already written for Windows. The IBM strategy, moreover, could backfire. Since OS/2 had been designed for the PS/2 range of computers, their images were indissolubly linked. If customers happy with Windows wanted to upgrade to newer, more powerful processors, they would be lost to IBM. A strategy designed to tie customers to the market leader could paradoxically set them free.

The size of the threat to IBM was demonstrated by its fierce reaction in the spring of 1992. Unable to break through by conventional means, IBM started to give away the latest version of OS/2 – 'bundling' the software with some versions of its PS/2 computers. This was presumably a would-be pre-emptive strike, aimed at cracking Microsoft's hold on the market before the improved Windows NT appeared. But you can't make money from free gifts.

Various estimates suggest that even when charging for OS/2, IBM lost money heavily. Material costs of $25–30, added to royalties to Microsoft of another $25–30, plus $50–100 of advertising per copy sold, amounted to at least $100 of expense for a product that yielded only a $50–$75 price. Jack Schofield of the *Guardian* had seen OS/2 on offer for a mere $39, or less than the cost of materials and royalties.

OS/2 had thus already cost IBM great sums, and the bundling expedient looked too much like bungling for comfort. In truth IBM had locked itself into a costly war with Gates which was quite unnecessary. If the object was to cut the Microsoft magnate down to size, OS/2 had failed abysmally. Some industry observers (though a minority) still thought that OS/2 would break through in the long run. But in mid-1992, it wasn't clear that IBM had time to spare.

The agreement which allowed IBM to use future versions of Windows would expire the following year. Without such an agreement, it would be OS/2 or nothing for IBM. One report described the choice in apocalyptic terms: 'IBM has until next year to make its peace with Bill Gates . . . or face the prospect of annihilation in the world personal computer market.' To forestall apocalypse, in July 1992, IBM swallowed its pride and made a truce. The two companies would continue to allow each other use of their patented technology – while fighting with might and main to achieve market dominance.

If it lost, IBM would only have itself, and in particular its atavistic drive towards building quasi-monopolies, to blame for the reverse. The company's software strategy wasn't even single-minded. To break away from its dependence on Windows, and to intensify its assault on Apple, IBM made deals with Next, created by Steve Jobs – the expelled father of Apple – and lost $50 million; with Apple, in a complex deal, hinged on software, whose consequences weren't obvious to anybody – including the customers; and with Metaphor Computer Systems, where IBM dropped a mere $10 million.

The company gave the impression of striking out (in more senses than one) in all directions to avoid following one of them – the route taken by Microsoft. Scott McNealy, the free-wheeling entrepreneur who built up Sun Microsystems, remarked on the outcome: 'OS/2? That one's already buried. There's grass growing over the grave.' Sun, of course, is a trade rival. Its workstations and RISC chips compete with IBM. But a software developer, a convert from OS/2, expressed the same thought in a different way: 'DOS and Windows are going to own the desktop.' Very certainly, they weren't going to lose it.

In the *Wall Street Journal*, writer Paul B. Carroll argued that the billion-dollar market for operating system software was only the front line of a much more important engagement – the battle for $40 billion a year in sales of new machines and applications. Whoever owned the dominating operating system, said Carroll, agreeing with Bill Gates, would take a commanding lead into this race.

No prediction is safe in a field of fast-changing technology, though. That's why technological bets so often fail – especially if they bear no clear relation to market needs. The Apple Mac succeeded because the technology that Steve Jobs backed, after seeing the future at Xerox's Palo Alto Research Center, met the market need. The technology gave users an operating system that worked both better and far more easily than MS–DOS – the perceived advantage in the customer's eyes was real.

The IBM developers earn full marks for their persistence in attempting to achieve a like Unique Selling Proposition – a wonderfully distinctive product advantage unique to IBM. When the PS/2 first appeared, the PC management was convinced that they had hit this jackpot with something called MicroChannel. This was a 'bus', the internal route that speeds data round the PC. No doubt, it represented a substantial advance – only the customers couldn't *see* MicroChannel; they didn't even know either PC's contained 'buses', nor understand what they did.

That being so, IBM felt forced to launch costly promotional campaigns to persuade people how miraculous MicroChannel truly was. But customers buying Macs (or later Windows) didn't need persuasion – they could see for themselves, and wanted what they saw. Many corporate customers, in contrast, were encouraged into buying PS/2 computers by the selling of MicroChannel, while frankly admitting that they had no idea of its meaning or use.

For most purposes, anyway, the faster bus was of only academic interest. So what if it could work faster in networks of personal computers? The great majority of users, to their own great disadvantage, hadn't networked their PCs as late as 1992. By then a host of network products were available, and the MicroChannel brouhaha had passed into the mists of history. Nobody else took up the innovation in which IBM had invested such high hopes.

In retrospect, the OS/2 saga is a rerun of the MicroChannel incident. At one stage in the British market, IBM's publicity in the personal computer field even hinged, not on the hardware, but on OS/2. Instead of selling the PS/2 on its own merits, IBM was trying to promote it through the software. The campaign, oddly, used a cartoon elephant as its prime image. But it was an elephantine tactic, anyway. Once again, a company that was supposedly customer-led was trying to lead the customer – and the lead wasn't being followed. And there are two of Gerstner's biggest problems in a single sentence.

VII

THE RESISTIBLE RISE
OF JAPAN

19

Fujitsu & Co:
The Dark Cloud
in the East

As the Nineties unfold, opinions remain divided on the strength of the Japanese challenge to American leadership of the computer industry. The optimists maintain that the US still holds all the hardware aces; its labs are the supreme well of new technology; its installed base of computing power round the world dwarfs all competition; and its hardware makers still lead the market in current sales in almost all sectors. In software, the US supremacy is uncontested – and soft power, not hard, will dominate the future.

Since these facts are mostly uncontestable, what can possibly explain this jeremiad? 'We have this inexorable drift toward being a techno-colony by the end of the decade.' Nobody could accuse the speaker, Andy Grove, of ignorant defeatism. He's the chief executive of Intel, whose 286, 386 and 486 microprocessors (now joined by the Pentium) have been synonymous with the explosive growth of the personal computer in numbers and powers. No Japanese has dared enter the lists against Intel. Its chip designs are shining symbols of the industry's success. Its leadership in world semiconductor sales has forced the Japanese into also-rans.

It's a success in which IBM shared, both as the prime user of Intel's microprocessors and as the investor whose benevolent shareholding had given Grove's company the springboard of success. So what explained his dismal prognosis? The answer was spelt out in the *Chicago Tribune* in an excellent article by R.C. Longworth. Its burden was statistical. In key sectors (like Intel's microprocessors) the US led comprehensively. But the overall figures showed broad retreat.

For instance, the American lead in hardware (78 per cent against a mere 11 per cent for Japan in 1984) was still substantial, but the gap had narrowed by 1990 to 59–25. The trend pointed to a crossover in the reasonably foreseeable future. Nor could the Americans rely on new inventions to rebuild their position – ominous data for portables and laptops (the newest and fastest growing sector) showed Japan with 60 per cent of the market.

For flat panels the picture was even bleaker – Japanese firms had 95 per cent of the market in a technology invented by the Americans (which US companies are now striving, with some difficulty, to improve). The Japanese author and politician Shintaro Ishihara (author of *The Japan That Can't Say No*) put the issue neatly, if obviously: 'Brilliant breakthroughs in the lab are useless until engineers and lathe operators turn them into products.'

If chips are taken as the product, the Japanese had converted a percentage ratio of 57–27 to their disadvantage in 1982 to a 50–36 advantage ten years later. In one particular chip technology, that of dynamic random access memory (DRAM), the Japanese share was 60 per cent against America's 11 per cent. Two-thirds of silicon wafers are Japanese made. The US, with 2 per cent, barely has a look-in. In ceramic packages, the US does a little better – 3 per cent. The rest of the market belongs to Japan.

In other words, while IBM slugs it out with competitors in the brand-name markets, the process is beginning to resemble Napoleon's retreat from Moscow. As IBM retrenches, its true market share (percentage of all hardware sales) is being picked off by well-armed and trained guerillas. Increasingly,

American firms are battling each other with Japanese ammunition.

Longworth cites Compaq's LTE laptop – made largely by Citizen Watch. His article was illustrated with a photograph of Apple's John Sculley, holding another laptop, the Powerbook – reliant on Sony. The personal laser printers sold by Hewlett-Packard are Canon-made. There's a Sony disk drive in workstations sold by Sun Microsystems. Note that the latter market, for powerful PC configurations used originally by engineers, but now spreading to other users, including managers, is another where the US reigns supreme.

But the colossal growth won't be in these top-end products. If that super-growth, as expected, is based on miniaturisation, the Japanese are in pole position. Actually, the race looked like a foregone conclusion as the Nineties began – witness the turning of Compaq and Apple to Japanese suppliers. Companies like Citizen Watch treasure the engineering talent that has brought the national, cultural fascination with miniaturisation into the forefront of a great industry.

These skills are not widely matched in the West, and it would be unrealistic to expect any speedy catch-up from this point. Much of the industry has yet to pull its head out of the sand. One of Longworth's interviewees, a software manager, used the language of bereavement counselling to express the industry's state of mind – it was 'still in the denial stage'. Deniers are unlikely to take vigorous and effective action. The evidence of technological leadership seeping away is pervasive and strong. For instance, lithography, the key to chip manufacture, has become a Japanese preserve. None of this has been accomplished by magic, and little by fundamental Japanese innovation. The technology has sometimes, alas, been stolen. Mostly, it has been begged, borrowed and bought in two senses. Straightforward licensing has given Japan essential technology. But so has acquisition of all or part of companies with valuable technological resources.

By 1992, some 363 high-technology firms had passed into

Japanese hands. In computers, they hold eighty-seven out of 133 American businesses bought wholly or partially by foreigners. Longworth gives the example of Semi-Gas Systems Inc of San Jose in California. Its expertise in purified gases passed into Japanese ownership, along with the benefits of $5 million in US Federal Government support.

'There's an economic war on, and we're losing it,' was the grim verdict of Papken Der Terossian, the chief executive of a chip-maker, the Silicon Valley Group. Accepting his description, is the war being waged on equal terms? The Japanese ability to buy up key players has no parallel the other way round. Japan's capitalism doesn't create a host of buyable businesses: American capitalism does. It's a marvellous method of starting up new businesses and rapidly developing their markets. But the transition into medium scale (let alone major size) is far less easily achieved.

Start-up stars may well find that the optimum moment to optimise their personal wealth comes shortly after the first moment of fruition – when the company is still riding high on its initial surge. At that stage, the entrepreneur either goes public, or sells out – perhaps to the Japanese. The long building process that created IBM itself has become much harder to finance.

Most Silicon Valley start-ups (or upstarts) rely on venture capital funds. That's quite patient money. The funds usually run for a ten-year period, but their purpose is to yield abnormally high gains on their investments. For these yields to materialise, profits must be taken. The rule of thumb for a successful investment is ten times your money after five years – at which point the successful investor looks for an exit, via public flotation or outright sale.

This process had served the US (and world industry) magically well until the Nineties. Apple, Intel and Compaq are amazing, seemingly final testimony to the effectiveness of venture capitalism in this venturesome, capital-intensive technology. Yet the degree to which America's flagship industry is still

American becomes increasingly doubtful as the century draws to an end.

Outside advanced ceramics, the Japanese have an inferior record in innovation. They have over-compensated for these failures by an astonishing run of successes in application. Liquid crystal technology, which lies behind the flat screens of the laptops, is only one among the fields where the Japanese have soared far above the competition. In many cases (as with this technology) the basic discoveries were made, and under-exploited, in the West.

Supremacy in the applied technique of miniaturisation has seen Japanese companies, like Canon and Citizen, fighting with each other to build PC printers, no wider than A4 sheets of paper and ultra-light, that fit neatly into briefcases. Small wonder (you might say) that Apple Corp turned to Sony in producing its Powerbook laptop, one of 1992's most successful new products of any kind. Small wonder, again, that Apple's potentially revolutionary keyboard-less Newton electronic diary was produced in partnership with another Japanese company, Sharp.

The Newton's microprocessor comes, not from Silicon Valley, but from a small British company. This trend away from the Valley won't reverse. The US is no longer the overwhelming source of the hardware of the computer age. The fields in which near-total dominance was once achieved – mainframes and minicomputers – are those where IBM and Digital reigned supreme. The old kingdoms have lost power as growth in older products has faded and the industry has proliferated fantastically in both numbers and products.

No industry has ever evolved so rapidly, and from so many different starting points, as computing. Even the name 'computing' has been left far behind. The technological flowering has created not the hundred flowers of Mao's blooming, but hundreds of thousands. The Chinese dictator, unable to control the blossoming, crushed the plants underfoot. The giants of computing, faced with myriad known and emerging uses of burgeoning developments in hardware and software, have no chance of doing likewise.

In other global industries, such as automobiles, the pattern has been initial proliferation, followed by national consolidation, followed by globalisation. It once seemed certain that computer hardware, if not software, would follow the same route. How could small makers of PCs survive against global successes like Apple and Compaq, let alone the sovereign power of IBM?

For every head lopped off by market forces, at least two more have grown. Every day new developments testify to this vitality. The *Wall Street Journal*, not long ago, would never have bothered with product releases of high-tech companies. But the issue of 3 June 1992, one random example, routinely reported developments from companies as diverse as Data-General (a new high performance personal computer); Seagate Technology (two new miniature computer disk drives); and LaserMaster Technologies (products to improve speed and quality of printing).

There was also a routine report from a Japanese company – Hitachi (note the miniature emphasis) had developed 'the smallest ever computer chip'. Note, too, that the development came from a multinational giant – for better or worse (in the long run, possibly worse), Japan's pace is set by conglomerates that lead in size as well as technological resources. Not so in the US, where small is technologically beautiful.

In *Business Week*'s 1992 list of America's fastest growing companies, half the top twenty were engaged in the broadly defined computer industry. They ranged from A to X. Artisoft stood at number one. After three years of 171.3 per cent annual growth it had $64.3 million of sales, or precisely one-thousandth of IBM's. The company made both hardware and software for networking personal computers by 'peer-to-peer' links. The latter do away with the need for powerful 'servers', such as an IBM mini or workstation. They are yet another threat to larger machines and their makers.

As for X, number twenty was Xilinx (growth 39.9 per cent to $94.3 million over three years). Its reprogrammable chips had doubled profits in three years. As the A to X companies flourish, innovation bubbles up from the bottom. So far, efforts to direct it from the top have foundered. This is a serious problem for IBM and other leaders of the Western industry – these leaders are too often being led. But the giants of Japan are no better placed.

Their problems are symbolised by the largest top-down project of all – the Fifth Generation Computer. Eager to seize the lead from America, Japan captured world attention with this combined multi-company operation. Its grand design was to realise the supreme ambition – to approximate the workings of the human brain in the ultimate supercomputer. In 1983 Edward Feigenbaum of Stanford University wrote a book on what he called 'Japan's computer challenge to the world'. Others echoed the view that this bold vault would overleap competitors and give Japan the global lead.

In June 1992, the grandiose project was laid to rest after a decade of doomed endeavour and dreadful cost. The Fifth Generation stayed earthbound. 'In terms of applications for the world market they fell well short of the goals,' Feigenbaum said. 'It's like they gave a very expensive party, and nobody came.' The essence of the defeat was rubbed in by Nippon Telephone & Telegraph. The country's telecommunications monopoly ordered its supercomputer not from Japanese makers, nor from American mainframe suppliers, but from Intel.

The microprocessor company's bid had undercut all contenders. The 'massively parallel processing' already described in an earlier chapter is the key to Intel's success. Its most powerful chips are combined to tackle different parts of major calculations at the same time. While the Fifth Generation approach was similar in concept, American technology was simply superior at solving the hardware and software problems.

The $400 million spent by the Japanese generated a mass of

software – but you can judge its merit by its fate. The head of MITI (the much-vaunted Ministry of International Trade and Industry) made the software available to all and sundry absolutely free. As a US computer scientist remarked, 'Nobody would pay for this stuff. It will only run on the machines they built for this project, so who can use it?'

The machines were one-off computers created by Hitachi, Toshiba, Mitsubishi and Oki Electric, giants who otherwise steered clear of the project. As the Fifth Generation spending ground its way towards collapse, so the goal of humanised computer reasoning lapsed, too. 'Intelligent' computing will certainly materialise one day, but probably not via the top-down route marked out by MITI.

The temptation to crow over the Japanese failure, while understandable, is dangerous. The Fifth Generation was only a fraction of the totality of Japanese research and development. The spin-off from the failed project, in technology and experience, could conceivably prove valuable, and it never pays to underestimate your competition, especially if it's Japanese.

Western competitors have a tendency to create comforting myths about the Japanese. In cars, the myth was, first, that they couldn't compete with Detroit or European engineering; when that comfort failed, it was styling at which the invaders were doomed to flop; when that myth collapsed, it was luxury executive cars that were beyond Japanese competence – today, try telling that to the buyers of Toyota's Lexus or Nissan's Infiniti.

Much comfort has been drawn from Japanese inability to match Western genius in software. In mid-1992, even as the Fifth Generation project folded, one expert reported on Japan's formidable progress in tackling the *process* of writing software. The work promised to speed up software production – just as Japanese engineers in cars and consumer electronics have accelerated new product development to overwhelming competitive effect.

The Fifth Generation failure is not the end of the road for Japan's computer scientists. For the first time, people from government, business and the universities have combined on a project. New and arduous disciplines have been learnt in the field of artificial intelligence. And $770 million of spending will go over the next decade on 'the Real-World Computing Project', which will attempt to generate 'neural network' systems that can recognise patterns (at which existing computers are notoriously inept).

That attempt may be no more successful than its predecessor. Development doesn't take place in a competitive vacuum. The top-down Fifth Generation project failed primarily because of the breakneck speed of bottom-up development of microprocessors in the US – and not just by Intel. Its dominance will not prevent a growing echelon of competitors, from start-ups to IBM, from continuing to tackle the leader head-on.

This rivalry unquestionably guarantees a stunning pace of development. The Japanese lag far behind it. Their dominance of the technology of chip-making contrasts oddly with the lamentable lag in making microprocessors. They would have been better advised to concentrate on closing this mysterious gap. But the Fifth Generation may close another lacuna: Japan's lack of any equivalent to the academic research fuelled by US government money – channelled through the Defense Department's Advanced Research Projects Agency.

'Everything America has has come out of a small group of dreamers supported by DARPA,' according to John Gage, director of science at Sun Microsystems. 'Building a similar community was vital for Japan.' It does not, of course, follow that the community will conquer. The primary mechanism of success was the American propensity for spinning off, not technology, but technologists. The main contribution of large US firms, in key respects, has been their inadvertent nurture of brilliant breakaways.

In a straight bet between Japanese heavyweights and American upstarts, punters who know their computer history would always favour the latter. Fight commentators, however, have always swung between two extremes. On one side are the deniers who chant what *Business Week* described as their mantra: 'The Japanese do not understand marketing. The computer industry moves too fast for the Japanese. The Japanese can't write software.'

At the opposite pole are the Cassandras, who point to the Japanese edge in chip-making tools, memory chips and six other key technologies, and to their rising sales of both PCs and mainframes in the US. According to one report, NEC, 'fully integrated and positioning itself to take on IBM and AT&T', had US companies 'shaking in their boots', and a 'strong challenge' to IBM and AT&T was being mounted by another Japanese conglomerate – Fujitsu.

Compared to other markets, the penetration of Japanese brands in computing, in fact, has been pitifully small and slow. But that's not the whole tale. The threat is reality. Fujitsu, maker of the world's fastest conventional supercomputers, its lightest laptops and its largest memory chips, has the second highest sales of computers, topping DEC, Hewlett-Packard and Unisys. By buying into companies like International Computers Ltd in Britain, Amdahl in the US and Nokia Data in Scandinavia, Fujitsu has heavily reinforced its own market-leading strength in Japan.

Other Japanese conglomerates have used other strategies to add global power to their local assets, not least through the proliferating alliances struck with their US rivals – above all others, with IBM. The Cassandras can, with some ease, construct a scenario that shows Japanese penetration in computery following the same pattern as in other industries, from cars downwards.

In 1989, Edmund J. Reilly, then president of Digital's Japanese company, warned that, 'There is a graveyard of companies that have given technology to the Japanese.' Scott McNealy, the CEO of Sun Microsystems, observed that the Japanese were taking their profits from memory chips 'and sinking them into software, artificial intelligence and computer-aided design tools'. He concluded that, 'If you have all those profits and a monopoly in computer components, you own the computer industry'.

McNealy's own company, the world leader in workstations, had felt obliged to give Fujitsu access to its technology 'in return for help in establishing [it] as a standard'. The debate over Japan's potential was thus over by the beginning of the Nineties. In a way very different from IBM's, hydra-headed and far less conspicuous, Japan Inc has become the largest, though not the leading, force in the world computer industry. Its American competitors need to recite a new mantra: 'The Japanese understand marketing. The Japanese are moving as fast as the computer industry. The Japanese can write software.'

That's the reality. Anything else is self-delusion.

20

IBM Japan:
Flawed Jewel
in the Crown

'If US . . . companies continue business as usual, they will either fail outright or become, in effect, local design and marketing subsidiaries of Japanese companies that will dominate a $1 trillion world hardware industry.'

None of the Cassandras warning the US computer industry about its fate have been more scholarly, persuasive or downright alarming than Charles H. Ferguson. Once an IBM analyst, Ferguson was a research associate at MIT's Center for Technology, Policy and Industrial Development when he published those ominous words in the *Harvard Business Review* (July–August 1990).

His detailed argument assembled facts and figures, none comforting, which showed that, far from differing from previous assaults on world industries, Japan's attack in computing was following the same pattern – and with the same success. The previous chapter delineated the same developments – how Japanese companies first establish leadership at the lower end of technology, then advance to become dominant suppliers of components and sub-assemblies at all technological levels, and finally move into complete systems.

Ferguson shows that 'the digitisation of everything' has played into the hands of Japanese conglomerates. Strengths in one field (consumer electronics or photocopying) have been used as springboards into others. He also lays great emphasis on the power of the super-conglomerates, the *keiretsu* of linked industrial and financial companies, in generating co-operation within a competitive culture – egged on by the corporate state.

His thesis was that, unless US (and European) companies mimicked the *keiretsu*, the 'endangered list' included 'most of the US computer, office equipment and imaging industries, from high-flying newcomers such as Apple, Compaq, Conner Peripherals and Sun Microsystems to established giants such as DEC, Xerox, Hewlett-Packard and Kodak'. Conspicuously not among those present was IBM.

Ferguson's view was that the Western industry's future depended on its ability to coalesce into larger, interlocked groupings. IBM, in addition to acting vigorously to maintain its own technological independence, had led the way in attempting to create vital collaborative strategies. He rejected the popular view that the future hinged on the vitality of smaller companies (many of them still to be born). If that were true, it would follow that America's dominance no longer hung on the superiority of IBM.

That superiority had once been a source of great comfort for those contemplating the relative decline of America in several key industries. In computers, apparently, America had nothing to fear from Japan – thanks to IBM. In mid-1990, Ferguson still regarded IBM as the citadel of America's defences, although he was concerned at its tendency to ride two horses – collaboration on one side and 'overly individualistic patterns of behaviour', seeking 'narrow, short-term advantages' on the other.

For all that, IBM's strength, even after the consistent pattern of failures and setbacks since 1986, compared impressively with most of its big business peers. True, other American industries were strongly placed vis-à-vis the Japanese as the Nineties began; for example, drugs, aerospace and entertain-

ment (though Sony and Matsushita had made up for that defi-
ciency by buying into Hollywood and the music industry at
multi-billion-dollar price tags). But IBM outdid most other
large companies and industries in one respect – it had won big
not only outside Japan, but inside that trickiest of markets.

IBM Japan Ltd was a jewel in a crown studded with gems. At
one point it was the unchallenged Number 1 in the world's
fastest-growing economy, the source of 10 per cent of the corporation's worldwide profits. Every commentator pointed to
this most excellent example as a demonstration to other
Western businesses of what truly effective management could
achieve. The Japanese themselves were apt to cite IBM as the
company they most admired, an American firm that was 'more
Japanese than the Japanese'.

If the compliments were meant to lure IBM into a false
sense of security, they succeeded. In 1979, aggressive pricing
and technological prowess in mainframes took Fujitsu past the
100 per cent-owned US subsidiary in the domestic market.
Seven years later NEC followed suit, this time under the impetus of minis and micros. To some extent, the Japanese were
exploiting the innate advantages of indigenous producers who
could rely (as IBM could not) on orders from public bodies,
and from their associations of like-minded companies, the
above-mentioned *keiretsu*.

But these innate Japanese advantages had always existed,
so they couldn't have been decisive. What was? *Fortune* writer
Joel Dreyfuss listed six gross errors of omission and commission by IBM.

1   Developing a 'reputation for arrogance and poor service' –
    both of them anathema in the Japanese culture.

2   Over-reliance on mainframes in a down-sizing market.

3   Getting leapfrogged in new product development:
    Dreyfuss cited an office computer that could handle

Japanese text, a first that was rapidly overtaken by local rivals.

4   Refusal to discount prices, which allowed Fujitsu to under-sell IBM by up to 50 per cent.

5   Feeble efforts in the small systems market, where NEC's 36 per cent share was nine times that of IBM.

6   Failure in entry-level PCs, where NEC seized 70 per cent of the market, and where IBM's competitive series, intro-duced in retaliation in 1984, flopped – four out of five models had been withdrawn four years later.

'We didn't know the market, and we didn't have the sales channels,' confessed an IBM Japanese executive. In a way, that sixth error is almost forgivable. The analogous PC Jr flopped in the same chancy market back home (just as Japanese mak-ers failed in efforts to market home computers in Europe). But IBM's first five errors were made from the same cloth as its defects at home: disregard for customers, sluggish innovation, obsession with mainframes and fixation on high profit mar-gins. These formed the global pattern of IBM's relative decline.

The attitude which Armonk took to this most symbolic of markets fits that same pattern. Japan is unique in IBM's uni-verse – the only non-American market to possess all three elements of the IBM mix: plants, product development facili-ties and research labs. In 1984, the Asia/Pacific Group (or APG) was created and housed in Tokyo. There, 200 plus non-Japanese exercised responsibility over Australia, New Zealand, southeast Asia, China, India – and Japan. The Japanese oper-ation was staffed, in contrast to APG, almost entirely by locals.

The extra layer of management introduced at APG was well-intentioned. It saved the local IBM boss from having to visit Armonk once a month (for what should surely have been the unnecessary task of 'selling Japan in IBM'). But the new structure raised obvious possibilities of conflict with APG's boss. That was Richard Gerstner (brother of Lou, the future chief executive of IBM, then still making his reputation at American Express). The missionary task, and the monthly visits, now fell to Gerstner.

'The biggest challenges,' he said, 'are conveying the demands of the Japanese customer, the intensity of the competition, the time it takes to get a return on your investment.' Gerstner added that the task was getting easier. But it's something of a mystery that the Armonk executives should have needed persuading of any of these familiar truths. After all, IBM had operated in this market for decades. Still less should IBM have needed to add another tier to its already top-heavy establishment in order to deliver the message.

The logical response to the Japanese dilemmas – the way in which they might have been averted – was to encourage the affiliate's free-standing role in the IBM community. It was IBM Japan that needed to be more Japanese than the Japanese, or less IBM than the rest of IBM – for instance, by indulging in joint ventures and discounting. One initiative in particular was especially important for the Japanese customer; enabling IBM products to connect with those of other companies in integrated systems.

In 1993 that integration was still not a reality. Dreyfuss told his readers that Sony relied on IBM for its worldwide word processing and data network. But Fujitsu, DEC and NEC machines were in use for Sony's engineering and design, production control and electronic mail. One Sony executive, Hiroshi Adachi, said that his ideal was to access files in the IBM system from a Fujitsu terminal. Dreyfuss concluded: 'IBM's future in Japan may be determined by how long Adachi, and executives like him, have to wait.' They are still waiting.

Of all markets, Japan is the one where keeping customers in suspense is most dangerous for IBM, simply because its main competitors are much larger than IBM Japan – and no midgets compared to IBM worldwide. The uphill Japanese struggle was as ominous for IBM as its previous success had been hopeful. As long ago as 1983, another *Fortune* article, dealing with IBM's loss of Number 1 position in Japan, laid down this pregnant challenge: 'In the US, IBM can sell good but less than extraordinary equipment at a premium simply because of those famous initials. In Japan IBM is more like any competitor, forced to keep its manufacturing efficient, strive for broad distribution, and price carefully. It remains to be seen whether IBM can come out on top in this unusual situation.'

A decade later, the answer was emphatic: IBM was Number 4. Over the intervening years, IBM had intermittently been the subject of reports about its latest Japanese comeback. Their publication parallelled the comeback stories back home. In all instances, in both worlds, putative delight was followed by positive disappointment. Thus in 1992, IBM was turning 'tougher in Tokyo', with a president, Takeo Shiina, who was 'bent on making blunders a thing of the past'.

In early 1991, however, Armonk had turned to an American for Japanese salvation. World Trade president Ned C. Lautenbach, brother of Terry, the former IBM US boss (who quit abruptly in 1992), was 'sent to get our business going again' in Japan. That December a 'sweeping reorganisation' coincided with the corporate upheaval in the US. The Oriental orientation, however, differed markedly – there were no large-scale lay-offs. IBM Japan (IBMJ) 'consolidated product-marketing groups to better serve broad customer requirements' – for example, serving large customers with all their needs across the IBM range.

The programme of reform mimicked what CEO Akers was attempting in the US. Autonomy down the line was increased, to speed up deals and lift some of the burden from Shiina, who claimed that the fifty-nine 'major decisions' passed upwards a year before had come down to twenty-five. A new focus on software and services was supposed to help IBM's mainframes to climb back to prime position from third. In

PCs, IBM was resuming the attack with new vigour, featuring workstations, laptops and a willingness to share technology with local rivals.

Lautenbach, like the many IBM cheerleaders before him, was feeling 'very positive' after a restructuring that 'has been like turning on faucets of energy'. The taps weren't powerful enough – IBM Japan achieved only a small advance up a steep hill. Fujitsu was outselling IBM in information systems three to two, and NEC and Hitachi also had significant leads. Their rise has been inexorable, a victory for the national strategy of using IBM's strictly controlled entry into Japan as a foundation for the local industry, and then using government support for collaborative ventures to build all-round competitors.

At Fujitsu, in consequence, initial dependence on Siemens of West Germany was rapidly reversed. The company capitalised on its growing technological and financial strength by allying with Amdahl (a thorn in IBM's mainframe flesh) and ICL (the rival which had always resisted IBM's rise in the UK market). ICL now plays a pivotal role (and a successful one) in Fujitsu's empire.

It has been strongly reinforced by the addition of Nokia Data, the Scandinavian computer group. Like Nixdorf of Germany, Nokia had been blown into losses and a dubious future by the ice-cold winds of technological change. Medium-sized firms which live by selling specialised EDP solutions built around minicomputers have no future in a world of high-powered, PC-based workstations and proliferating, comprehensive software packages.

In that new world, however, Japan had assumed new significance for IBM. Its Japanese company had worldwide responsibility for development and manufacture of laptops and small disk drives. And Armonk's new global strategies, such as the thrust for service revenues and technological alliances, have been tested in Japan. The essential difficulty, which explain's IBM's years of Tokyo travail, is that efforts to penetrate the Japanese markets by American companies inevitably increase the competitive power of their hosts. For a major example, Japanese manufacturers have no important proprietary position outside their home market in PCs other than portables. That's because the leader, NEC, with a traditional half of sales, insisted on maintaining an exclusive architecture – and its local rivals insisted on keeping their own operating systems, too.

In early 1991, IBM lined up eleven Japanese computer companies for an assault on NEC. They were licensed to use key technologies that would make their machines compatible with IBM's and thus with each other's. Opinions differed as to whether the ploy would bear any real fruit, but in terms of their ability to compete globally, the IBM licensees could only benefit – especially since compatibility would open the door to American software.

That would please those in the US who see software, not hardware, as the golden key to future markets. Provided that this vision is true, and that the US keeps its premier position in software, the national strength in information technology might even be enhanced – and Cassandras like Charles H. Ferguson would be disproved. In early 1991, the US share of world software markets was estimated at 57 per cent, or $62.7 billion – almost out of sight from the nearest competitor, Japan, with 13 per cent (the three European leaders had 21 per cent between them).

No non-American comes anywhere near the industry leader, Microsoft. The latter's strength, however, like that of the US as a whole, lies in packaged programs, including operating systems. Other countries are on much better terms in custom-written and specialised programs – and Brad Cox, co-founder of Stepstone Corp, which makes advanced software for workstations, sounded as apocalyptic as Ferguson when he pronounced that 'The only industry we have a leadership position in is software. And I think we're losing that like all the others.'

Ferguson himself dismissed the software argument as irrelevant: 'According to this view, Japanese producers will specialise in commodity manufacturing, while US companies will continue to lead by virtue of their command of the higher-value-added activities of design, software, systems integration, and marketing. This argument is appealing, but wrong.'

Whatever happens in the much smaller software market, gains there (and the US was hardly likely to expand so large a market share) can't compensate for losses in hardware. That's simple arithmetic. The idea that Japan is condemned to lag in adding value is just simple-minded. Ferguson cited LSI Logic and VLSI Technology, start-ups which in the early Eighties licensed their technology to Toshiba and Hitachi respectively. Japanese producers, by 1990, held half the world market in the products concerned – application specific integrated circuits.

In software, American technology is equally accessible – through acquisition. Half a dozen Japanese firms, including Hitachi, had taken major stakes in US software houses by 1992. 'We can't ship our product to the US because software is culture,' said Kazuhiko Nishi, president of ASCII Corp, the largest Japanese software company. 'Our only choice is to take a stake in established companies.'

At the same time, Japanese companies are exploiting their own skills in other ways – for example, in setting up 'software factories', which adopt manufacturing methods to produce software with much lower defect levels than American equivalents. Much of the Japanese excellence in software is hidden from view, anyway. As Microsoft's Bill Gates has said, 'The reason the US is ahead is not because the Japanese can't write good software.' Every electronic gadget that emerges from Japan, from Nintendo games to auto components, relies on brilliantly efficient software which is packaged into the product. That has a double significance.

First, it rules out any prospect that, in Ferguson's words, 'Japanese companies will lose digitised consumer industries to superior US computer companies.' As he writes, this is 'fantasy'. Second, much computer software is already bought, not by consumers, but by hardware manufacturers. Few of the millions who use the MS–DOS operating system, for example, have ever seen the product.

Increasingly, PCs are being sold with software 'bundled' into the hardware package, although in the early Nineties, true, most packaged programs are still being sold unbundled, in boxes of floppy disks whose prices are often extortionate. But as the power and memory of PCs continue to soar, it is easy to imagine a future in which advanced word processing, data-base, spreadsheet and other programs will be packaged within the hardware, all set up and ready to go – with easy-to-follow computerised manuals thrown in.

It's by no means certain that hardware will be the commodity market and software the value-added end. Software piracy is rife (to the tune of $10–12 billion of illegal copying a year). Production costs are very low in relation to prices that are dropping or being heavily discounted. So packaged software looks very much like becoming a commodity itself. Probably the market will divide, like that for hardware, between high-margin products with smaller volumes and low-margin mass markets – the kind in which the Japanese have specialised.

Whether this prediction comes true is beside the point. For in the whirling world of information technology, prediction is never better than an informed guess. Nothing stays the same. Two years after Ferguson published his *HBR* article, for instance, Japan's dominant makers of random access memory chips, on whose prowess he laid great stress, were suffering much financial grief. Also, what he saw as a 'model alliance' between IBM and supercomputer designer Steve Chen had died the death.

More seriously, IBM's 'extraordinary and exemplary' role in forming Sematech, a co-operative venture to protect the US interest in chip-making capital goods, had been overtaken by events. In August 1992, the issue was whether the Pentagon would withdraw support, as proposed. Asked by the General Accounting Office if they would continue funding Sematech in that event, ten of the consortium's dozen industrial members said no.

On the credit side, Sematech had achieved its goal of reversing the drop in domestic use of American-made chip-making equipment (once in free fall). On the other hand, the consortium members were uneasy about the return on their investment. IBM had pumped $100 million into the consortium, and was being optimistic in seeing a return by 1996. Other companies weren't sure they would ever see their money back.

The point is less the rights and wrongs of investment in Sematech itself, rather that this was the sole example of the industry trying to 'emulate Japanese industry-government co-operation'. The core of Ferguson's hopes for rolling back the Japanese tide remained IBM and whatever alliances could be built around that core. And the race was on to see whether a wider industry structure could be created before that core was fatally weakened.

21

Partnermania:
If You Can't Beat 'Em . . .

Through all the years of its dominant success, IBM followed a straightforward policy – if you can't beat 'em, beat 'em. The all-out drive for market supremacy was accompanied by product exclusivity. An IBM product was made only by IBM, from its own designs, in its own plants, with its own components, often on its own equipment – and none of these assets were available to outside companies.

Outsiders were let in only as suppliers of those necessities which IBM chose not to manufacture. Few outside products got as far as the final assembly lines. There, an enviable design policy gave the finishing touch to a homogenous product range that heavily reinforced the main marketing message – IBM is best of the best. Whether that applied to its production processes and costs is another matter. Exclusivity made that irrelevant.

If 'IBM-only' is the rule, even if outside suppliers are capable of undercutting IBM's internal sources, they can't. Indeed, a weird logic drove the process towards higher costs. Where IBM led the market and prices (it did, across most of the product range), Armonk could (and did) dictate gross margins to its manufacturing plants. Working on a cost-plus basis, these had no incentive to reduce costs – the higher the cost, the greater the absolute yield from the same percentage mark-up.

What applied down the line governed the results for the entire corporation. Small wonder that IBM could report the highest overall margins of any multinational manufacturing giant. But in the Eighties, and especially at the lower end of the market, the comfortable equation no longer applied. High prices meant low sales. To get competitive prices, IBM needed competitive costs. Inevitably, this demand exposed the frailties of the cost-plus culture, and enforced wholesale cuts in a bloated labour-force.

By this time, starting from the mould-breaking decision to source the personal computer outside, IBM had become a giant consumer of outside components and assemblies. That was one breach in the wall of exclusivity. Increasingly, IBM has become a contractor, buying in a bulging array of hardware and software to keep abreast of rapidly developing markets. These imports, however, have been offset by increasing exports – like any nation state, the corporation must try to balance its external trade.

The decision to sell IBM microcircuits to outsiders, announced in 1991, was another watershed in the corporation's history. Another landmark decision, revealed in 1992, was to assemble finished products for sale under labels that wouldn't bear the three magic initials. That followed inevitably from a strategic change that breached exclusivity even further. The great loner would welcome allies – even from among its own enemies.

At times, hardly a week seemed to pass without some announcement of a new IBM alliance. Take 22 April 1992, and an agreement under which Thomson-CSF, the French electronics giant, would use IBM's high-speed RISC microchips. Earlier in the year, IBM had agreed to invest about $100 million in the state-owned computer maker, Groupe Bull. RISC (reduced instruction set computing) chips were again involved: at the heart of both agreements represented an astonishing reversal of past policies in more senses than one.

The French government was welcoming the very company against which Gaullist defences and offences had been mustered in the past. To complete the irony, Bull contained the relics, not only of French computer chauvinism, but of two long-term mainframe rivals of IBM's – Honeywell and General Electric. But there was more to the French deals than wheels turning full circle. The Thomson agreement allowed IBM to market real-time workstation systems to be developed by the French company, and envisaged both groups launching their first products using the Power PC RISC chips at roughly the same time (end-1993).

The latter chips, too, had not been developed by IBM in isolation. Here its partner is Motorola – the deadly opponent of Intel, IBM's main supplier of microprocessors. Intel is the partner in yet another IBM deal, as licensee for screen graphics technology. New Intel chips will incorporate the new IBM technology, which is aimed at achieving an industry standard. IBM was thus hoping to bolster market dominance through proprietary technology – its old strategem, realised in a new way: through alliance.

The financial terms for the Intel graphics deal were not disclosed. That applies to virtually all the alliances of the Akers years, so great in number that no IBMer can rattle off more than a few. In one sense, though, the deals pay tribute to IBM's immense strengths, above all to its technological and marketing attractions.

These alliances and partnerships, however, haven't been taking place in isolation. For example, the very next day's SGS-THOMSON (a Franco-Italian micro-electronics alliance) was linking with Philips of the Netherlands to devote $200 million to developing 'state-of-the-art technology for CMOS, a fast-growing material technology for computer chips'. The specific objective was to wrest market share from American manufacturers (the easy leaders with 47 per cent) and the Japanese in high-speed, portable chips for autos, telecommunications and consumer products.

With one tentacle, the French partner in this venture was thus seeking to haul back part of the Euromarket in chips, while with another arm it was pulling IBM and the Americans through the door. These are merely a few examples of the bewildering pattern of technological and marketing deals which now criss-cross the electronics world. The lattice is impenetrable even to insiders. No deal is more intriguing, though, or less clear in its implications, than the partnership between IBM and Apple.

The piquancies abound. Apple is the only significant maker outside the IBM-compatible world (though that drawback has recently been eased by technology). IBM had also earlier signed up with Next, the Apple rival created by its ousted founder, Steven Jobs. According to Jobs, chatting to none other than Microsoft's Bill Gates for the benefit of *Fortune,* 'somebody at IBM a few years ago saw our Next Step operating system as a potential diamond to solve their biggest and most profound problem, that of adding value to their computers with unique software' – hence the deal, priced at a modest $50 million.

Unfortunately, IBM wasn't the cohesive monolith which Jobs (and the world) imagined. 'It is a very large place with lots of faces, and they all play musical chairs. Somewhere along the line this diamond got dropped in the mud, and now it's sitting on somebody else's desk who thinks it's a dirt clod. Inside that dirt clod is still a diamond, but they don't see it.'

There's no reason to suppose that Jobs' discouraging experience is atypical. In this procession of deals (as in the Next case), IBM sometimes gave the appearance of following every highway, and not a few byways, without a clear, agreed plan. It was travelling hopefully, the hope being that the journey might arrive at somewhere worth reaching. In the Apple deal, the objective was nothing less than the entire future of PC technology. The alliance would be the gateway to another stupendous revolution, in which micro-electronics would infiltrate, even take over, activities across the entire spectrum of human life.

RISC technology in general, and the Power PC in particular, play a crucial part in this alliance, too. Unveiled in 1993, the chip is crucial for Motorola, which has depended almost wholly on Apple for its presence in the personal computer market. The new RISC chip will be the core of the new generation Macintosh, but it will presumably also be the heart of new IBM PC's. The present sharp differentiation between the two firms must theoretically wither away.

Who will gain most is an open question. But Apple had the most powerful incentive to sign this bundle of pacts (five in all). Adopting the IBM/Motorola chip, rather than buying from such rivals as Sun Microsystems and MIPS (or Motorola alone, for that matter), set Apple firmly in the IBM-compatible world. That was the unifying theme of the whole deal. The nearer IBM and Apple draw together, the easier it should be for Apple to attend to the business customers who are IBM's province.

Part of the joint venture, called Taligent (from 'talent' and intelligent'), is designed to give both the companies a new operating system that will make writing new software much easier. Taligent brings IBM funding and independent software writers to an original Apple project called Pink. The project is a front-runner in 'object-oriented' program writing, which promises much faster speeds.

Another joint venture, named Kaleida, is developing technology in multi-media, the combination of sound, data, graphics and video that is a hot new play in the dizzying world of micro-electronics. In addition, there's 'PowerOpen', a project which aims to update the Unix operating system. Success here will take IBM deeper into workstations and other more powerful computers. Apple will also be able to serve business users more effectively as IBM-compatibility takes it into networking. Compaq (among others) currently has a powerful 'server', which can look after several PCs at once. Apple has none.

Whichever way you cut it, the deal is remarkable. Whether

the result will swing towards corporate users (the IBM tendency) or individuals (Apple's mainstay) is only one of the unanswered questions. The biggest, which applies to most of IBM's new alliances, is simply whether the project will work out, commercially or technologically. High-flying projects (especially joint ones) have a bad but inevitable habit of aborting – partly for inherent reasons, partly because of unpredictable outcomes in the outside world.

IBM's multiple link-ups echo its old, obsolete policy of betting on every technological horse in the race. If they back every available source of the next breakthroughs, the IBMers are insured against being left, as before, on the outside looking in. They are bargaining their own present technological riches and vast marketing reach against an assured position in the future.

Two disadvantages are self-evident. Back every horse in the race, and you must win – but you make no money. All those alliances, with their unknown financial commitments, involve sharing profits. That must reduce the potential for IBM itself, especially as a prime objective for its partners (explicitly declared by Apple) is to benefit from IBM's greater credibility. In any event, IBM can't back all the horses; for their number is increasing all the time.

The new explosion of technology is reminiscent of the Big Bang that supposedly created the universe. The discoveries are creating wider and wider bands of more and more new materials from which more and more new products and classes of product are emerging. If the Apple forecasters are right (which is debatable), the universe of the electronics companies will reach $3 trillion of sales by 2002 – that's $3,000,000 million, or the equivalent of forty-six IBMs.

The vision, as Andrew Kupfer wrote in *Fortune,* is of an age in which 'the borders dissolve between telecommunications, office equipment, computers, consumer electronics, and media and publishing'; the 'digital technology gadgets focused on the intersections of those industries', which Apple is starting to produce, will become an awesome flood of things like 'electronic books, electronic organisers, electronic note takers, display telephones, personal communicators'.

It's a world quite far removed from that in which Apple grew and flourished, and light years away from IBM's large corporate womb. The sea-change from million-dollar mainframes to PCs costing thousands (and heading downwards) has already caused IBM the worst pains in its entire history. What part can it play in these new mass markets? Where does it draw the line? How does it gain the places in the sun that will be created by suppliers and technologies still to come into sight?

The alliances are slowly creating a new role for IBM, as a kind of Queen Bee, a huge amorphous shape, the focus of the hive, fed by the other inhabitants in return for its vital function. The corporation has far more of almost everything than its competitors, Japanese, European or American: more installed machines, more technologists, more patents, more products, more projects – and now, more alliances. Like the Queen Bee, it has imposing mass; but the insect model is also conspicuously inert.

The number of worker bees around the queenly IBM, though, is anything but static. On one count, IBM had in a couple of years paid more than $100 million for equity stakes in some 200 software and computer-services companies. That was in addition to the $100 million, mentioned earlier, that brought IBM 5.7 per cent of Groupe Bull and enabled the French company to use IBM's RS/6000 microprocessor.

That chip deal is one of 130 which clearly marked out a grand strategic pattern. The company that once kept its components to itself had determined to sell them to all-comers – and as many, and as much, as possible. The strategy sounds aggressive, but is actually defensive. IBM's European performance has bettered that in the US, but still shows lamentable slippage in market share – from 32 per cent in 1985 to 22.6 per cent in 1991. That's equivalent to a $10.8 billion loss of sales.

The components drive won't make much dent in that formidable number. The company will do well to win $900 million of the European market for computer components by 1995 – that's only 3 per cent. Japan, accounting for perhaps two-fifths of the market, has stolen much of the market position that could have belonged to IBM – had it started earlier. As it is, the catch-up is both belated and costly – half a billion dollars, for example, is earmarked for dynamic-random-access memory (DRAM) chips.

The plant involved will be the first in Europe to produce 64-megabit DRAM chips (together with 16-megabit ones). More important, Siemens of Germany is involved, coughing up a further half-billion dollars in yet another alliance. The IBM grand strategy evidently goes beyond expanding its European sales, badly though it needs the boost. The few remaining European computer makers need to form a family – and who better to serve as mother than Queen Bee IBM?

Siemens, after all, owns Siemens-Nixdorf, which, however troubled, is still a significant computer company. Bull is already in the IBM camp, so that leaves only Olivetti, which has been in negotiation with IBM from time to time. Provided that a number of political hurdles can be surmounted, the strategy could create a Fortress Europe as a powerful companion to a Fortress America. You can see the vision – two citadels protecting the indigenous computer industry by multiple alliances between companies which have IBM pacts as their common denominator.

They will also have bridges to Fortress Japan. On 13 July 1992, IBM and Siemens joined with Toshiba to announce another grand design. This one will probably require eight years and a billion dollars to create a memory chip with 256-megabit capacity – four times that of the joint IBM–Siemens project. As *Business Week* described it, 'The goal is a twenty-first century chip on whose tiny silicon surface will be etched what amounts to a street map of the entire world.'

Whether these chips (which 'will store . . . about two copies of everything Shakespeare wrote') will arrive on schedule, on cost, or on performance nobody knows. Nor is it clear how the technology will compare and compete with other devices, unborn, planned, or yet to be conceived. Other combines are at work. On the very same day, 13 July, Fujitsu and Advanced Micro Devices announced collaboration (shared plant cost $700 million) for electrically programmable read-only memories and flash chips.

Toshiba was also in partnership in memory chips with Motorola, as Texas Instruments was with Hitachi, and AT&T with NEC. In flash memory chips, Intel had teamed up with Sharp. And Motorola had a both-ways tie-in with the IBM–Toshiba–Siemens union. The latter is located at IBM's East Fishkill site (at the new Advanced Semiconductor Technology Center) under a Toshiba manager. How the 200 engineers, drawn from all three partners, would talk (let alone work) together, was left to hope rather than experience.

The initial result of the chip alliances, however, was still more 'COMPLEXITY!!!'. The exclamation marks are those of Michael J. Kami, a consultant of great insight. Long ago, he worked at shaping the strategy of IBM (he quit to perform the same job for Xerox). One of Kami's slides is a map of computer industry alliances that resembles a subway network gone mad. It has four large nodes, or hubs, of which IBM is only one.

The others are Apple, Digital and Microsoft. That makes two crucial points about a putative Fortress America. First, it won't and can't merely be IBM writ large. Second, even firms which aren't directly connected by alliances will probably be linked indirectly through mutual relationships. Thus, lines connect IBM with everybody else on the map, by one route or another – quite apart from the companies in which it holds shares and those that conform to its software guidelines.

The confusions are infinite. Apple is a platform partner to Digital, meaning that it conforms to the same software guidelines. But, as noted, Apple is developing software in partnership with IBM. Another batch of partners group under the name Accumaster – they support AT&T's network management standards. The phone company, by virtue of its NCR acquisition, is now a significant force in the computer industry. In this cat's cradle, nobody is without partners, because nobody can afford independence.

Neither can they afford dependence. Intel's great strength, an astonishing feat of self-control and long-range intelligence, was to stay at arm's length from its shareholder, IBM. The price of independence, however, has to be paid. In 1992 the *Wall Street Journal* reported that the live-in affair between the two companies, with Intel acting as sole supplier of chips for IBM's PCs, had moved into a new phase: 'IBM and Intel aren't splitting up. But the computer giant wants to spend more time alone, and it wants to see other people.'

The living-in was changing, wrote Laurence Hooper, but love hadn't fled (or turned to hate, as in IBM's relationship with Microsoft). Yet the profound development described in this book, in which the microprocessor has become the computer, has shifted the balance of power between the two parties. As the then IBM President, Jack D. Kuehler, said, 'When you sell a personal computer today, the people who make the money are the microprocessor maker and the operating system supplier.'

That single sentence explains why IBM went into competition with Intel. That competition didn't stop at selling PCs with IBM-made chips. Competitive logic pointed towards encouraging Intel rivals and selling IBM chips against Intel to third parties, including chips which clone Intel's code, and copies which improve on Intel's performance – and those policies are being pursued. Intel's CEO Andy Grove put a brave face on the change. His shareholder had pursued a 'variety of strategies . . . some favourable to us, some not'. But theirs was 'the best real-life example of a strategic alliance' that had once been a customer-vendor deal.

For the countless executives round the world who were

involved in IBM alliances at all stages of inception and progress, the writing on the wall was clear enough. No one knew which, if any, of the deals would ever reach the sovereign importance of the Microsoft and Intel relationships. But would IBM, sooner or later, again be tempted to believe that its self-interest lay in an opposite direction to that of the partner – or the thousands of partners?

By mid-1992 the company had more than 20,000 business alliance relationships worldwide, including almost 400 equity investments and joint ventures – and more were being created almost weekly. The task of keeping tabs on the equity deals, let alone the alliances, must stretch even IBM's bureaucracy. The strategy could easily make managerial nonsense. But does it make technological sense?

The answer of Professor David B. Yoffie of Harvard Business School is not encouraging. 'This is a roulette strategy. They're putting chips down on every major technology and hoping the ball will fall in the right spot. The risks are high.' And the auguries are mixed. After seven years of joint venture with Toshiba, the latter had gone for a different small screen technology – and had outperformed and underpriced an IBM portable using the joint development.

The Queen Bee, after all, remained royal, and very much larger than most of the workers in the hive. The IBM of 1992 was searching for new ways to defend a size, strength and status that could no longer be preserved by market domination, price leadership, technological supremacy, or any other traditional means. Maintaining control through a complex, interlocking network of alliances might look like a feasible alternative. But it was no easier than networking all of IBM's different, incompatible breeds of computer. And that, as late as 1992, had defeated IBM.

VIII

THE TROUBLE WITH MAINFRAMES

22

The Mainsales
Mentality

Everything is understandable about IBM's dominance by 'the mainframe mentality'. The phrase covers not only the large hardware systems themselves, but the customers – the great public service organisations and the biggest commercial institutions from which the first Tom Watson had drawn his first customers. The Census Bureau was the breakthrough customer for the Hollerith punch card machine in 1890, long before Watson arrived on the scene. Sixty years later, the 1950 census gave the same opportunity to Univac, the pioneering electronic computer invented by J. Presper Eckert and John Mauchly.

Since the Eckert-Mauchly wonder displaced some of its own existing hardware, IBM had to recognise the arrival of new competition. True, IBM discounted Remington Rand (which had bought up the Eckert-Mauchly) as a serious competitor in business machines. IBM's own business was booming along (placing forty electronic calculators a month in late 1950 and 100 a year later). Tom Watson could apparently afford to be complacent – but something, maybe the Census Bureau contract, stimulated his old belligerent reflexes.

He ordered a start on scientific computers. The consequent 701, while technically inferior to Univac, won enough success to convince the younger Tom Watson (and through the son his father) to launch a whole family of computers. The colossal cost would have bankrupted any lesser company. Between 1950 and 1956, long-term debt quadrupled, rising from 40 per cent of revenues to a peak 52 per cent of sales in 1955 – and turnover had more than doubled in the meantime.

Watson Jr, after taking control, added as much in sales ($333 million) in three years as his father had achieved in four decades. The 700 range, moreover, had powered past Univac. Well behind after its late start, IBM had seventy-six installations against Univac's forty-six by 1956. By then outstanding orders numbered 193, more than treble those of its rival. As IBM consolidated its unique strength with its clientéle in big business and big government, a torrent of riches flooded in.

This experience lay behind the thinking which launched the greatest gamble in business history – the young Watson's mega-bet on the 360 mainframe. The formula was basically the same. A research-led drive of great expense would leapfrog the opposition and propel IBM to undreamt-of levels of turnover. Capital spending duly soared to three times the previous peak in 1965. The next year it ballooned by a further 60 per cent, reaching $1.6 billion.

In six years the value of IBM's plant and property more than trebled to $6.6 billion. But the impact of the 360s was equally phenomenal. By 1965, IBM's net profits matched its total sales at the end of the older Tom Watson's reign. Gross revenues had grown fourfold since 1956 under the inexorable, irresistible impact of the 360s.

The formula seemed equally inexorable. Ride the whirlwind of the new technology for its five years of dynamic life. Build up cash reserves to finance the next big technological push. Take the next great leap forward in sales and profits. Repeat to taste. There was only one drawback: IBM never repeated its history-making achievement with the 360s. As Robert Sobel observed, Tom Watson had in mind a family of advanced computers that would 'provide IBM with a lead in technology, expand its markets, ward off competitors, and unite his company'. Far more of this grand strategy came to pass than with most. But unintentionally 'Watson had opened his own Pandora's box'.

The 360s magnified, broadened, transformed the market. The 11,700 computers operating in the US in 1963 doubled by 1965 and doubled again by 1969. With the world outside America following fast, the computer was moving at great speed out of the large organisation and into the world of medium-sized users – and smaller ones still. While this created far greater sales potential, the proliferation of markets made them less susceptible to rigid IBM control.

That didn't seem to matter as the 360s worked their wonders, not only on the customers, but the competition. The effort to produce rival third generation computers, while not beyond the technological reach of IBM's many competitors, over-stretched their finances. They couldn't stay in the new game. It was an honest version of the knockout that Watson Sr had practised illegally with rival vendors of second-hand cash registers.

Unfortunately, the old, dishonest knockout appeared to resurface in a new guise. As noted earlier, IBM's top-of-the-line 360/91, a direct blow at Control Data Corp, was announced long before it was ready. It's irrelevant to explore whether or not IBM was using its famous (or infamous) ploy, robbing competitors of sales by premature announcement. The impact on Control Data was certainly savage, but that on IBM was ultimately far more severe.

In an industry rife with litigation, the small rival's suit set off the Justice Department and stimulated a series of legal cases, some potentially very damaging, all highly vexatious, that bedevilled IBM's Seventies. The 360/91 had a further baleful effect – its failure as a product left IBM vulnerable to supercomputer competition at the top of the market. Some of it came from the prodigious Gene Amdahl.

In 1970, when IBM turned down his project for a very large

machine using fully integrated circuits, Amdahl popped out of Pandora's box – and out of IBM. His allies included Fujitsu, the Japanese company that was to break the American stranglehold on mainframe sales. Still vulnerable at the top, IBM had also left too much room beneath the smallest machines in the 360 range. Its first effort to crack the 'entry level' market, the System 3, was, by IBM standards, a failure.

If the European markets (where smaller users were predominant) had called the tune, things might have been different – a smaller German-designed calculator had been a hit. But Pandora's box had released another demon. The 360 had bound IBM together as one homogenous, indivisible multinational whole. Now all its forces marched to the same drum. Inevitably, the pace was slower.

To cope, IBM embraced 'matrix management': or was it vice versa? Did the matrix act like an octopus to stifle some of the corporate vitality with its many tentacles? The matrix gave IBMers different bosses for their functional, product and marketing roles; they moved into a complex world of committees and crossed lines. The increase in internal complexity was compounded by the complications in external markets that had sprung from Pandora's box.

Companies which couldn't afford 360s still badly needed computing for competitive purposes. Up popped a new breed of companies which would 'share time' between their customers. IBM might have attacked this intermediate market itself. But with money pouring in from sales, rentals and service of the 360s and their software, there was no pressure, nor much apparent need, for new lines of business.

When a hot-shot Dallas salesman named H. Ross Perot proposed that IBM should enter the computer services business, the idea died somewhere in the depths of the bureaucracy. Perot went ahead on his own. His foundation, Electronic Data Systems, joined the swelling number of computer intermediaries, and to famous effect. Of those go-betweens, however, the most harmful were not the bureaux (to some extent, they were training up future customers for IBM) but the leasing firms.

Their economic coup fittingly became a classic business school case. One of the leaders, Saul Steinberg, was at B-school when he spotted the gap created by IBM's accounting policies. To generate profits as rapidly as possible, IBM depreciated leased computers over a five-year period: the lease charges, of course, reflected this depreciation. Over the rest of the lease, the rentals rolled in as pure profit.

As Steinberg *et al* spotted, the 360s would not be superseded in a hurry – not after so enormous an investment and up-heaval. The formula was elegantly lucrative. Buy a computer from IBM (forced to offer both sale and lease by the 1956 consent decree), depreciate it over ten years, and you could safely undercut IBM – stealing its business (and some of its profit) while it obligingly provided the ultimate customer (yours) with service as part of the 'bundled package'.

Once the leasing companies had appeared, IBM was bound to lose out. Whichever way the manufacturer cut the cake, the result was lower profits. Like nearly all giants attacked by price-cutters, IBM preferred to lose market share, which affected only a segment of its profits, rather than sacrifice margins across the entire product range.

Sooner or later, though, the latter sacrifice must be made, and the damage inflicted by the undercutters is thus doubled. But this double jeopardy lay well in the future when the leasing companies first arrived. So did the main impact of another attack on IBM's high prices – from smaller, cheaper machines which IBM simply didn't make. The 360 architecture couldn't be adapted to this lesser level of computing.

That opened the door to rivals (notably Ken Olsen of Digital Equipment) who kept prudently clear of IBM's commercial stamping ground. They concentrated on scientific and academic markets. Again, the arguments for inertia were powerful. Small markets and low prices were not attractive to IBM, and the competition was tiny – it was many years before DEC's total sales reached the same level as IBM's profits.

Somebody might have reflected that scientific uses had led commercial applications in the history of computing. IBM was by no means alone in its vision of the future. Stand-alone machines of limited capacity were no part of that vision: nor was linking them with others in networks to multiply their power. Rather, the corporate mind was dead set against such thinking, anyway. IBM's future belonged instead to increasingly powerful mainframes, accessed through terminals, that would meet all conceivable needs.

It was a convincing vision. But the post-360 IBM developed a disconcerting habit of failing to cover its flanks. By avoiding this failure when the electronic computer appeared, the Watsons had robbed Univac of its just reward for pioneering. After the 360, IBM's tracking of rival, non-mainframe technologies was too desultory. It therefore couldn't mount effective competition from its own resources, even after the challenge had become too obvious (and serious) to ignore.

The issue of mind-set was decisive. In one magnificent stroke, with the 360 family, IBM had rendered itself invincible on the battleground of its own choosing. Demand for mainframes was certain to grow as far as anybody's eye could care to see – and growth duly did continue right through the Eighties. The pricing and profitability on mainframes stayed wonderfully attractive, and their installation locked in the customer, probably for life.

In the honeymoon years of the 360s, the hardware and software could handle every task which, at that point, IBM's customers wished to automate. As new tasks developed, anyway, new technology would be available to cope – and IBM was trusted to provide it. Beside this all-embracing picture, everything else was peripheral, and the peripheral profits could safely be left to peripheral companies.

In the meantime, IBM could learn from the negative lessons of the 360 launch. The company's greatest success had threatened to be its fatal disaster as monumental production and development snafus all but swamped the programme. Watson and his triumphant management were plainly right to make sure that the company would never again run such unnecessary risks; right to guarantee that order and control would supersede disorganisation and confusion.

The systems were duly refined. But that had the uncovenanted effect of making deviation more difficult in a technology which is deviant in its very nature. Start into the future too late and you may never get there. A major part of the problem, though, is knowing where to start. Uniquely among the century's dominant technologies, that of the computer has fed on many sciences and innumerable talents, with a cross-fertilisation that has enormously magnified the impact of each contribution.

Time and again, the injection of new ideas from unexpected sources has kick-started computery into dramatic transformation. The result of this time-compressed, kaleidoscopic process has been, not only the creation of the world's third largest industry, but a price-performance curve of unprecedented shape. Take ENIAC, the Eckert-Mauchley brainchild from which Univac sprang: building it cost almost $3 million in today's money, where today a few hundred dollars buys vastly more powerful hardware off the shelf.

The headlong fall of hardware prices as performance has surged upwards is no more amazing than the accompanying explosion in software. That has left the original limited uses as far behind as the Dark Ages of a thousand years ago. Yet only four decades have passed since Univac first showed its paces publicly, on the November night of President Eisenhower's election in 1952. All these processes – cost reduction, performance enhancement, and use expansion – are still galloping on as new generations of scientist and engineer continue the cross-fertilisation.

The computer is evolving (some would say, has evolved) into a thinking machine. It began as a creature of thought, springing from Alan Turing's insight into mathematical logic, which postulated a logic-driven, problem-solving machine.

Turning the insight into reality took one brilliant contribution after another, always coming from different directions, countries and people – like Konrad Zuse of Germany, who thought of applying binary numbers and logic gates, or another engineer, Tommy Flowers (a Briton, like Turing), who proved that valves would work the gates much faster and more reliably.

John Von Neumann, a Hungarian-American, and like Turing a mathematician, made a dazzling intellectual leap into the concept of stored memory and then on to the basic design of all computers. The cast-list of brilliance goes on and on. Doug Engelbart, an American engineer, prefigured the personal computer in 1968; Ted Hoff, a physicist at Intel, took the inspired step of putting many integrated circuits on a single one, thus creating the microprocessor. Who would have guessed that these two approaches, when combined, would crack the iron grip in which IBM held the corporate market?

Hoff's original corporate client also ignored this historic opportunity. The company was Japanese – which makes the valuable point that tunnel vision isn't simply a Western ophthalmic disease. But what if the next unpredictable lurch of the technology were away from the mainframe? Was it even remotely conceivable that the mainframe could become obsolete, save for a few specialised uses?

The answer to that last question wasn't self-evident even in the early Nineties. But by then mainframe obsolescence was a definite possibility. Inside IBM, though, it long remained simply unacceptable. Nor was this a question of mind-set alone. For all the growth elsewhere (much faster in percentage terms), mainframes still provided the dominant share of IBM's sales and by far the largest proportion of profits.

Yet another business school classic was in the making. What does a great company do when its basic market is declining through inexorable economic and technological forces? The crude arithmetic should have been as obvious inside IBM as outside – in 1989, the cost of a million instructions per second (mips) on a mainframe was $116,786. On a mini, the figure was $10,975. On one of IBM's own PCs, the number was a mere $369.

But the prognosis was even more alarming (or should have been). By 1995, the mainframe-mini-PC scale would be $39,490 per mips, $738 – and $17. On that crude calculation, a mainframe would be 2,323 times as expensive as a PC. IBM stalwarts would continue to maintain that the mainframe had many calculating and storage powers that were beyond microprocessors. But that argument looked increasingly untenable when linked microprocessors were forming the world's largest super-mainframes – and taking orders away from IBM.

Some people within IBM may have been blinded by the mainframe mentality. Others were well aware that their staple product was under threat. According to Chposky and Leonsis: 'Over drinks or on the golf course and always well beyond earshot of IBM loyalists, many of the more astute mainframe marketers cursed [chairman] Opel for bringing the PC into IBM.' So long as the threat was on the fringes, with fringe competitors like Apple, the mainframers hadn't worried – now they did.

They saw that 'backed by IBM, the PC was actually *inside*. It was like a Trojan horse within the Big Blue walls'. At least one ex-IBMer reported that, even before IBM launched its PC, several mainframers saw the danger precisely – that the structure of the industry would buckle as customers flocked after the price-performance powers of the micro. The worries could spot that mainframe growth would never again match the glorious past; and that, as big system demand fell, IBM's profitability, intimately linked to its dominance in a diminishing market, would likewise fade away.

Personal computers, said this ex-IBMer, 'are inherently inimical to that dominance. The mainframe people saw the PC as IBM's worst enemy – bar none.' The analysis, while absolutely accurate, smacks of hindsight. Very few people outside IBM foresaw that trend before the PC appeared in August

1981. Inside IBM, though, John R. Opel, the chairman at the time, was visionary enough to take pre-emptive action.

When fears for the future were laid on his desk 'by men whose opinions he respected, the chairman did not waver'. According to one source, Opel knew that the threat would come some time, from somewhere – if not from America, from Japan. 'So Opel chose to keep the Trojan horse within his own walls, which meant the short-sighted in his company had to be prevented from harming the PC.'

It's certainly true that Opel 'placed an unprecedented umbrella over the entire project'. But, of course, it wasn't the short-sighted inside IBM who were leading this supposed opposition. The true myopics dismissed anything other than mainframes as having little present or future importance. It was the long-sighted who saw how great – and threatening – that importance was going to be.

But how could anybody be so foolish as to take the next mental stumble: to imagine that the tide of technology could be withstood simply by IBM refusing to enter the water? The reality is that selling mainframes rather than itsy-bitsy PCs appeals to every emotion inside the lifelong IBMer, including greed – for itsy-bitsy PCs earn itsy-bitsy profits, while large systems paid the huge commissions which were the driving force in the IBM marketing ethos.

Nobody in IBM, from Opel downwards, was immune from the mainframe mentality. The mind-set dogged the efforts of the corporation to capitalise on its greatest achievement apart from the 360. That computer family automated American big business. The PC and its emulators were to change the way in which people worked – and lived – right through society. By the early Nineties, however, it still hadn't sufficiently changed the way in which people worked – and thought – inside IBM.

What would IBM be like today if its fate had fallen into the hands of the PC mentality? The question is fantastical, but the fantasy suggests a company much more akin to the entrepreneurial business John Akers was trying vainly to create in the

Nineties. The mainframe mentality stuck IBM with methods, mental sets and economic road blocks that retarded its development. They left it vulnerable to competitors who had far less investment in the past, and far greater commitment to a revolutionary future.

23

Technology Manoeuvres: Saving Akers' Ass

IBM's failure to maintain its quickly won dominance of the personal computer market, and its loss of middle ground to Digital Equipment, had deeply pernicious results. They were mercilessly summarised by *Business Week* in a mid-1989 cover story that was otherwise highly favourable to IBM and John Akers. It was the last major story in any periodical to feature the latter as hero manager.

Hands in his trouser pockets, he was photographed wearing a broad smile, jacketless, and posed in front of the massive striped letters, IBM. The headline read, 'A Bold Move in Mainframes'. As the text explained, IBM's growth had slowed as PCs and minis had become the Number 1 and Number 2 products, vaulting past the mainframes that had been its mainstay. At the start of the Eighties, IBM had enjoyed five years of super-growth that nearly doubled revenues and profits. Half the sales and 70 per cent of the earnings had been milked from mainframes.

As their market subsided, so did the financial performance. Yet in 1989, 44 per cent of sales and half of profits still stemmed from mainframes. Any further erosion would fatally damage chances of returning to growth. The 'bold move' was to upgrade and remodel the System/370 mainframe (so old in industry terms as to be antique). Buyers could then 'store more data, including electronic images, voice messages, and even video'.

That was only half the battle. IBM planned 'to make the mainframe into a hub that will anchor vast information networks in the 1990s'. The master key to saving the mainframe from becoming the dinosaur of computing was called Systems Application Architecture. This grandiose scheme had been announced over two years before the cover story. It was a highly complex answer to a deceptively simple ambition: 'Make the mainframe lord of databases. Connect it to all the smaller machines, and have it hand them any piece of information they demand even if it's in another small machine half a globe away'.

This wasn't just a pleasing dream, but a 'strategic imperative', to quote William F. Zachmann of Canopus Research. He argued that IBM urgently needed 'to maintain account control by linking personal computers to its high-profit mainframe systems'. The innocent phrase 'account control' meant ensuring that customers bought from IBM and nobody else. They had been reducing their dependence on their mainframes. Now that trend would be magically reversed.

Nobody expressed this point more bluntly than Earl F. Wheeler. In April 1988, as software czar, he took charge of SAA and an army of 30,000 programmers – that's three times as many as Microsoft's *total* employment even four years later. In 1989, Wheeler said that 'IBM would like to see SAA accepted as an official standard.' For 'like' read 'love'. If that were to happen, IBM's core product sales would boom as SAA demanded 'more mainframe power and more storage'.

You can't create an industry standard out of thin air, though. As Wheeler spoke, that's all SAA was. In that rarefied atmosphere, it was perfectly possible to make impressive announcements. On 16 May 1989, the company announced a crucial part of SAA called 'OfficeVision'. It would link the mainframes with IBM's AS/400 minis and its PS/2 personal computers. All of them would work harmoniously in 'co-operative processing'.

OfficeVision was the answer to an information manager's dream. Unfortunately for IBM (and the customers) that's what it remained, a dream. In 1991, *Business Week* returned to the subject of SAA. But now the trumpets rang with a different sound. OfficeVision had 'become a symbol of SAA's shortcomings'. The critical linkage between PCs and mainframes, due in March 1990, had been postponed twice, and its appearance was now *sine die.*

Some customers reckoned the day would never come. One said that 'I've already written off OfficeVision because it has been delayed so many times.' During the delay many other suppliers plunged into the networking market – and their products were not tied to IBM's, or even to mainframes. IBM itself had been forced into deals with two independents (Lotus Development Corp and Novell) simply to stay in the networking game.

The OfficeVision fiasco was only part of the wider, and graver, failure of SAA. What had been designed to keep customers was losing them. Some who were interested in minicomputers turned to other makes on discovering that IBM's couldn't communicate with its own mainframes – because the SAA promise hadn't been delivered. At Pacific Bell, Jack L. Hancock, the executive vice president for technology, was looking for other solutions because 'SAA is late'.

He added that 'It represents a loss of revenue and ego on IBM's part.' How big a loss can be measured partly by the slow growth of IBM's software sales between 1986 and 1990, when they merely advanced from 11 per cent of the IBM total to 14 per cent; and partly by the huge investment bogged down in SAA. That meant not just the pay of 30,000 expensive programmers, but $500 million of minority stakes in software and service companies. The money was a *quid pro quo* for supporting SAA.

The SAA enterprise had been a disaster from any point of

view – save IBM's. 'I would not categorise SAA as a failure,' said Joseph Guglielmi, an IBM vice president on the personal computer side. It's hard to think of a better description, especially since IBM had been absolutely right in identifying the customer need. The information-handling needs of the Nineties did indeed require software that would link all a company's computers in precisely the interactive way that IBM envisaged.

But those needs didn't require that all the hardware, or for that matter the software, should come from IBM. On the contrary, as the years went by the demand for 'open systems' became more and more insistent. By 1992, NCR (now owned by AT&T) was abandoning all its proprietary systems in favour of a hierarchy of computers, all built round Intel microprocessors, that would cheerfully communicate with each other and with any programs and peripherals the customers wanted.

Even with its much smaller installed base, NCR incurred a financial penalty in changing strategy. But the alternative to losing some of the proprietary benefits was to lose them all. As the open tide rolled on, IBM began increasingly to look like a computerised King Canute. Had SAA delivered, the tide would at least have been slowed, but Wheeler's army ran into what one consultant called 'software gridlock' for reasons that ran deep into IBM's past success and present philosophy.

What Zachmann described as 'the proliferation of hardware architectures in IBM's product line' presented the programmers with unique difficulties. He traces the problem in part to the anti-trust suit, which from 1969 onwards hung the threat of break-up over the heads of the men at Armonk. In case that nightmare came to pass, IBM installed a partial break-up internally: large systems for large customers came under a different division from smaller systems for smaller customers.

The mainframe policy applied with the 360 had been simple and supremely effective. The same architecture applied throughout the range, and the same programs could be run on every machine. Had smaller machines stuck to the same architecture, IBM would have cannibalised 360 sales. It could, though, compete just as effectively with the rising minis from Digital, Prime, Data General and Hewlett-Packard by selling proprietary systems that were incompatible with the 360.

In the world after 1982, with the anti-trust suit abandoned by the Reagan Administration, the PC brought the self-created crisis to a head. The PC was also incompatible with the rest of its computer family – an inconvenience (especially for customers) which became a serious threat when Digital's VAX line of minis, linking efficiently via the VMS operating system, leapt past IBM into the new world of the network. 'SAA,' wrote Zachmann, 'is to a very large extent IBM's response to Digital's highly successful competitive efforts.'

But there's a world of difference and difficulty between writing brand-new software to link a brand-new line of computers and 'defining a set of standards to create common user, programming, and communications interfaces' across a raft of existing incompatible architectures. Small wonder that 'software gridlock' developed as the 30,000 IBMers, no doubt in endless committees, wrestled with technical problems seldom tackled before, and never on such a gigantic scale.

These difficulties were obvious from the beginning. First, the SAA idea ran counter to the increasing demands of customers for open systems that would allow them to have many suppliers, not just IBM. Second, the inevitable long lead-time gave others, both rival manufacturers and specialist database companies, the chance to beat IBM to the punch – and, wrote one observer, 'If it is too late to market, IBM's grand scheme could fall flat.'

Third, the strategy was aimed at the thousand or so big corporate customers, who had already spent billions of dollars on IBM mainframes and the associated software. These companies accounted for perhaps half of IBM's profits. The new ploy might or might not succeed in stopping the inroads that Digital minis (and desktops from other sources) had made into core IBM territory. But it might also leave the hosts of lesser customers for others to harvest.

That weakness was compounded by the fourth – the defects of OfficeVision, above all its premature announcement. You wouldn't have guessed that anything was amiss from the publicity. A thousand programmers had toiled away in eight laboratories all over the world for two years, spending an estimated $500 million to produce the software applications. Terry R. Lautenbach, then US general manager, said proudly that 'we broke our collective backs to deliver'.

Deliver what? On announcement day, there was nothing to buy. Promised goodies like electronic mail, an address book and a phone directory, plus all the user-friendliness of the Apple Macintosh, sounded wonderfully attractive. But the wait was at least a year, even if OfficeVision met its schedules (it didn't). True, in the meantime they could just buy a PS/2 with its proprietary OS/2 system and wait for the applications to catch up.

With OfficeVision, said senior vice president George H. Conrades, 'you may finally get the "Aha!" of why OS/2 is important.' The importance and the Aha! meant more to IBM than to the customers. In mid-1989, they were still resolutely unmoved by OS/2. IBM was asking customers to back its vision by spending at least $7,300 per workstation on the promised software. They would also have to buy a PS/2 PC, which didn't exist, with enough internal memory (four times that of the most powerful machine then current) to handle OfficeVision.

Those super-PCs would cost $11,000, making a grand total of $18,300 of new business for IBM. A company equipping a thousand desks with the marvel would thus generate turnover of $18.3 million for the company – a price tag of mainframe proportions – while binding itself to IBM for evermore. SAA czar Wheeler was sure the customers wouldn't feel a thing: 'Instead of sitting down to a computer the way I look forward to the dentist, they'll enjoy using it – and be more productive.'

Three years later the enjoyment was still theoretical. To

connoiseurs of IBM strategy, the train of events recalled the pre-emptive non-strikes of the past. The mere announcement of a new IBM product had been enough to cause corporate customers to keep their power dry and to wait for whatever IBM had to offer. If the product arrived successfully, the customer was tied to IBM. If it didn't, the customer was still tied to IBM, because the competition had been shut out of the game.

The strategy had always run the same risk as the boy who cried wolf. Some day, the customers, disappointed once too often, would refuse to believe the cry – 'IBM is coming' – and buy somewhere else. To some extent, IBM was relying on the notoriously short memory of the human being. Who in the Nineties, apart from a few journalists and industry experts, would remember the ballyhoo over SAA and OfficeVision and lose all faith in IBM's promises?

The British magazine *Computing* took a robust view of the situation: SAA, it declared, 'is confusing most of the company's biggest customers as it desperately tries to hang on to them in the face of increasing competitive pressures in the mainframe market. In the US, some people refer to SAA as Save Akers' Ass, referring to IBM chairman John Akers' attempts to retain large customers with the elusive and nebulous promise of SAA.'

Companies, said the magazine, 'refer to SAA as a riddle'. Worse, it appeared that 'IBM itself is unable to provide the answer' to the riddle; although the clues weren't encouraging, such as an estimate that it would take customers 'at least three years' to move over to SAA. IBM was trying to ride two horses at once. It would enable companies to bind all their hardware and software together (a highly praiseworthy aim), but it would also tie them irrevocably to IBM systems.

Those who ride two steeds often fall between them – if they don't get torn apart. In any event, on Zachmann's analysis, the dual ambition was impossible to achieve. 'Unfortunately for IBM but fortunately for personal computer users, the form that SAA is taking makes it likely that, even if IBM stems com-

266

petitive losses to Digital, dozens of more aggressively priced microprocessor-based systems will find it easier to take even more business from IBM.'

That followed ineluctably from a basic fact. The IBM programming army was writing applications that could be used across every system manufactured by IBM. Those applications, by definition, would work just as well on compatible systems made by others. Zachmann thought that IBM could be repeating its historic error when it 'inadvertently and unwillingly set a *de facto* industry standard' for PCs. The chances were that SAA would also result in a situation where IBM could neither exert control nor profit sufficiently.

The analysis conjured up a vision of its enormous investment fuelling the profits, not of IBM, but of an army of other vendors. But that rested on an assumption that IBM's proprietary operating program, OS/2, would 'soon be provided by virtually every personal computer vendor of any consequence'. Four years later, OS/2 had made miserable progress (although the latest version which arrived at that point was far better technically), and SAA was regarded by many as the living dead of the computer world.

'Officially, IBM will never disown SAA,' said *Business Week* in mid-1991, 'because of the enormous amount of money and energy it has sunk into it – and because of the customers who are still waiting for it.' That, said the magazine, was 'a little like waiting for Godot'. Yet, if Zachmann's diagnosis had been partially falsified by events, his prognosis had not. Vendors other than IBM had continued to make hay in all the areas the prophet had foreseen: aggressively priced workstations, based on microprocessors; network servers; and similar equipment.

In addition, other software suppliers had seized the market opportunities which IBM had lost through the non-appearance of its dream. The 'bold move in mainframes' which IBM planned to make the 'key to networking', and 'so restore its growth', had been overtaken by IBM's own failures and by the unremitting advance of the technology. By 1992, customer companies could achieve what IBM was still only promising, in established and proven ways. They could use the relatively expensive solution provided long before the SAA announcement by Digital's VAX machines, or get there far more cheaply with linked PCs.

Already providing computing power at a hundredth the cost of mainframes back in 1989, PC workstations have continued to get cheaper and more powerful. Dearer than its competitors, because of its huge mainframe investment and massive overheads, IBM lost power in the marketplace as its position eroded and its stratagems misfired. 'Are IBM's glory days gone forever?' *Business Week* had asked in that May 1989 cover story. The answer seemed to be yes: SAA hadn't Saved Akers' Ass – and, in the end, nothing could.

24

The Rocky Road
to Supercomputing

The absolute triumph of the 360 range had one consequence which couldn't have been easily foreseen. Instead of feeding IBM's appetite for the great leap forward, the 360 sated the urge. After the unprecedented, fearful expense and upheaval of replacing its entire product line with new technology, the company understandably needed time to digest its own achievements. But digestion became a way of life – and for sound economic reasons.

As Robert Sobel wrote, 'That part of the computer revolution at IBM had ended: from the early 1970s onward evolution was the order of the day insofar as mainframes were concerned. The industry had achieved stabilisation in this area at least, in large part because of IBM's leadership.' But where had IBM led? The 'stabilisation' lay in the marketplace, rather than in the technology.

The focus of technological advance was moving away from mainframes – dramatic progress continued elsewhere. But the 360 had established a customer base so large, broad and powerful that IBM had no call to rock its own boat with new changes: 'IBM balked at suggestions that it reinvent the computer or consider anything that would disturb the 360 client base.' For their part, the clients, having shared so expensively in the 360 upheaval, were in no mood to incur the expense all over again.

Against this background, the decision to dodge creation of a 'Fourth Generation' computer was intelligent. The 370 series, unveiled in 1970, was cleverly promoted as a 'new generation'. It was indeed a marked advance over the 360s on some parameters – speed, price per calculation, flexibility, etc. But apart from a radical improvement in memory, the 370 contained little novelty. Even with this important change, Sobel reported, IBM had been motivated primarily by the usual need to keep out competitors: 'Independent computer engineers, after exploring the new internal storage system, concluded it had been designed more to discourage users from taking memory banks from manufacturers of peripheral equipment than anything else.' As with memory, so with pricing policies: IBM leased its entry machine at rates that made it far more difficult for independent leasers to achieve a warming profit margin.

The IBM 360 has been truthfully described as 'one of the grand product success stories in American business history' – despite the sloppiness of its development process. Distressed by the disorder, which nearly caused catastrophe, chairman Thomas Watson Jr asked vice president Frank Cary to 'design a system to ensure us against a repeat of this kind of problem'.

Cary, though, found his own system too cumbersome and restrictive, and abolished it when he became chairman. The product-development structure had prevented a repeat of the 360 blunders: 'Unfortunately, it will also ensure that we don't ever invent another product like the 360.' In fact, IBM never did – unless, that is, the AS/400 minis and the mainline PCs, both phenomenal sellers, are included in the same league. In both these cases, however, IBM was following. With the 360, it unequivocally led.

IBM dodged dramatic innovation primarily to protect its profitability. In so doing, it ignored a lesson that Japanese electronics companies had already learnt – that surges in new product introductions are accompanied by leaps in profit. Technological stagnation, on the other hand, leads to stagnant profits – as IBM found. Domestic revenues didn't surpass the 1968 record for three years. Only the continued gains abroad (and interest on its growing cash hoard) kept IBM's earnings on the rise.

The process was a foretaste of the Eighties, when rapidly growing foreign revenues concealed the domestic stagnation of other companies, too, such as Apple and Compaq. The question asked by *Business Week* in 1989, 'Are IBM's glory days gone forever', is an echo of the *Forbes* demand of the early Seventies: 'Are the days of IBM's great growth behind it?' Whoever asked that question, though, couldn't have dreamt that, nearly two decades on, the 370 series would still be the bedrock of the company.

That was partly because no mainframe rival – apart from RCA, whose effort ended in ignominious failure, a half-billion dollar loss and retirement from the computer industry – tackled IBM with a new technology range. IBM had no competitive pressure, no reason to listen to Gene Amdahl, possibly the most distinguished designer to work for the company.

Just as Amdahl had been overridden on the issue of large scale integrated circuits, which he favoured for the 360, so he was vetoed over his ambitions to build a genuine fourth generation machine. There's a vein in the older-line American high-tech companies that favours keeping new technology on ice until the market for the next stage is hot – to put that another way, until the old technology no longer sells. And the 360/370 line went on selling.

Amdahl in short order lost his laboratory and quit the company. This didn't halt work on future systems: 'Future System' was the actual name of a replacement product. It aimed at overcoming the 370's technical drawbacks in the fast-growing market for mainframes that were fed by, and in turn responded to, hundreds and thousands of terminals for users like banks and airlines. It's said that some $3 billion was spent on 'FS' before its summary execution in 1975.

The reason was fear. Would customers rewrite their 370 programs to suit the radically new architecture of FS? IBM's conservative bent made the answer all too certain, and the results of the next five years, it seemed, applauded the decision. Between 1975 to 1985, as world mainframe sales multiplied more than threefold, so did IBM's revenues. The 370s had intrinsic drawbacks, which have been blamed on a design governed by the need to handle batches of punch cards. On one theory, the inefficiencies simply meant, happily for IBM, that customers had to buy more machines.

There's an analogy with Volkswagen, which for years persisted with the Beetle. Its technological shortcomings became more and more pronounced as its obsolescence increased. So long as sales stayed high, though, profits were far above the potential of a replacement line. The policy eventually and inevitably exploded in VW's face. It led to financial crisis and emergency action. In one heroic, traumatic year, the entire product range had to be replaced and the Wolfsburg factory totally revamped.

VW emerged from that appalling crunch with a strong product range, reflected in some excellent years. But its starring position in the US market (where the Beetle had been fourth best-selling marque) was lost for ever – at the nadir, American sales were a tenth of the peak. Nor did VW recover European supremacy until the Nineties, and then largely because three of its rivals, Fiat, Renault and Ford, fell over their own feet. In the short to medium term, dropping the FS made IBM many mints: in the long term, the move created irreversible harm.

The well-placed FS veterans in IBM did their best to limit the damage. They included the Number 2 to John Akers, president Jack Kuehler, who held the chief technologist role. Another FS graduate, Carl J. Conti, was placed in charge of mainframe development. That meant primarily intensifying the upgrades to the basic line, which by the early Nineties was less ageing than downright aged. Advances in memory, optical fibre cables, disk drives and file-tracking were among the blood transfusions pumped into the old chassis.

Super-cooled gallium arsenide microprocessors were in the pipeline as the Nineties began; so, deceptively, was the work of Steve Chen. A brilliant designer who had emigrated from Cray Research, Chen was expected to make a breakthrough in supercomputing from which IBM, his backer, would benefit. By 1992, however, the serious doubts being expressed about Chen's progress (coincidentally, the great supercomputer designer, Seymour Cray himself, seemed to reach a dead-end at the same time) were increasingly ominous.

What one insider called 'baby steps' could certainly make the IBM mainframes still more formidable tools. Baby steps were perhaps made inevitable by the intimidating amount of software rewrites needed for each pace. Without the revamping, inherently much harder than starting from scratch, IBM had no hope of making its mainframes the hubs of corporation-wide, worldwide information systems – gigantic spiders at the centre of webs stretching out to computers of all shapes and sizes, and brands.

If that could be achieved, thought one of Conti's assistants, it would 'cause an inflection point' in mainframe sales: the IBM-ese, being translated, means a new boom. Behind the sluggish sales performance actually lay a rapid rise in demand (30 per cent to 35 per cent) for mainframe power and storage, which customers could meet by upgrading their own computers. But if the spider's web concept materialised, faster growth still would surely follow – 40 per cent to 45 per cent. That meant rich sales of many more mainframes.

Absurd predictions of a 10–13 per cent growth in IBM's mainframe revenues in the early Nineties must have heartened Akers and his executives as they pursued the 'baby steps' strategy. The actual decline, while partly the result of recession, also reflected fatal flaws in that strategy. As noted in the previous chapter, the spider's web wasn't the only means of meeting the needs of corporations to communicate with themselves and with each other across thousands of channels.

In these competitive areas, IBM's inhibitions against launching new technologies were beside the point. The pace of change was constantly narrowing the gap between mainframe, mini and micro. For instance, the target for System 370 in 1989 was 400 million instructions per second. Intel's Pentium microprocessor, unveiled three years later, had a capacity of 250 mips, and the company was talking confidently of selling 'bips', a *billion* instructions per second, well before the end of the century.

Despite such contradictory facts and figures, the sense of power and glory remained at IBM – but this didn't guarantee progress. Take Chen and his supercomputers. This was the market on which Tom Watson Jr had turned his back, arguing that, on the analogy of General Motors and Ferrari, the high-performance special could and should be left to niche players. But by 1992, supercomputing had begun to loom large in IBM's plans, for a simple reason.

Machines that once largely served scientific and governmental markets were now becoming important for the prime commercial customers – the last redoubts of the mainframe. Wal-Mart Stores, the world's most sensationally successful retailer, used a supercomputer (and not an IBM product) to handle the 1.8 trillion chunks of information from which it could glean inventory and sales trends. The supercomputer market was relatively small ($2.5 billion, a twentieth of the commercial mainframe business), but it was potentially another vulnerable heel for the Achilles of IBM.

The corporation had two-thirds of the mainframe market. But it was just another player in supercomputers – though a reasonably successful one. Elsewhere, the IBM story had been one of sinking earnings, huge write-offs and failed turnarounds. But some observers thought that, moving with unaccustomed quietness, IBM was becoming a major force in supercomputing, even though in 1992 it didn't, in point of fact, make a supercomputer.

By brilliant technology, its labs had developed 'vector processors' that could soup up the top-of-the-line mainframes. In certain calculations they could match or even beat the genuine super-articles from Cray Research and other suppliers. From 1986 to 1992, IBM sold a thousand or so of these boosters – and their estimated annual sales value was a useful $480 million.

But vector processors, despite their top speed of 2.7 billion instructions per second, were not the ultimate answer to super-computing. Only an IBM supercomputer – abandoning the Watson inhibition – could provide that. The failure of IBM's not-so-secret weapon, Steve Chen, was a major disappointment. His plan – the ultimate in vector processing – cost IBM $100 million or so. But schedules slipped badly, and what exactly Chen's machine would do, and when, was still unclear after four years. Small wonder IBM dropped Chen in 1993.

General opinion in the industry held that a different route, massively parallel processing (or MPP), was the key to the future. In 1993, IBM itself bowed to the generality by announcing an MPP product line. Traditional supercomputers and mainframes alike are menaced by this new technology, in which chip-maker Intel has a clear lead, with other hot competitors pressing hard. They include one group, AT&T, working through its NCR acquisition, whose purse is notably deeper than IBM's.

Nevertheless, IBM's financial strength was seen as its greatest asset in the race for this vital prize. One market researcher noted that the company 'had sufficient resources to fund multiple efforts. They're in an enviable position'. This exaggerated IBM's lessened financial powers. Anyway, IBM's efforts were multiple in a sense other than parallel processing – they were split over five different parts of the empire.

In Kingston, New York, the 'Highly Parallel Super-computing Systems Laboratory', financed by several IBM divisions, was in the van – heading for speeds of more than a trillion instructions a second (beguilingly known as 'one teraflops'). IBM had got into bed with the government's Argonne National Laboratory for this project. It was designed to speed the way towards achieving a saleable product linking hundreds or thousands of IBM's own RISC microprocessors.

These were also used, however, by the Advanced Workstations Division, which had united up to a dozen of its products to generate supercomputing speeds. Chen's outfit, Supercomputer Systems Inc, over in Eau Claire, Wisconsin, was to lose IBM's support. But in Yorktown Heights, New York, the Thomas J. Watson Laboratories, part of the Research Division, were also involved in mainframe enhancement. The big push in that area, though, was at Somers, also in New York, where the Enterprise Systems Division was making and selling its vector processors.

This catalogue makes it evident how dispersed IBM's effort had become. For certain, its competitors (including small specialists like nCube, Thinking Machines and Oracle) were better able to concentrate their work. The roll-call also points to the difficulty that IBM's diversity imposed in organisational terms. Several divisions, apart from those engaged in the supercomputing researches, had interests in their outcome. How could they all get what they wanted – especially if their autonomy, as the December 1991 reforms envisaged, was to become much greater?

That autonomy was contradicted by the reforms themselves. The central management that ordained the reorganisation also ordered cutbacks in the supercomputing marketing and sales teams. The team that had been selling half a billion dollars worth of vector processors annually was more or less disbanded. The main IBM sales force would thus be competing in this highly specialised market against the specialised teams of Cray, Intel, etc.

Even with market support specialists at their side, this looked like giving IBM salesmen too heavy a task. Nor was the change made because the new sales method seemed more effective. Top management was merely trying to save money in the short term, in a way that threatened to undermine IBM's long-term need. It surely had to win the supercomputing lead before others – probably using massively parallel technology – started to pick off its mainframe customers.

The work with Argonne promised an impressive build-up towards the one teraflop nirvana in the later Nineties, but IBM would do well to start deliveries before the end of the decade. Before then many more customers with gigantic data-bases would be following in Wal-Mart's footsteps. Or would they? In fact, supercomputers are losing out on some important orders.

A Cray machine in Lawrence Livermore National Laboratories has been replaced by a network of advanced workstations – basically, very powerful desktop microcomputers, a bunch of which cost a mere $1 million in this instance. British Petroleum has been spending $700,000 on another cluster, intended to save $2.5 million on Cray leasing fees. BP planned to eliminate the rest of Cray's bill by buying three more workstations. The financial logic sprang from technological catch-up. According to a University of Tennessee scientist, in fifteen years workstations had improved their speed 1,000 times: supercomputers had only quickened by fifty-fold.

The performance gap had been closed further by the software advances that link workstation clusters in parallel – as at Livermore. Its workstations, and those of BP, all came from one supplier – IBM, with its RS/6000. They offered a massive price advantage over the supercomputer alternative: the $700,000 for BP's three-station system, compared to $20 to $30 million for a top-end Cray or similar configuration. Quite apart from the huge cost savings, desktop solutions are more popular with staff, who gain greater control over the work and don't have to wait for supercomputer time.

That all sounds like good news for IBM workstations,

though not for the other corporate interests that have been working to drive the company back into the supercomputer race. To the extent that RS/6000s take away supercomputer sales, IBM is cannibalising its own future market. So many of its commercial clients are investigating workstation clusters that exponential growth is a real and enticing prospect. The pleasure, though, is not without pain.

The ache of getting $700,000 for a bunch of IBM workstations, instead of $20 million and upwards for a supercomputer, is greatly eased if the displaced machine is made by Cray Research. But the potent competition of the RS/6000 and its many non-IBM rivals doesn't end there. If workstations can compete on quite even terms with the most powerful computers on earth, what can they do against humbler mainframes?

IBM President Jack Kuehler put a brave face on the threat in a 1992 interview with *Datamation*. The hardware, he suggested, didn't matter so much. 'I would not be surprised if you didn't see workstation technology over time become more of the underpinning of that high-end software . . . And we're working down the path.' To that the *Guardian*'s computer editor, Jack Schofield, commented, 'Quite right, too.'

But 'what happens to IBM's bottom line if it swaps $100,000 workstations for high-margin $2 million mainframes?' There are no prizes for the answer. Dataquest projections show that workstation revenues grew from a bare billion in 1987 to $8.7 billion in 1991, four times the value of the supercomputing market. Workstations were outgrowing supercomputers by two-to-one, and by 1996, workstation sales were expected to pass $32 billion – eight or more times supercomputer sales.

As one of the workstation leaders, though not *the* leader, IBM can expect a fair share of this enormously expanding sector. But there's a catch – every dollar it takes from the market's hide will be matched, and more, by the dollars it removes from its own.

IX

THE MANY
REINVENTIONS OF IBM

25

Spinning-off:
A House Divided . . .

A variety of the old legal maxim, *de minimis non curat lex*, applies in very large companies like IBM. Just as the law doesn't care about little matters, the corporation tends to lose interest in little businesses. The trouble is that a little business in IBM terms may be colossal by other standards – like, say the two-hundredth largest company in the US.

That was the size of what's now known as Lexmark. Before, it was the typewriter and printer business of IBM. In the spring of 1991, IBM divested itself of the bauble, a very rare event in itself. The company had sold off Rolm, but that was a recent and rotten acquisition. IBM had created its typewriter interests. Moreover, it had built the division into a market leader whose prestige reinforced the group's status at the top end of the business equipment market.

IBM's electric typewriters, perceived as the best on the market, carried the highest prices. It was no use grumbling about the cost – if you wanted to recruit or retain a top secretary, you gave them an IBM. It was the Mercedes-Benz of the executive suite. Every machine paraded the name and fame of its maker before the same people whose multi-million dollar orders for mainframe computers built the profits and progress of the main business.

What went wrong? *Fortune* writer Brian Dumaine thought that 'Over the years IBM had gotten so big that its typewriter business, with a mere $2 billion in revenue, had suffered from neglect.' He cites the lack of interest among salesmen, who 'understandably pushed expensive mainframe systems and peddled typewriters only as an afterthought.' But that wasn't the real problem. The managers of the typewriter business had other sales outlets, actual and potential. It was management's neglect that ruined one of IBM's best businesses.

That neglect is all the more remarkable because its worst damage occurred in the area where IBM should have been strongest: technology. In the progress of typewriter technology from manual to electronic, IBM achieved its greatest success in the electro-mechanical stage. It added ingenious ideas like the golfball type font to the basic principle of operating the keys by electric power. Yet the world's greatest powerhouse of electronics technology missed the next and crucial stage – adding electronics.

IBM did give memory functions to its typewriters, making them even more expensive. But the Japanese were allowed to lead in producing all-electronic machines. They shattered the price structure and took office typing into a new era. The old leader still had a chance to recoup. The word processor, the ultimate in electronic typewriters, was an early life-form of the personal computer – yet IBM left this market entirely to Wang.

Its progenitor, An Wang, was a former IBM associate. Hhe used his IBM rewards (for inventing the magnetic bubble memory) to launch this instant-hit product. IBM's people must have noticed the flood of orders, $1 million in all, taken for the Wang product on its first showing at a 1976 trade fair in New York. The lack of reaction to these market changes can be partly explained by the typewriter division's relative unimportance in the IBM world. A second factor was surely the lack of cross-fertilisation, taking expertise from one part and injecting it into another.

A third and fundamental factor was that competent management, instead of being helped by the IBM system, was positively hindered. The size, centralisation and control mechanisms of IBM simply got in the way. With the creation of Lexmark, the surviving employees moved into a luckier way of life. Its breakaway management, though, wasn't headed by some genius imported from outside. CEO Marvin Mann had worked for IBM for thirty-two years. Yet he knew exactly how an entrepreneurial business should be staffed and organised.

He employed half the former numbers in manufacturing, administration and development. By separating out four units, respectively in printers, keyboards, typewriters and printer supplies, Mann exchanged the fuzziness that clogged IBM's information flows and marketing for focus. Marketing was entrusted to a dedicated sales force of 900 people. Meetings and formal presentations were slashed even more severely than the work force.

Executives attending the fewer meetings no longer needed, as in their IBM days, to overload themselves with all the transparencies they might need to answer questions from their superiors. Mann emphasised the importance of having people who are 'working in units where they feel they can make a difference'. He dismantled a superstructure that, far from adding value, was subtracting it – and that applied to both tactics and strategy.

The strategic damage was the greater. The typewriter division was neither given its head nor integrated into the group's mainstream strategy. Otherwise, IBM might have broken into the PC market far earlier. A clearly laid out technological path ran through electronics and memory. If it had been followed, the PC operation wouldn't have started as a sideshow. IBM might also have avoided the trap of leaving its PC system wide open to imitators.

That is hypothetical. The unleashing of Marvin Mann and the powerful abilities that had been bottled up inside IBM was not. Sell-off shouldn't have been the only way to unbottle the talents. That raises the fundamental issue behind the reforms which John Akers set in train in late 1991. A *Wall Street Journal* writer saw the early experiences of Lexmark, the entirely freed typewriter and printer business, as a good omen for the reorganisation. He thought it might 'turn out to be a model for the quasi-independent business units that are at the core of IBM's plans to decentralise'.

There was, however, nothing quasi about Lexmark's independence. IBM retained a 10 per cent stake in the company and a seat on the board. But the shots were ultimately called by Clayton & Dubillier, the investment firm that arranged its leveraged buyout. For five years, Lexmark had the right to the IBM trademark – an asset of incalculable value. IBM was still by far its largest customer for printers, keyboards, etc. Otherwise it was strictly and absolutely (and at the start unprofitably) on its own.

That loneliness was a virtue. One consultant observed that as an IBM business, the future Lexmark had everything ('a factory that was state of the art') except the ability to escape from an imposed problem: 'that the parent is busy and neglects the kids . . . Also, the overhead costs of any organisation that big is a tax that burdened their ability to play in the low-end, commodity price business. They couldn't compete effectively. Something had to give.'

The first fruits of the rebirth, a new range of laser printers aimed straight at Hewlett-Packard, were well praised. But IBM had long been at least HP's equal in the technology. It had lost the war in the marketplace, where the concentrated HP sales forces had run several rings round the IBM organisation. As usual, the latter represented a range of products. In setting free other, much larger parts of the company, would IBM destroy the unified sales force that had once been the envy of the office machinery industry?

That was the logical conclusion of other independent initiatives. In June 1992, a company known as Individual Computer Products International made its bow in Britain.

Nothing about ICPI's name hinted at IBM. Nothing about his dress style connected the company's leader to IBM, either. He launched his baby while wearing a plaid jacket and yellow tie. The man alongside, his boss, was in neat IBM navy blue from shoulders to trouser bottoms.

The dress clash was self-consciously adopted to point up the independence of ICPI from IBM, which owned the fledgling lock, stock and barrel. This was IBM's latest tactic in the war against the clones: the ploy was 'if you can't beat 'em, become one yourself'. Like its low-priced competition, IBM would have most of its cheap PCs made (would 'source' them, in the jargon) by Far Eastern suppliers and sell them, not on features, but on price.

There was no shortage of sources. Taiwan alone is supposed to have 3,000 clone-makers, cashing in on the elemental fact that one man can box an Intel microprocessor as well as another. If the other man is IBM, though, his overheads and R&D costs will cripple him in a price war. The lower end had become a commodity market, in which all low-cost PCs were virtually the same. So what would differentiate IBM? Ads appeared at once in the British press for a computer brand named Ambra, but giving no answer to the obvious question: Ambra Who?

This was IBM's (or rather IPCI's) brand-name. A budget of $8 million had been earmarked – a sum vastly beyond the reach of any other clone-maker – to propel the brand into the pubic consciousness without any benefit from the IBM association. By setting up new companies in France, Britain and Canada to market its anti-clone clones, IBM, wrote one commentator, 'aims to gain entry to highly price-sensitive segments of the PC market in which its own brand-name products *cannot compete*'.

That presumably included the bottom-of-the-range PS/1, which was aimed at the value-for-money buyer. The symbolism was awkward. Was that the underlying problem? That, where meaningful competition existed, IBM simply couldn't compete? Was ICPI, set up outside the colossal framework, and presumably outside its overheads, a recognition that only similar escape and lightening of the load would place most of IBM's operations in a position where they *could* compete?

Plainly the brand would be competing in part against the Personal Systems Business Unit, IBM Europe (whose very name identified its bureaucratic lineage). The point of stressing the new company's independence wasn't management philosophy – the fashionable and attractive idea that autonomy and identification are the keys to success. It was commercial necessity. An IBM low-end product would have taken away from (or cannibalised) higher-priced sales; the giant felt it couldn't afford that loss in Europe.

Its share of the European PC market had stumbled from 40 per cent to 12 per cent in a decade. In the country where Ambra kicked off, the UK, a 26 per cent share in 1989 had become 15 per cent. Much of the damage came at the cheap end, which at 45 per cent a year was growing twice as fast as overall sales. The clones were exploiting direct sales channels, by phone and mail order. Ambra would do the same. It was the ultimate in me-toos.

The only thing special about the product was something missing: IBM. Not a single component was scheduled to come from an IBM plant. The suppliers were scattered around Taiwan, Singapore and Malaysia in the East, with some contribution from Germany and the UK – and software from the US (coming from Microsoft, with which a life-or-death struggle was being waged in the mainstream market).

Thus had IBM, the mightiest, most coherent manufacturer of all, become, in this instance, a 'hollow corporation'. ICPI was purely a marketing company, wholly dependent on outside businesses to have anything to market. IBM's new model was not National Cash Register, the colossus that inspired Tom Watson, but Liz Claiborne, the fashion business, which likewise has no manufacture. The paradox, however, is that the classic hollow companies had no assets save the all-embracing corporate brand, and IBM's hollow company wasn't using that asset at all.

ICPI and its phantom independence became a sideshow to the main event. Jim Cannavino, head of the entire PC operation, and a coming man at IBM, made a public bid for real independence in early 1992. He wanted a PC business modelled much on Lexmark lines, except that IBM would still own all the stock (which didn't rule out a future spin-off). Cannavino's reasoning was that the PC business needed the freedom of action to compete in a ferociously combative marketplace.

The creation of a separate company in September 1992 revolved around granting it total responsibility for every aspect of the business: R&D, manufacture and marketing, all would be under the same roof. This would reverse the historic destruction of independence that brought an end to the original and wonderful saga of the PC start-up. When marketing was removed from Boca Raton's control, it ripped the heart out of the operation. And that removal had been ordained by John Akers.

Now, he announced a transplant. Nothing had really changed in the intervening years, except that the separation of marketing had failed. In an anti-bureaucratic industry, the bureaucracy took charge. To repeat an earlier sentence about the typewriter failure, 'the size, centralisation, and control mechanisms of IBM simply got in the way'. They retarded PC sales and profits as they had those of typewriters. But centralisation of marketing was the essence of the old power structure. Remove it, and what was left of IBM?

Total separation of PCs from the rest of IBM raises many grave and weighty problems that didn't arise with the relatively small typewriter business. None of the latter's products were integral to networks that link families of other IBM machines and depend on the same massively expensive software developments. Workstations, the most powerful and lucrative end of the PC market, had to be kept separate, and so was software, although the fate of the OS/2 operating systems is umbilically linked to sales of the PS/2 personal computer.

The need for radical change in the PC business, though, was plain in 1992. By failing to match rival cuts in the great price war, and delaying its major response until the appearance of new models in September, IBM suffered a sharp and shocking drop in market share. It wasn't the best of backgrounds for the cocky Cannavino's achievement of independence from Armonk – unless the episode was meant to demonstrate how much the division lost, compared to its rivals, from lack of freedom of action.

Without question, the $10 billion IBM PC Co makes far better sense than its predecessor – including financial sense. In the first quarter of 1993, losses of $1 billion were converted into small profits, and market share recovered from its 10.9 per cent low to nearly 15 per cent. Before independence was granted, the notorious three-year product development cycle had already come down to six months, the result, not only of breaking R&D away from the parent, but of eliminating functional barriers within the PC operation itself.

That had still left Armonk with a dead-man's hand on other aspects of the operation: for instance, as in taking anything up to sixty days to authorise a price change. Now the five units into which the new company is divided decide their own prices, and are free from the debilitating IBM process of concurrence and non-concurrence all the way up the hierarchy. Those units, however, point to a more debatable aspect of the PC Co – the complexity of its line-up.

There's Ambra and there's ValuePoint (the IBM low-end brand introduced in October 1992 in the US); then there's the PS/1, which also aims at cost-conscious domestic and small business users, the top-of-the-line PS/2, and portables. With each unit having several variants, overlaps are inevitable. Each unit, moreover, develops its own brands and controls its manufacture and marketing, as well as its prices.

Philosophically, that's the best way to run the businesses, but it's unlikely to make the most economic sense. The new pricing policy does, however. IBM's differential over low-price, mail-order competitors came down by two-thirds in early 1993, which readily explains the jump in market share. The previous poor performance flatters the improvement, though – a rise from awful to moderate isn't the same as achieving excellence.

For example, *Business Week* reported that IBM had sold 100,000 of its excellent new ThinkPad 700C laptops in fifty-three days, more than IBM's total laptop sales in the previous two years. But Apple sold a million Powerbooks in their first year – and got a little windfall from one recent ThinkPad success. A major European insurance group ordered 1,000 of IBM's babies for its salesmen. The laptops came without vital carrying cases, which IBM couldn't supply. So the customer had to buy the cases from Apple . . .

Laudatory stories about a current renaissance at IBM, like their predecessors, need to be treated with a certain reserve. But as the PC numbers became much better, just as important, the intangibles visibly improved. Bucked-up PC executives began to talk about a rebirth of the start-up spirit, the come-back of Camelot. The management, led by Robert J. Corrigan, had abandoned the old insularity. The new outwardness was symbolised by an extreme change in the notorious 500-page non-disclosure agreement on which IBM used to insist with supplies. It's now three pages long.

Could the PC Co be a model for rebirth of the entire corporation? Restructuring alone isn't the answer, and can't be, given the complexities of the technical interrelationships between IBM's components. The PC Co, argue though it may, still bears a heavy excess of corporate overheads. Behind the new deal in PCs, and the separation of Lexmark, though, lies a half-perceived but vital need to make IBM a new kind of company, different not only from its own present and past, but different from any other in the world.

The best pointer to that kind of rebirth lies in a PC venture that antedates the PC Co. IBM's joint ventures with Apple Computer and Motorola aim at producing by 1995 startling new operating software (Taligent), powerful microprocessors

(Somerset) and dynamic multi-media software (Kaleida). The three partners have contrasting images – the white-collar salesman, the quality-conscious engineer, the Silicon Valley whiz-kid. It could be an appetising mix.

According to *Business Week*, the culture evolving from the trio, each with a few hundred employees, so far leans towards Apple: 'The style is pure Silicon Valley: flexible hours, small teams, and pizza bashes to build team spirit.' At Kaleida, the head man is former venture capitalist Nathaniel Goldhaber; he says 'The hardest challenge for the IBMers is to take on more responsibilities . . . engineers meet directly with customers to hear what's needed in new products, instead of relying on a marketing staff, as IBM does.'

In modern management, that's standard practice. Nor is there anything revolutionary in the success formula proposed by Joseph M. Guglielmi, the IBMer running Taligent: 'Put smart people in charge, motivate them, and get out of the way.' The Akers regime never applied that simple recipe, never appreciated that a real and deep cultural difference had to be led by, and most pronounced at, the summit of IBM.

Men who had prospered under the old order were being asked to create the new. It was like asking the Ancien Régime to launch the French Revolution, or the Politburo to create a democratic and economically progressive Soviet Union. The *Wall Street Journal*'s comparison of an earlier Akers attempt at revitalisation with Gorbachev's *perestroika* and *glasnost* comes back to mind.

The Soviet Union broke apart, but the awful problems bequeathed by past failure had not been resolved. The IBMpire hasn't split asunder like Gorbachev's. But its fissiparous tendencies are obvious and, as at Lexmark and PC Co, promising. That places a momentous, mountainous choice before the new CEO, Lou Gerstner. Akers was the Gorbachev of IBM. Gerstner dare not be the Yeltsin.

26

Right Disease,
Wrong Cures

The magazine writer who coined the phrase 'reinventing' for the American corporate shake-ups of the Eighties and Nineties struck a rich vein. It put a brave face on hard facts. Some once-great business had become mired in stagnant sales, declining profits, lagging technology and limping competitive prowess. Now a management reared in obsolete traditions was expected to match, better still surpass the achievements of the best performers in Japan.

The phrase 'reinvent' perfectly suited the situation and the public relations need. The corporation had been 'invented' by some founding genius like Thomas Watson Sr. Now his heirs had to start, like him, from a blank sheet of paper. They might write off much of the inheritance, they might throw some of it away – just like an engineer re-engineering an engine. The end result would be a new corporation – reinvented, free of the lumber of the past and fully possessed of the virtues of management renewed and reinvigorated.

The reinventors, in drawing a line between themselves and the past, were by implication stressing the faults of their predecessors and their own virtues – something to which managers are never averse. Up to a point, the blame truly does lie with their inheritance. But after a period of grace the heirs are on their own. That period is measured in years – but not eight of them. The agonies of IBM as the Nineties began belonged wholly to the existing management.

The reinventors had constantly been forced to go back to the drawing board, confronted by irresistible evidence that the 'new' IBM worked no better than the old. With each successive disappointment, comments on the reinventions became more grudging and guarded. Long before, however, IBM's business peers had withdrawn their blessing. They did so in a manner which neatly charts the ebbs and flows of the reinventions of IBM.

Every year *Fortune* magazine polls nearly 6,000 business executives to discover how they rate the largest companies in the US on eight criteria: quality of management; quality of products or services; innovativeness; value as a long-term investment; financial soundness; ability to attract, develop and keep talented people; community and environmental responsibility; and use of corporate assets. Year after year, on the combined scoreboard, IBM came triumphantly top.

In 1984, chairman John R. Opel commented on this top ranking: 'I think this is the finest industrial enterprise in the world.' His self-satisfaction was marred by only one blemish – IBM wasn't placed top for innovation: 'I don't really understand it. We've got a portfolio that testifies to our technical innovations, and we have got a remarkably successful marketing organisation that does some very creative things every day.'

A year later, IBM still came top overall, but the innovativeness ranking was down again, this time to thirty-first. Even in its own industry, with ten runners, IBM was only fourth. A still larger slump on this ranking, to seventy-eighth, didn't prevent the champion from retaining top position in 1986. But on 16 January 1987 came the bombshell: 'The king is dethroned; IBM, No. 1 since the survey began, drops to seventh place.' The slide continued: thirty-second in 1988, then thirty-fourth, then forty-fifth. In 1992, it was placed 206 out of 311 runners.

The judgement wasn't simply that of IBM's peers, but of its

major customers. The very people who should, had Opel been right, have seen evidence of IBM's innovation in products and marketing, had turned thumbs down while the company's general reputation was still riding high. *Fortune* rightly tied these warning doubts to the fate of the PC Junior, which marked the real turning point in IBM's fortunes. But journalists in general were still prepared to give IBM the benefit of the doubt.

The demotion edition carried an article on 'IBM's Big Blues', which struck the reinvention note: 'A Legend Tries to Remake Itself.' Opel's successor, John F. Akers, was characteristically and wrongly expecting 'that in the not-too-distant future we will be back'. He didn't diagnose innovation (where IBM dropped to 158 the next year) as the root of his troubles: 'Amazingly, chairman John Akers says the quintessential marketing company lost touch with the buyers.' He was, however, 'reprogramming the troops'.

That involved in successive years:

1 Boosting the sales force by several thousands, redeploying many of the thousands from headquarters.

2 Revamping the product line and improving 'responsiveness to customers', internal housecleaning and management reshuffles.

3 A $2.3 billion cost-cutting drive that would cut 10,000 jobs.

Yet for all the reinventing, the customer/peers still seemed to think they were facing the same old, self-satisfied IBM – and they hadn't liked the new. They can't have been any more enthusiastic about what they now saw – a whole string of reinventions. IBMers themselves were no more pleased. In 1987, 15,000 of them departed semi-voluntarily, while another 21,000 were redeployed. In this churning, 8,200 staff and 16,000 manufacturing jobs were lost; 11,000 retrained IBMers were added to the sales force and 7,700 to the programming army. And still the winds of change blew about their heads.

The corporation was about to impose its fourth major overhaul of the sales organisation in five years – a frequency which (a) demonstrated the size and persistence of the ailments, and (b) proved Armonk's inability to find the cure. Early in 1988, Armonk tried the most radical therapy to that date. It imposed a new grand design. Five supposedly independent business groups were created. Each was placed in the care of a general manager who reported to a single superior – Terry Lautenbach, general manager of IBM US.

Any management expert (or tyro, for that matter) could see at a glance that Lautenbach's responsibilities were impossibly large. He also had authority over US marketing and services. Yet he ranked below the summit. Chairman Akers, two vice chairmen and an executive vice president shared 'review responsibility' for the activities that reported to Lautenbach. The four also reviewed the overseas marketing and manufacturing arms. Since the writ of the five general managers for product development also ran worldwide, though, Lautenbach's remit wasn't strictly confined to the US.

This cumbersome structure was supposed to be an improvement, and was in two respects. The omnipotent eighteen-member Corporate Management Board had itself been set up only in 1985. Ironically, it was intended to make product strategy more responsive to customer demands. Now it was shunted aside in favour of the four-man Akers group. The 1988 reforms also abolished the Information Systems Group (ISG), a strange creation whose written consent was required before any hardware or software could be introduced.

The idea was to integrate decision-making across the entire product range. The actuality of ISG was to create a massive bottle-neck. The irony could hardly be greater. The first Akers reforms embodied a deliberate, deeply considered policy of centralisation. They sought to impose horizontal control across the vertical product divisions in the fervently held belief that the technology was becoming universal, and that the customers wanted integrated solutions to their information needs.

Battles between the product groups and ISG were inevitable, and the hierarchical structure made matters worse. With the right to 'non-concur' in operation, many of these battles ended up on the chairman's desk. One mid-range computer was held up for four years until Akers, it's said, resolved the matter – too late. The delay resulted in failure. The 1985 reinvention, intended to create a more responsive, dynamic system, had produced a costly, constipated and rudderless result.

The January 1988 reforms were designed to regain control by reversing engines – by decentralising. They were welcomed round the world as an imaginative response to the corporation's size and spread. Like the 1985 reorganisation, though, the reforms had a limited shelf-life. In December 1991, the entire scheme was scrapped as the five decentralised product groups became nine, and four overseas marketing and services companies were created.

By this point, understandably, the journalists had joined the business executives – IBM had lost the benefit of the doubt. In mid-1992, *Fortune* delivered a verdict on the latest and most sweeping of the reinventions. Akers was finally attempting to 'uproot a structure and culture formed when IBM had no serious competition . . . But is he pressing the message hard enough to permeate this immense organisation? Probably not'.

A couple of months were spent interviewing analysts, consultants, customers, employees, leaders of competitors and top IBM executives before reaching the verdict. How did they rate the widest-ranging reorganisation and rehabilitation ever undertaken by a major corporation? The Akers plan unveiled late in 1991 had eight constituents, listed below with *Fortune*'s grades:

1   Give more autonomy to IBM's businesses, divided, as noted, into thirteen – nine American-based in manufacturing and development, four geographically split in marketing and services. (Grade B+.)

2   Remake the culture of complacency, where progress has been most glacial. (Grade D.)

3   Retain a single sales force, which plainly has an impact on the autonomy of the eight manufacturing and development businesses. (Grade B.)

4   Shift the emphasis from products to services (following an industry-wide trend). (Grade B–.)

5   Emphasise customer satisfaction, another trendy strategy. (Grade C+.)

6   Cut staff without layoffs, which meant reducing numbers from a peak 407,000 in 1986 to some 300,000 at end-1992. (Grade A–.)

7   Reduce costs – to which the staff cuts made a huge contribution. (Grade B+.)

8   Share risk and gain expertise through partnerships, where IBM has been extraordinarily active. (Grade B+.)

The overall grade of B– hardly amounted to a vote of confidence. In part, that was unfair. The latest and greatest reinvention was too recent to have taken full effect. But the low score also reflected two criticisms that couldn't be explained away. First, the eight-point programme contained inconsistencies (like, obviously, keeping an IBM-wide sales force for supposedly autonomous businesses). Second, the interviews uncovered huge gulfs between words and deeds.

Whether divisional autonomy is real or illusory depends on freedom to compete, not just with the outside world but with each other. The nine non-marketing 'Baby Blues' started with Enterprise Systems, whose $22 Billion of sales was mostly in mainframes. It was roughly twice the size of each of the next three: Adstar, making storage devices, tape drives and related software, mostly for mainframes; Personal Systems, with $11.5 million in sales, mostly of PCs; and Application Business Systems, whose success in minicomputers had made it a star.

Below these giants were four relative minnows: one in printers and related software (Pennant Systems); one (Application Solutions) in software and services; Technology Products, one of the world's leading micro-electronic manufacturers; and Networking Systems, whose links to the mainframe business were especially close. But the overlaps throughout the roster were countless – and risky.

Was Personal Systems free to undercut the AS/400 minicomputer by four-fifths with an RS/6000 workstation – or wasn't it? The single marketing organisation would inevitably push the more expensive solution. 'I called the local IBM office in Augusta,' said a consultant, 'and they wanted to sell me an AS/400. They made me go around and around. It wasn't easy to convince them the RS/6000 was what I really needed' – at a saving to his client, and a loss to IBM, of $1 million.

There's even difficulty in converting IBM's huge revenue in services (the best part of $6 billion) into a business. The experts in various industry sectors, now drawn together in a gigantic global consultancy, spent their past lives as value-adding adjuncts to the hardware salesmen. A real services business hinges on the quality of service. IBM's performance here was seen by customers as poor. They blamed arrogance derived from a past when customers saw no alternative to IBM.

Cutting costs had stemmed the 12 per cent annual growth in expenses of the mid-Eighties to under 4 per cent in 1991, without tackling one of the largest lumps – the $6.6 billion spending on R&D, which so conspicuously failed to arouse the enthusiasm of non-IBM executives for the company's innovation. Too much of the cost-cutting came from shedding numbers, where the final bill had yet to be paid: 'Work force experts are only beginning to quantify the damage that layoffs and the accompanying resentment and fear can do to an organisation.'

Changing bad habits has been slow – as *Fortune* noted: 'As recently as last year, temps hired in one Westchester office got only forty-five minutes of work each day. When one asked to do more, she was told to bring a book like everybody else.' That example, like most of the other defects that brought IBM its low grading, sprang from a culture that was still awaiting reinvention.

The magazine's David Kirkpatrick was fierce in his attack on a company that is 'deeply complacent', a CEO who seemed 'insufficiently concerned' by the complacency, the collapse of morale among IBMers ('The people are lost.'), the parochial thinking that still called the PC business 'Entry Systems' (implying that one day buyers will grow up and graduate to a proper computer), and the paltriness of the cultural reforms.

There were signs of change. George Conrades had been removed from running IBM in the US, a step attributed to non-performance, and intended to encourage the others. Blue suits, white shirts and dark ties were no longer essential. More people were on incentive pay – 1,500 as opposed to under 100 before. The business units had been given $200 million in 1992 to lubricate motivation. In the US, all employees could add 3 per cent to basic pay if their unit beat its targets. To which you can only say, 'Big deal'.

The list is generally unimpressive. The eight-point Akers reforms were essentially top-down. The main fans of the greater autonomy given to 'lines of business', or LOBs, were their bosses, men like Robert LaBant of IBM North America: 'This has unleashed an unbelievable amount of energy and creativity . . . It's exciting. It leaves me breathless.' His counterpart in Europe, Renato Riverso thought that 'These are radical changes, not just a readjustment of company structures. It is changing the company from the base.'

Riverso was locating the base very high. The reinventions of IBM had devolved power from the top tier of management to the next. But what about the many tiers below? The lesser ranks were buffeted about in the winds of change. Yet their say in these momentous matters was limited to offers they could hardly refuse – of reassignment or 'voluntary' departure, with abnormally generous cash sums (for example, two years' pay plus $25,000) to grease their going.

Departures were also much in evidence at the top. Armonk had seen extraordinary upheaval. The five great units into which IBM was briefly subdivided in 1988 had been entrusted to four men and one woman. It was thought that a successor to Akers might be among them. In 1992, only one, Ellen Hancock was running a Baby Blue; another had retired, and a third, Conrades, had been forced out. Two had become senior vice presidents, as was Terry Lautenbach who left in 1992.

Two of Akers' top triumvirate had also departed: Kaspar V. Cassani by retirement, and Allen J. Krowe for a top job, chief financial officer, at Texaco. By any standards, this was formidable attrition. The swift succession of organisational and personal reshuffles only made sense on the theory that shake-ups themselves, irrespective of their nature, have beneficial powers. A less charitable view would be that both the new organisations and those running them had failed in the appointed task of reinvention.

That wouldn't surprise the more perceptive observers of the 1988 effort. *Computer Industry Report* noted the paradox: 'When one looks closely at IBM's new organisational layout, one is struck by its similarity to the pre-Akers corporate arrangement.' On Akers' own diagnosis, its competitive problems had sprung from that organisational form. Ralph Emmett Carlyle wrote in *Datamation* about customer complaints, for example, that 'the mainframe division has locked itself into an inflexible product development structure that rewards predictability, and penalises innovation.'

He added that 'Still others sneer at what they refer to as "warmed over" products.' IBM was attempting to regain 'account control' by offering large customers products for all their needs and 'bundling' in more add-ons with primary sales; but that was rejected by the customers themselves. That only led IBM to redouble its marketing initiatives (hence the four sales reorganisations in five years). 'It's significant,' said one astute commentator, 'that around 90 per cent of all IBM's organisational innovation in the past five years has been on the marketing side.'

The unfortunate result, however, was that the marketing people were constantly selling products that the product sides hadn't yet developed. Even the billions of investment poured into low-cost production had contributed to the innovatory log-jam. One customer wisely remarked that 'In its efforts to become low-cost producer, IBM has settled into a pattern of substituting predictability for innovation, of minimising design risks.'

Another observed that low-cost production demanded long, stable product cycles. 'Since these don't exist in the real world, IBM has had to create them artificially. It does this by opting for 10 per cent to 20 per cent improvements to existing products rather than for new products.' The product divisions, irrespective of who ran them or how much control was exercised from Armonk, were locked into 'programmes that stretch out for years'. Another customer sneered at this 'planned mediocrity'.

Against these comments, the slippage in IBM's rating by its peers for innovation, and its rapid degeneration into a precipitate slide, assume far greater importance than IBM's leaders saw at the time. Baffled and miffed, they continually appealed to IBM's massive R&D spend (more than Apple or Compaq's turnover), its patent performance and its scientific distinction (its labs boasted three Nobel prize-winners in

1992). And there's no discounting the excellence.

One mid-1992 assessment placed IBM seventh in the world, led only by Eastman Kodak in the US, in technological strength. The criterion was the number of US patents won in 1991 and the number of times IBM's patents are cited when new patents are sought. True, on 'technology cycle time', the survey (by CHI Research and *Business Week*) found IBM outranked even within the computer group – led by Intel, Fujitsu, Motorola, Hewlett-Packard, Tektronix and Zenith. The giant was replacing one generation of inventions with another more slowly than these competitors.

That's scant reward for over $6 billion a year of spending. One competitor claims that he once compiled a list of all the research projects which IBM had announced in recent years. Not one had resulted in a commercial product. Maybe that's an exaggeration, but it's only a partial one. The successes like the PC, remarked this critic, were the work, not of the labs, but the engineers who, in the PC example, used not a single outcome of IBM research in developing a world-beating product.

'IBM's problem has never been inventing wonderful stuff,' observed *Fortune*, 'but rather getting it out of the lab into a profitable product.' Was it possible that, in reinventing IBM, Akers had missed the most important area – invention itself?

27

The Blame
in the Boardroom

The ouster of John Akers as chairman of IBM was a long time coming. That's no surprise. Boards have historically been unwilling to dethrone CEOs. They are even less eager when, as at IBM, no successor is in sight. None of the members can have relished the prospect of what actually happened – conducting a public search, in the full glare of the media, until they finally settled on Louis V. Gerstner.

Left to themselves, they might have stuck with Akers until his mandatory retirement, a year or so on, at the age of sixty. External pressure removed this option. The ground swell of opinion was merely expressing the obvious: Akers had failed. In the week after Robert C. Stempel's boardroom discomfiture at General Motors, *Business Week* noted that the restructuring and refocusing of IBM under Akers hadn't 'done much for investors'. Their investment had fallen in value by 9.2 per cent between 1987 and 1991.

'Sounds like GM. No wonder it's on California Public Employees' Retirement System's list of poor performers. Still, "Akers has the board's full support", says a spokesman. Most observers agree. But he's on a red-hot seat.' Akers endured the heat for nine more months, until it became unbearable. As at GM, the heat should have been shared by a board, which 'fully supported' Akers through all the false dawns. They even backed the absurd last fling, when two senior retirees were brought back to bolster the CEO's indefensible position.

A glance at the board's composition in the 1991 annual report readily explains its shenanigans. It was almost a parody, rather than a paradigm, of the boardroom system that has helped lower the flags of many large US corporations in the past decade. The board was far too large for an effective committee (eighteen members); it was headed by a chairman who was also chief executive; it was stuffed with retirees (a third of the number, including former chairman John Opel); and it was short on relevant business experience.

Eight members were drawn from other industries. None of their companies manufactured or marketed in manners remotely analogous to IBM's processes and needs. Three of the fifteen non-executives came from health care and two from chemicals – which would have given a visitor from Mars a very odd idea of IBM's business. Two were media and entertainment executives. The total was made up by four representatives from academe, two lawyers and Stephen D. Bechtel Jr of the plant construction business that bears his family name.

Whatever their qualifications, most held little ownership stake in IBM. In a letter to *Business Week*, a Florida correspondent told the editor he could 'rest assured that shareholder discontent with company performance will never affect the majority of IBM's board. Ten of its seventeen members own less than 1,500 shares each. Collectively it is not in their interest to challenge the lacklustre performance of CEO John Akers, an action that might jeopardise the maintenance of their $55,000-per-year retainers.'

The non-executives may regard that as unfair criticism, a blow below the belt. But their collective ability to ride herd over Akers' performance, or even to judge it intelligently, was limited to the point of futility. This type of boardroom construction only works for a company that's running well, is led by an executive team which knows where it's going and why, and produces satisfactory results for investors and employees alike. In such cases, little is required of outside directors.

In cases like the IBM of the crisis years too much is required of them. Even if the board had been smaller and possessed more relevant and current experience and skills, how could its members have grappled with such deep-rooted issues? Product and process, culture and principle, competition and commercial strategy – the corporation was in broad disarray. These were the issues which beset, and indeed bewildered, Akers and his two executive partners on the board.

The issues couldn't be resolved at that level, anyway. The fate of IBM would ultimately be decided in the mighty units, and not only in the US. All over the world, people like Nick Temple, general manager of IBM (UK), were striving to adapt to their changed industry within the constraints imposed by the organisation. People were changing, too. The new leaders weren't necessarily of the familiar breed. 'The huge man with a turned-up collar and untidy hair does not look like an IBM type.' So began a profile of Temple, published in Britain's *Independent on Sunday* in the spring of 1992.

Temple had been publicised as that contradiction in terms, an IBM revolutionary – somebody who wanted to reshape the corporation's culture. IBM (UK), was seen as a flying test bed for new approaches that might revolutionise the entire corporation. Temple's ascent to general manager and chief executive had been uncommon: 'I am a bit extraordinary, I suppose I am unusual in the sense of having come from the technical and software side. I have never sold anything in my life.'

That's rare indeed. The company's ethos has been dominated all its life by the salesmanship of which Thomas J. Watson Sr was a supreme exponent. The issue from which the boardroom was so remote is whether the revolution is real. From one viewpoint, Temple's programme in Britain differed neither in need or nature from the Akers approach in the US.

He was forcing through heavy, orthodox cutbacks in employment, against a background of unprecedented, large financial losses. At the same time, he was talking about unorthodox modes of managing the colossus.

In 1991, IBM (UK), long the cynosure of Britain's American transplants, lost £124 million, a sad retreat from the £420 million profit of the previous year. Taking out costs had become essential – not least because it had been ordered from on high, by Armonk. Temple (a much less rumpled figure than that profile suggested) cut 2,600 jobs, leaving fewer than 15,000. Some of these were moved from administration to the front line. Over a thousand found themselves in the software and services operations.

But beyond this standard retrenchment, Temple claimed, his company was 'pioneering change both culturally and structurally'. The change follows the prescription of all the management gurus who are trying to lead organisations along new roads into the twenty-first century. Temple attacked the hierarchical pyramid, creating a flatter structure in which individual businesses can be picked out. The style is deliberately not 'top-down'. Hierarchy is a means of passing orders downwards and imposing control, and that isn't Temple's expressed objective.

'My job is to create space and leadership, not to tell people how to do their jobs. That would be highly arrogant. The top of a company is not the fount of all knowledge.' The diagnosis and the prognosis are reasonable enough. But whether they, and the similar rethinks all over IBM, will achieve results to match the triumphs of the past depends on many unknowns – and on the break-up of many old, resistant realities.

First, IBM (UK), like all the corporation's satrapies, is a sprawling empire, with facilities spread from Havant near Portsmouth in the south of England, to Greenock in Scotland. The London telephone book alone listed seven addresses at the time of Temple's profile. His 15,000 people, moreover, were all trapped, like flies in amber, within the IBM matrix.

Some responsibilities, like sales, were clearly delegated to Temple's care. Others, like manufacturing and the development activities which developed his own career, were not.

Dealing with the company still presented outsiders with an uncertain choice of which official in which office had the power of decision. For the officials themselves, bureaucratic channels laid down what they could and couldn't do on their own initiatives. Change programmes had been under way for some time. They aimed at directing the culture away from the old mainframe-dominated mentality, bent on selling the costliest possible configuration to large customers, and towards the new age of multiplicity.

But anybody dealing with the salesmen on the ground could sense that they still believed in the old processes and still strove for the old prizes – the big commissions that came from the big sales. Even when it came to shedding some of these hard-liners, IBM couldn't help reverting to its habitual style of haughty benevolence. Many were set up as independent dealers, apparently solving the redundancy problem and strengthening IBM's sales network at a stroke. Ill-equipped for independent business, they were given favoured treatment by their former IBM colleagues, and this undermined and alienated the existing dealers.

Procrastination, too, has been built into IBM, not by would-be strategists, but by the matrix management system (with threefold, overlapping command structures) and the other means by which IBM kept its armies marching in step down the decades. Temple's career throws a revealing light on one such means. He spent his early years on the development side in the UK, before leaving for the US in 1981 as a consultant in software and telecommunications. The next post was in Germany setting up two units – one a software laboratory, the other in business banking.

Posted to Paris, Temple was the first head of European product development who wasn't American, which says a great deal about past attitudes at Armonk. Lip service was paid to multinationalism as to all other supposed corporate virtues. In practice the dominance of Armonk was maintained as thoroughly by appointments as by anything else. The 'I've Been Moved' syndrome filled jobs – it was also an effective means of imperial control.

This Roman-style imperium is cracking under commercial pressure. The IBM board has been presiding, unwittingly, over a spiritual break-up that can only be intensified by the ideas and efforts of new men like Temple. The issue is how far and fast they and the ethos they represent can penetrate through the organisation. Will the depth and the speed be great enough to save IBM from further decline, even disintegration?

The question once sounded unthinkable. It certainly wouldn't have been thought by a board whose business experience was either negligible, or confined to other big battalions. An equally unthinkable headline appeared in the *International Herald Tribune* in 1992. 'What's Good for GM May Be Fatal.' David C. Munro, the authority quoted, was the auto giant's chief economic forecaster for ten years. When he left, the company had already halved in size since his arrival – and he wasn't sure 'what will be left when the company enters the next millenium'.

Munro diagnosed two main ailments – 'elephantine mass' and insularity. 'GM doesn't have a very good history of pulling in information and ideas from others, and at the top it has a history of resisting change from outside. There are an awful lot of people in that bureaucracy who only know what others are thinking down the hall.' The same painful observation could have been made of IBM at any time, including the present. Down the postwar decades its managers have created a company at once far too large and much too introverted.

All the surgery and medicaments of the crisis years were supposed to cure both conditions – to turn IBM's thinking and actions outwards and to bring down its size. Some of the slimming was unwanted. For the first time in its history, IBM began to experience a steady haemorrhage, not of frustrated genius lower down, like Ross Perot and Gene Amdahl, but of seasoned executives at the very top. No less than thirty corporate officers left between 1986 and 1992.

They included the director of software strategy, Mike Maples; executive vice president and director, Allen Krowe; president of IBM World Trade Asia, Ed Lucente; chairman of all IBM World Trade, Mike Armstrong; and the head of corporate marketing, George Conrades. The latter, as noted earlier, was carrying the can, fairly or not, for IBM's difficulties in the US market, and resigned after what was seen inside the company as a public execution.

The others, however, left for pastures new and green: Northern Telecom, Texaco, Hughes Aircraft (where Armstrong became CEO) and Microsoft – to whose summit, ominously enough, software king Maples headed. Presumably, the board of directors felt some concern over this exodus. Perhaps, like the pressurised Conrades, they took a sanguine view: 'John Akers is investing in the next generation of executives, in their mid to late forties. It's important that everyone be pulling in harness.'

Others were not so sure. Another veteran emigré remarked that 'Not everyone agrees with all the strategies and tactics that the company is taking. After a while the fun goes out of it. You go through so many reorganisations that the objectives keep changing, and you get frustrated.' The dichotomy of view goes to the heart of the matter. Within IBM, the reorganisations had met with widespread cynicism. Would putting old bureaucrats behind new desks make any real difference?

Akers had certainly reorganised too often and too clumsily. Clumsiness is in a sense unavoidable when reorganising – as the displaced managers play musical chairs, many are bound to fall on the ground, and some won't find any seats. There's a crucial trade-off between the gains of a reorganisation – matching responsibilities and authority to the needs of the market, say – and the losses in morale and security.

Many desired and desirable benefits of reorganisation, like greater flexibility and speed of decision, can be achieved within unchanged structures by changing processes and principles – for example, leaving reporting systems intact, but changing what is reported. The drift of Akers' thinking in 1992 was to place the prime emphasis on financial reporting. He saw IBM as an emerging portfolio of companies, which would be measured by cash-flow and return-on-asset goals.

Consequently, IBM executives would need more financial skills, and the previous supremacy of sales and product management expertise would count for less. If that meant more outsiders, thought Akers, so be it. That would certainly meet the prescription of ex-IBMers – one believed that 'inbreeding' was 'stifling' the company's 'ability to think any new thoughts'. Akers ought to start hiring people who 'don't come from the IBM school'. But the most prominent member of that school, of course, was Akers himself. Could he really think enough new thoughts – and turn them into new action?

The action had become particularly urgent in the spring of 1992 because of the spate of top-level departures. With three years to go until his own retirement, Akers had run out of clear potential successors. The company's president, Jack D. Kuehler, was in the same age bracket, while the departure of Armstrong and Conrades had removed the two likeliest contenders. The situation, which the board should never have allowed to develop, was reminiscent of a previous crisis point in IBM's executive suite.

IBM chieftains like to boast about the stability of the succession – only six leaders in seventy-eight years. Akers himself noted that 'Many American companies seem to have a tenure for the CEO of only four to five years. That's not the way IBM has historically approached the challenge.' But his numbers grossly exaggerate the stability. Tom Watson Sr and his natural successor, his son, ruled the company for fifty-seven of those seventy-eight years. Since then, five CEOs have averaged five and a half years apiece.

The average is raised by the eight Akers years, cut short though he was, and brought down by the tenure of T. Vincent Learson, who was at the helm for less than two years. Like the pre-ouster Akers succession, that of Tom Watson Jr was complicated by age. Learson was older than Watson, and only the latter's heart attack and early retirement gave Learson his brief moment at the summit. He was the boldest of the 'wild ducks' (in Watson's phrase), a man who 'seemed incapable of being tamed'.

The latter quotation comes from Robert Sobel's *IBM*, which portrays Learson as a 'quintessential IBM man, one devoted to the company, tough, shrewd and energetic', a 'corporate troubleshooter . . . a tough taskmaster and a brutal opponent'. Learson modelled himself on General Patton. He was the driving force behind the 360 range of computers which utterly transformed the industry and ultimately IBM. He stood for a rougher and tougher culture that died with his departure.

Watson gives an entertaining portrait of this formidable corporate freebooter in *Father, Son, and Co.* 'Vin worked best by himself, and despite his great intelligence, decisiveness and drive, he was not at all contemplative or methodical . . . He ducked meetings whenever he could, put very little store in staff work, and favoured executives like John Opel who knew how to take shortcuts across organisational lines.' Under Watson, with the highly methodical Al Williams as president, Learson formed a powerful team.

While it was doubtful whether, at fifty-eight, Learson had new ideas to offer, his successor, Frank Cary, 'had been considered an able bureaucrat who for all his good qualities was deficient in imagination'. In the description by Watson (who hand-picked Cary and warmly praised his tenure), Cary was 'a brilliant business analyst, cool, impartial and totally self-confident. He rarely spoke up at meetings, and it wasn't his style to step in and save the day the way Learson and I did.'

Cary began a succession of leaders who were as devoted to IBM as Learson, but who, for both good and ill, lacked his drive and ferocity, and played things safer. To quote Watson again, Cary 'didn't make heroic moves, and didn't make glaring mistakes; when he ran into a problem he simply figured out how to fix it'. The company needed in its top team, and in its executives at large, a synthesis between the Learson and Cary moulds – and Akers was attempting to achieve that synthesis (lower down, but not in his own environs) in the early Nineties.

The division of IBM into thirteen business units, some of them gigantic, had given opportunities to much younger people (many in their mid-forties) to demonstrate their talents in ways which had not been possible before. As you would expect, Akers spoke highly of these up-and-comers: 'I think the people coming along now are all more highly skilled than the generations before that. That's been true all the way along.'

Nevertheless, members of all generations were joining the queue of IBM executives who saw better opportunities outside – better than those in IBM. It was, after all, undergoing continuous upheaval against a background of deep uncertainty about its future and therefore their own. The departed Conrades observed that the product mix and manufacturing capacity problems faced by IBM persisted, and used a striking metaphor: 'We'll work that pig through the python.' Unfortunately many IBMers saw themselves as pork rather than as its consumers.

'Akers,' said Conrades, 'is bound and determined to see that through.' In the end, the board deprived him of the opportunity, although it's unlikely that the pig would have got through the python under his regime. The new man, Gerstner, moved quickly to replace that regime with men who, like him, were new to the company. Akers and those most closely identified with his reign were history – and unhappy history, at that.

Tom Watson delivered no verdict on their performance in *Father, Son, and Co.* Unlike Frank Cary, however, they had attempted 'heroic deeds'. Their agenda for all parts of the business was always ambitious, conceived on the grandest scale, dedicated to perpetuating the dominance of the corporation. Unlike Cary, they had achieved little result save 'glaring mistakes'. That's what happens when bureaucrats try to play buccaneer – and find that 'elephantine mass' and insularity (including their own) obstruct them at every turn.

X

THE NADIR
OF THE NINETIES

28

Compaq: Come-Uppance and Comeback

The traumas which hit mainframe and mini makers in the Nineties were easy to understand and wholly predictable. They flowed from the technological revolution created by the microprocessor. As its computing power soared, but its price fell, the competitive position of larger computers was eroded, undermined and finally tumbled. But the traumas were just as painful for two microstars – IBM's personal computer business and Compaq.

Their common weakness was price. Both companies sought to use branding and reputation to stay clear of the proliferating, cheaper and absurdly numerous competition. Both strategies failed when the price gap yawned too large. The premium price structures were built on a fault-line. Since microprocessors and many other components were identical or easily imitable, how could IBM or Compaq or anybody else justify charging much more for similar boxes?

They couldn't. The full shock of this truth hit two undercover men from Compaq when, in October 1991, they toured the Comdex computer trade show in Las Vegas. The pair had a secret mission – to discover what it would cost to assemble a computer from the components on display. Posing as entrepreneurial clone-makers, they obtained low enough quotations

315

on enough components to mock up two models in their motel – and very cheaply.

'In some cases,' reported the *Wall Street Journal,* 'they were able to get price quotes . . even lower than giant Compaq.' In this fragmented, hotly competitive business, the economic advantages available, even to IBM, through placing mammoth orders are not significant – nothing like large enough to offset vastly higher costs for overheads, advertising and organisational delays. At Compaq, for instance, the lead time for a low-priced PC had been planned at eighteen months. It was *halved* after the undercover operation.

The two men's mission wasn't only secret from the suppliers. It was also unknown to their chief executive, Rod Canion. In one of the least easily credible stories of an incredible industry, excellently reported by the *Journal*'s Michael Allen, chairman Ben Rosen had gone behind his CEO's back – and plunged in the knife. Canion was fired during a fourteen-hour board meeting, almost immediately after the Comdex episode (though his ouster was probably already in Rosen's mind).

Rosen is a small, bespectacled, inconspicuous man, whose soft manner belies a sharp, hard intelligence. It has put him among the wealthiest of a rich breed, America's venture capitalists. His role at Compaq, which he had steered from opening days to success as a $3 billion-sales company, is a special pride. Canion and his co-founders owed Rosen plenty. Even before the start, he steered them away from initial, inadequate product plans and towards the portable computer concept which launched their rocket.

Acute sensitivity to industry trends is one of Rosen's strengths. His unease had mounted as Compaq, instead of leading the trend, had become a follower – notably in 486 computers, built around the latest Intel microprocessor, and in laptops. Rosen had lived through all the roller-coaster rides of the industry, and he sensed that the PC business had changed fundamentally. The cheap manufacturers were representing a new reality – a box was a box was a box.

That was essentially confirmed by Rosen's undercover agents, marketing manager Sean Burke (half Rosen's age at thirty) and engineer Jon Thompson. But their discovery cut across the grain of the Compaq culture. Like IBM, but in far fewer years, Compaq had developed an all-embracing internal view which governed its external actions. In this mental model, Compaq was the high-quality, high-end champion. It was the preferred choice of people who were serious about their personal computing needs.

IBM's mainframe business was being squeezed between superior supercomputers and increasingly potent minis and PC-based workstations. Compaq was being sandwiched between the latter (at the top end) and the low-priced clones. In another similarity to IBM, Compaq didn't see its collapse into loss in the first quarter of 1992 as a failure of the system. Sales had fallen by 17 per cent, true, but there was a recession on, after all. The system needed tightening up, by reorganisation, layoffs and other cost-cutting, but radical changes in the engineering-led culture weren't necessary.

The chairman's subversive intervention changed all that. From this radical step, others flowed naturally. The low-end line was entrusted to an 'independent business unit' or IBU. It was placed outside the Compaq mainstream as a deliberate means of avoiding the product development system. In only an eight-year history, that had become too conservative. Dedication to top quality has its virtues, but also its vices – over-engineering had become a revered part of the Compaq culture.

The irreverent low-end team, working under the codename Ruby, were housed away from the campus (twenty-odd glass and steel buildings in landscaped surroundings). Kept apart from other Compaq people, they made their own rules. The company's purchasing department placed price seventh in a list of priorities. In contrast, as to priority Richard Swingle, the product developer who headed the Ruby project, went direct to suppliers and hammered them on prices. The suppliers squeezed out by the pressure included Compaq's own production lines – when Taiwanese circuit boards came in 30 per cent cheaper, Compaq lost the job.

The Texas plant could have lost the entire computer to off-shore bids. But the *Journal* recounts an intriguing, even warming event. At a briefing of plant workers, Doug Johns, the new head of the PC division, was explaining the rationale for going offshore when one 'crusty old' employee (remember, the company was only founded in 1981) stood up and argued that Compaq workers should bid for the work.

'With all due respect,' said the veteran, 'you're kind of new at this, and you don't know what we can do.' Johns was a good enough manager to take the point. Further investigation showed that Compaq could cut its manufacturing costs to competitive levels, but not by sticking to the same methods. The Ruby engineers found, for instance, that by simplifying board manufacture you could produce the computer on a single line. The time came down from one machine in eight minutes to one a minute.

The cost savings that a supposedly efficient organisation could find were staggering – like $6 a box on packing cases by accepting a slightly lower specification. Then $10 a unit on chassis tooling fell to $1 'by using one size for a number of different models'. The quality was good enough to bear the Compaq label, but the appearance of the new machine ('wave-like front and turquoise buttons'), like its name of Echelon, shied right away from the Compaq connection.

That was too far for Eckhard Pfeiffer, the German chief executive appointed after Canion's overthrow. He held back $20 million of parts orders while he pondered the issue over the Christmas holidays. His decision, proved resoundingly right by the outcome, was governed by the need to sell low-cost solutions to the large corporate customers. They, he reasoned, still wanted a Compaq – and the Ruby team spent Christmas Day rushing through a redesign.

The team has since been reabsorbed, but so have its discoveries on cost-cutting and development time. According to one executive, 'The IBU changed the way this company did business forever.' The first months of the new ProLinea line were brilliant, and its continuing success (with 200,000 units a month being made in mid-1993) sealed the triumph of the change process.

The logic of Compaq's response, under Rosen's goading, can't be faulted, including its readiness to accept cannibalisation – that is, the loss of higher-priced, higher-profit business to its own new line. Swingle, promoted to head all Compaq's new product development, remarks that 'Either you eat your own children or somebody else does.' Faced with the threat of being devoured, Compaq had shown swiftness and ruthlessness of reform.

On its far larger scale, IBM found these qualities elusive; although the giant had, in part, set the precedent. The celebrated team that launched IBM's PC was the industry prototype of the 'independent business unit'. Their IBU, like Team Ruby, was freed of every corporate shibboleth in order to mount a crash programme. But while, like Ruby again, the PC operation was eventually absorbed back into the corporate mainstream, its lessons, unlike Ruby's, were not. The way IBM 'did business' didn't change, partly because of its paralysing inhibitions about running risks – cannibalisation, for example, had always preyed on the corporate mind.

That was one reason for the cheap design features and poor specifications which scuppered PC Jr. Similar errors gravely handicapped the PS/1 launch. But, then, IBM didn't have a corporate gadfly like Rosen to stir up everything and everybody – including the chief executive. The results in terms of business economics were spectacular. Although previous peaks of profit were unattainable, Compaq's sales soared as its prices sank. Share rose from a nadir of 4.5 per cent of the IBM-compatible market in the US to pushing 6 per cent.

IBM's share moved sharply in the opposite direction. As competitors introduced new models at prices cut far deeper,

IBM, preoccupied with internal factors, stayed helpfully inert – for a while. That's one reason why Compaq's problems hadn't ended – and may never end. Its giant competitor's inertia ended when the ValuePoint low-priced clone-fighters completed IBM's new range. Pfeiffer now faced a better equipped and organised opposition. After a terrible 1992, in which PC prices fell by 40 to 50 per cent, price pressure looked like becoming a permanent fixture – and net operating margins had shrunk in two years from 18 per cent to 5 per cent.

Until the great slide, the Texan company thrived on a strategy akin to IBM's in mainframes – to be a price leader, always somewhat below IBM, but notably above the other IBM-compatibles. The policy easily got translated into 'the sky-high prices of the past' when Compaq lost the technological aura that had sustained its market positioning. The quote comes from an advertising writer, Joanne Lipman, analysing the efforts of a new agency to put across a new message.

The advertising people had the tough job of promoting Compaq's new low-priced, clone-matching line without compromising the old image of quality and technological leadership. That image, however, had been partly compromised already. First, Compaq's perceived lag in laptops and in desktops using the new Intel 486 microprocessor had damaged its first-with-the-mostest reputation. Second, Compaq was sucked in by the irreversible shift of the personal computer towards commodity status.

Other branded goods have survived similar drifts by emphasising brand values through heavy advertising. Compaq, having spent $12.7 million in 1991, upped its budget by 76 per cent for 1992. The campaign kicked off with a twelve-page insert designed to pull off a difficult trick – persuading potential buyers that Compaq had changed, but without really changing. As Lipman wrote, the ad touted 'all the features Compaq has always been known for, including durability and engineering, plus a list of things it definitely wasn't that well-known for, like good customer service and low prices.'

The difficult straddling act between price cuts and quality image was epitomised by the later statement that 'you won't see . . . stamped-out, second -rate products with the Compaq name stuck on at the end of somebody else's assembly line'. That glossed over the fact that, while the company's note-book computer was definitely not second-rate, the Compaq name was stuck on at the end of Citizen Watch's assembly line. The 'things that make a Compaq a Compaq', to quote the agency, are not, in concrete terms, significantly different from what makes a Dell a Dell, or (for that matter) an IBM an IBM.

At the top of its range, however, workstations and other powerful microprocessor-based systems were burrowing away under the foundations of minis and mainframes. There Compaq needed to be perceived in the old light of techno-logical leader. Would Compaq be any luckier than, say, Cadillac when it risked (and failed with) a low-priced model? As the editor of *Computer Letter*, Richard Shaffer, said, 'Compaq has to be careful not to destroy [its] quality image. If they can deliver on the promise, fine. If they can't, they're dead.'

Until 1992, death had miraculously spared virtually all the 'new' computer industry's leaders – and the followers, for that matter. But for new technology companies, the opportunities for potentially fatal errors are coming thicker and faster. Compaq's plunge from star to fallen idol took only a couple of years, and came after less than a decade of life. In fiscal 1988, Digital Equipment made record profits of $1.31 billion. Four years later it lost $2 billion in a single quarter – and also lost its founder, Ken Olsen, in circumstances which left nobody cer-tain that this $14 billion company would survive.

Digital (and perhaps Compaq) shareholders could be for-given for looking nervously over their shoulders at the wreckage of Wang Laboratories. Like Olsen in minis, or Canion in compatibles, the late An Wang had pioneered a mighty market. Olsen had taken the minicomputer to second place in the industry by following a vision that outreached

IBM's. Canion had usurped product leadership from a rival which held all the trump cards. Wang had seen and seized the opportunity of electronic word processing.

As noted earlier, his first trade exhibit in New York in June 1976 had attracted a million dollars in orders. His product line had usurped the place of IBM electric typewriters in the well-dressed office. But like Olsen, and with less excuse, given the word processor's close relationship to the micro-computer, Wang had been late into the PC market. Neither company succeeded in building a worthwhile share.

The result in Wang's case was a three-year decline from $3 billion of sales and 31,500 employees to $1.9 billion in turnover and 12,500 people. The lifeline thrown out by IBM, a $25 million share purchase in exchange for Wang's selling of IBM equipment, was too thin. When the lifeline broke, Wang went into Chapter 11. Its bankruptcy was the biggest fatality of the personal computer age – to that point. There were special circumstances – there always are. The company had an incurable case of 'founder's disease'.

Dominating the business, as Olsen dominated Digital, An Wang, a man of real genius, had been reluctant to abandon the formula that made his proprietary millions to enter the new world of open systems. He sought to sustain Wang's position in the office without realising that the changing technology demanded a new formula. It was beyond an ailing and obstinate founder's reach.

You could argue that the troubles of IBM, Compaq, Apple (before the ousting of Steve Jobs) and certainly DEC also exemplified founder's disease – even though in IBM's case the founder was long gone. In their different ways, though, the Watsons, Wang, Canion, Jobs and Olsen had all created all-powerful cultures linked to a particular concept of the market and the technology.

Wang, for all his genius, never took a broad view of the office systems market. The big corporate market of the future will be dominated by networked personal computers.

Mainframes and minis were originally seen as the masters of the networks, but PC makers themselves compete here via the high-end versions sold as 'servers'. Now a new generation of super-servers has emerged, extra fast PC-based configurations that combine low cost with high, mainframe-style speeds – another line that demonstrates the new pressures on Compaq.

The Texans were creditably quick into the market, introducing the SystemPro in 1989. Typically over-engineered and over-priced (up to $26,000), it had under 10 per cent of the market in 1993. Its new ProSignia servers start from almost a tenth of the old top price – $2,600 in a market used to paying $11,500. This currently low-volume line wasn't expected to contribute even 10 per cent of Compaq's $4 billion of 1993 sales. But the prediction is that every appropriate PC will be networked by the end of the century. If the spider at the centre of the web is a Compaq, much of the web may well bear the same trademark.

But the competition is mounting. Each new opportunity produces a new star. A $51 million Californian start-up named NetFrame suddenly emerged as a leader, along with Tricord Systems and Compaq. NetFrame leads in a market that by 1995, according to International Data Corp, could be worth $1.7 billion. Other companies – Auspex Systems and Solbourne Computer – make servers for workstations. The leading station supplier, Sun, entered the superserver market in April 1992. Again, the stakes are large – servers for workstations may be worth $4 billion in 1996.

When market and technologies are changing so radically, only radical action – like that improvised by Rosen at Compaq – can change a company to fit new and deeply destabilising conditions, and to take advantage of the big new opportunities that abound in unstable technologies. But the corporate order imposed by the founder, and, in the cases of Wang, Digital, Apple and Compaq, maintained by his physical presence, inhibits radical action – even if radical managers are on the premises.

Jobs saved his foundation by hiring the outsider, John Sculley, who ousted him: An Wang, desperately ill, destroyed his creation by handing over to the wrong insider, his son Frederick. Wang's second choice, Richard W. Miller, probably came from General Electric too late. He compounded that problem by errors – such as taking too long to repair Wang's technological lag. At Compaq, Canion's departure could be safely engineered because Pfeiffer was waiting in the European wings.

The CEO from Germany inverted the price strategy. Compaq would still lead the market, but downwards. As turnover soared and profits returned, Compaq cut prices again – by up to 32 per cent. The process had an intriguing result. The lower-priced lines affected other products much less than expected. As often happens, cannibalisation proved more threat than reality. When you invert a fundamental strategy, however, you also change the foundations of the culture – and Compaq felt a cultural shock-wave.

A former employee told *Business Week* that success had spoilt the start-up: 'A slickness came into Compaq. All of a sudden, if you didn't have an MBA, red suspenders, and those little Gucci slippers, you were nobody.' The Pfeiffer plan to cut costs by 35 per cent to 50 per cent, and compete on price and performance, instead of performance alone, created a revolution. 'It was like a new election. New people were going to be running things. I couldn't have stayed around.' The speaker, an engineer, had been one of the first five people hired by the three founders.

One of them, Jim Harris, along with four other senior managers, quit at once. A bitter Canion had preceded them out of the door. At Digital, too, the decks had been cleared by the founder's exit. Looked at from that perspective, the departure of John Akers from the summit of IBM fits a pattern. In a world of extreme volatility, static leadership is a lethal liability. But Akers wasn't a founder, and more than a few IBM people needed replacement – an entire, elaborate, entrenched corporate system had become obsolete.

Its failures have fed into the marketplace. IBM consistently lagged behind developments in the PC market, after creating the industry standard by brilliant (though also belated) innovation. The lags are of a piece with Wang's mishandling of the PC revolution and Compaq's misunderstanding of the clone market which it had pioneered. The superservers mentioned above are yet another example. IBM had every reason to be in the market, for networks are the office of the future, and it sells PCs and workstations as well as minis.

Yet IBM's reaction in June 1992 was to buy a minority stake in another start-up, Parallan Computer. Its machines will be sold under an IBM badge. At least the reaction was reasonably timely, but it doesn't say much for the timeliness of IBM's R&D. One analyst believes that 'the superserver business is the last great opportunity to build a systems business.' The 'last' may be wrong, but not the great. There's something wrong when, yet again, the industry leader isn't first with the great. IBM shared too easily in the market miseries that caused the come-uppance of Compaq. Its far harder task is to achieve as complete a comeback.

29

Crisis of
the Corporation

The crisis of IBM is also critical for the large American corporation as a genus. The unprecedented downfall, not only of IBM's chief executive, but others at General Motors, American Express, Kodak and Westinghouse, reflects wide turmoil. But IBM's distress is the most disturbing. The company's managerial and technological reputation was exaggerated at its peak. Yet its performance and standards still surpassed most contemporaries in the US and Europe.

Comparisons with Japan, true, are less flattering. IBM is caught in a pincer between newcomers both global and domestic. The Asians, coming late into information technology, have concentrated primarily on components and sub-contracted assemblies, and their success at mastering complex technologies of product and process has won them enormous market share. New domestic competition, too, has ruthlessly exploited every gap which technology and IBM's inadvertencies have created.

In one sense, this is healthy – a seething collection of smaller firms will exploit the Information Age's boundless opportunities better than a global octopus. In February 1992, the perceptive *Guardian* computer editor, Jack Schofield, bluntly asked 'Do we need IBM? If so, what for?' If the idea was for all computers to work 'compatibly', IBM's didn't – and never had. Hence the gigantic project for Systems Application Architecture (SAA), which was only a partial solution: 'One consultant likened this to throwing an anvil to a drowning man.'

Nor is IBM required to set 'standards'. Today nearly every aspect of IT is governed, to greater or lesser degree, but always adequately, by international organisations. Their role, sometimes exclusively, is to set agreed standards. Where formal international agreement is lacking, agreement between competitors needn't coalesce round IBM. Nor is IBM needed 'to push back the frontiers'. For all its massive R&D spending, and for all the talent locked within its patents and labs, 'most of today's innovations have come from individuals or small companies or universities'.

These creative forces are technology-driven. The large corporations of America are mostly driven by non-technologists. Their CEOs have risen by selling rather than producing, managing rather than making. IBM, a salesman's foundation, naturally fits this pattern. It wasn't perceived as typical – because its products and achievements were technologically high. Closer examination of the power structure and reward systems in this technological cornucopia shows that selling ruled the company, and that technology was subservient to sales.

Subjecting technology to market disciplines, and to managerial expertise, is indispensable. That doesn't demote technology in the pecking order. A prime role of management is to finance, enable and ensure technological leadership; to see that, wherever the company chooses to compete, its products and processes equal or surpass the competition in satisfying the market and in timeliness.

Sometimes this means giving genius its head. IBM failed here with Gene Amdahl, the mainframe wizard: the former SmithKline French succeeded (if somewhat inadvertently) with Sir James Black. The brilliant pharmacologist proceeded to discover Tagamet, the billion-dollar anti-ulcer drug. Pharmaceutical companies like Merck – which years ago replaced IBM as America's most admired corporation – know the rules of the high-tech game.

Speed to market with market-leading products is the vital formula for drug firms, which are often (like Merck under Roy Vagelos) led by top-class researchers. Similarly, success after success in IT has been won by leaders whose leadership began in development: Bill Gates of Microsoft in programming, Ken Olsen of Digital in computer engineering, Robert Noyce in semiconductors. In new industries, high technology and management acumen often go hand in hand.

Virtually all Detroit's pioneers were automotive engineers, from Henry Ford downwards. Most of industry's founding fathers were technological founders as well. It doesn't follow that all manufacturers should be led by techno-executives. The genius of world-shaping entrepreneurs can lie in spotting emerging technology and jumping on the bandwagon – like John H. Patterson with the cash register, or his star pupil, IBM's Thomas Watson, with punch cards.

Thomas Watson Jr saw and exploited the potential of the digital computer. Another IBM chairman, John Opel, was the godfather of its personal version. As both men proved, IBM – like most large corporations – had (and has) all the resources needed to turn technological vision into rich reality. So why was so much leadership lost to small and foreign competitors?

The legendary PC team shot to fame (but not to personal fortune) as a group of engineers led by an engineer. They owed the corporation two things only – one irreplaceable, the other not. Without IBM's brand-name and reputation, the PC wouldn't have struck the market with such a thunderclap. Given its product advantages, the PC would have prospered under any name – but not so fast, nor so furiously.

The second contribution, finance, was available elsewhere. The PC depended centrally on a microprocessor from Intel, itself a venture capital creation. A continuing strength of the

US economy is its ability to mobilise large development capital outside the big-time corporate world. Whether independents would have had the courage, or felt the pressure, to force the PC project through in a year is another matter, but it's feasible.

Where IBM led, others could have followed. Within any Western car company, the talent lay ready, for example, to reduce model development costs and times to the Japanese standard. The four-year norm was conventional wisdom with no technical or economic justification – except that, on sloppy accounting principles, the longer basic models and engines ran, the more money you seemed to make. The fact that competitive power was steadily eroded carried no weight. It literally wasn't taken into account.

To many managements – and IBM was no exception – successful competition meant maintaining leadership by preserving the status quo as long as possible. The tyre industry resisted beyond the point of no return the new radial technology introduced by Michelin. Within IBM, powerful forces resisted first the personal computer and then its full implications for the same reason – the new technology upset the old order.

What are those 'forces'? They are human beings, professional managers. They rise through staff and line jobs, where they often have technological responsibility, but lack great knowledge. Some must end at the summits of organisations employing hundreds of thousands of employees. They are prisoners of the system; they also control and modify the system. Their power to create, or enable creation, is great, but so is their power to obstruct.

Contrast the fate of the Boca Raton group inside IBM with that of an independent business. The key PC people would today be senior officers of a leading corporation. Some would have fallen away as growth outstripped their abilities. The survivors would have sought to run the company with the same individualistic but collegial energy that served so well during the launch. As the company flourished, new talent would have been attracted by its growth. A significant, distinct, productive corporate culture would have evolved.

In real life, none of the inner group survived to lead IBM's future development in PCs. Only one, Don Estridge, their leader, would have risen further up the organisation, save for his accidental death. The PC company, as opposed to its product, died. In memory, it became a Camelot.

At US Ford, the team effort that triumphed with the Taurus was likewise dissipated. Ford had to start all over again to crack the compartmentalised, one-stage-after-another mentality which is a terrible handicap in world competition. Who is to blame? The technologists don't call these shots. That privilege is reserved for top management.

'Strategy' is determined by the corporate strategists, which doesn't mean the staff experts, often very clever, who do the strategic analysis and present the cases. The strategy that ultimately controls the layers of management descending the pyramid, the strategy that makes the columns of *Business Week*, is the product of the senior management. That strategy is not subject to checks and balances – especially if it's seeming to succeed.

After the Federal anti-trust suit collapsed, IBM's senior managers were riding high. Who would want to say them nay? It's hard enough to deny a CEO's wishes even in dire distress. At Compaq, the non-executive chairman led the moves that ousted the CEO, turned the business upside down, and may have saved the company. Events like those, however, are exceedingly rare. They shouldn't be.

IBM's management problems stem from a common cause, the concentration of strategic and operational power at the top. Even if all business chieftains were supremely competent technologically, thoroughly versed in strategic principles, deeply familiar with the business and its personnel, expert in all relevant management disciplines, concentrating on the true priorities of the corporation, and rewarded only for their success in achieving its top priority aims – even so, the task of 'managing' corporate giants would be beyond them.

As it is, too many have been left behind by technologies they never perfectly understood; have no prior experience and no present knowledge base in strategy; are remote from most people and parts in the business; have done little or nothing to refresh (let alone expand) their management knowledge since business school days; and spend more time on internal politics and external entanglements than on the vital business of their employer.

They are rewarded, not for any achievement that relates directly to their efforts, but simply for being there. Their power to create is paralysed, because they have become remote from the markets in which their people compete – and remote from those people. Their power to frustrate is enormous, though. Overnight, their decision or indecision can waste the destiny of products, plants and people.

The problem and the opportunity are highlighted by a dead plant that didn't die. It belonged, not to IBM, but to NCR – though IBM plays a pivotal role. The paths of NCR and IBM didn't cross during the first decades when Tom Watson was outshining his mentor. The digital era ushered in by Watson's son brought them into collision, for NCR's powerful position in banking and retailing was threatened by the computer. So NCR joined the heavyweights who mastered the technology but never mustered the marketplace strength to match IBM.

The Dayton company was even thrashed by IBM on its home ground, selling automatic teller machines to banks. But in 1980 strange things began to happen in one of NCR's feeblest facilities. Its Dundee plant in Scotland had once supplied cash registers to the British Empire. When James Adamson took over, the odds were heavily on closure – for Dundee had no profits or products of its own.

Its first ATMs, ordered by Dayton for two of Britain's Big Five banks, were sent back. Their awful standards launched Adamson on a new tack. Well ahead of other managers, he put overwhelming stress on customer satisfaction, even customer 'worship', and engineering quality. *Fortune* reported how 'Adamson asked his engineers to develop a machine twice as reliable as the competition's. They laughed. He persisted'.

The result? 'One day the director of engineering found a way to *triple* the reliability. That became the new target . . . The engineers redesigned virtually every element of the machines.' The customers and Dundee grew closer ('the more I talked to customers, the more rope they were willing to give me'). The closer they grew, the more ATM business was funnelled from Dayton to Dundee. In 1980, the factory made only some 1,000 ATMs: by 1983, it was NCR's only source worldwide.

From ninth position behind IBM and Diebold, NCR was moving up – fast. By 1984, its output had quadrupled, and that year's 4,000 installations took it to third place. Then IBM shot itself in the foot. The long-time philosophy of moving the customer up-market and up-price misfired. Superb specifications (the machine could read cheques and cash them) failed to impress a market which actually wanted 'an incrementally better, low-cost' replacement ATM.

IBM's sales slumped by over a third in 1985, as NCR took over leadership and piled on the pressure. Empowered workers increased output over ten times in the decade to 1990. NCR's base of installed machines – the vital statistic – expanded to two-thirds higher than IBM. That was too much for the ex-champion, which promptly surrendered, forming a joint venture that left Diebold in control.

Dundee had taken charge of the industry, setting its pace and its agenda. More important, like IBM's PC team, it had pointed the way to ending the crisis of the American corporation – and also the threat to its equivalent, the European multinational. The corporate genus has spread right across the American subcontinent and right around the world. It has spread beyond the reach of central control. It has not outreached the intelligence, initiative and ability of its members.

Not that far from Dundee, in Newhouse, another of IBM's

defeated opponents in mainframes (Honeywell) has similarly soared. Again, the surge has been led by customer service. Again, power has been devolved to the work force. Again, the initiative is local. Again, difficult transitions have been accomplished with a will – Newhouse has moved to flexible manufacturing in cells (in which workers in effect run large manufacturing businesses on their own) with remarkable impact on the plant's capabilities.

At General Electric, often the leader in American management fashions, CEO Jack Welch has launched a corporation-wide drive to 'empower' people at all levels. Their new powers and initiatives are intended to transform performance and improve the quality of management – for poor management created the corporate crisis. Just as quality can only be elevated by changing the factory system, so the management system must be changed to raise management quality. That must apply right to the very top of the corporation.

The overdue debate on chief executive payments in the US was sparked by their extortionate size, rather than deep concern over their impact on management. But if the greatest rewards go to successful corporate politicians, the means of climbing the greasy pole will dominate behaviour. At General Motors, Roger B. Smith faced no apparent dissent or disapproval during a decade in which GM's performance, poor to start with, steadily deteriorated. He even remained on the board after retirement.

It took two years and further rot before his fellows, alarmed by the outflow of GM's cash, at last sacked Smith's successor and gave power to another, unrelated, Smith (John). His solid, high-class achievements in turning GM's European losses into profit were his credentials. Such successes may not translate across oceans. They have a much greater likelihood than track records which include not a single victory in any major race. What preparation is that for the most demanding posts in the company?

Should they be so demanding? The scope of an IBM, geographically, commercially and technologically, is too great for a single group of executives to comprehend – in the senses of both understanding and 'getting the arms round'. Compaq, Digital and Apple are hard enough to manage, but IBM has several businesses of equivalent scale, and some vastly larger. Subdividing mammoths into businesses defined by products and competition makes far more sense.

If the principle is carried right through, what role remains for the centre? And what becomes of the corporate 'culture'? One reason for the spectacular performance of Don Estridge's PC team was his freedom to create a culture different from its paymaster's. The richest tradition of Western business is the invention of new organisational behaviours to suit new technologies and new environments. Unless people working inside large organisations can exploit that inventiveness, frustration and under-achievement will result.

Most writing on underperformance sooner or later mentions Japan. It's hard to avoid the comparison. After all, say, if your industry invents facsimile technology, but your country imports all its faxes from Japanese suppliers, they are outdoing you somewhere. More significant, Japan proves that alternative ways and exceptional methods exist – and that they can produce exceptional results.

An IBM isn't required so that America can compete with Japan. The policy of 'national champions' has failed in industry after industry, country after country. It's useless to give special support to a national company unless it is, or will rapidly become, superior in international competition. If it is superior, it doesn't *need* special sustenance. If it's inferior, the cosseting merely keeps inferior management in power.

The protection given Detroit by controls on Japanese imports only delayed the inevitable, at incalculable cost to workers, investors and consumers. Either the car companies competed effectively with Japan (at long last achieved in 1992 – 93), or they went out of business. Because of automotive economics, new domestic competition (other than foreign transplants) is impossible. In the broadly defined computer industry though, the opposite is true – there's an abundance of domestic competition.

Through the internal and external blockages created by its policies, IBM may have retarded rather than defended progress. The industry's exceptional volatility demands free-form, fluid management. Established corporations with rigid traditions and set procedures are not about to change their habits easily, especially under the leadership of men who prospered under an old system which buttresses their power and privileges.

GE's Jack Welch is intent on breaking free from those chains of the past. He believes that a full decade may be needed – and that backsliding into bureaucracy is a long-term danger, even for a company that has led US management practice for a generation. John Akers' IBM experiments with the 'strategic business unit' concept were about twenty years behind GE's pioneering of the SBU. In Detroit, with its lethal central controls over marketing, the argument is that products sharing common components and serving common markets require common management. That isn't the case with IBM – or Detroit.

IBM's products are notoriously incompatible, and its markets have been dividing and subdividing with the inexorability of fertilised cells. Peter Drucker notes that the same is true of Detroit. Its rare recent successes have mostly been in so-called niche markets where special products meet special customer needs. To maintain obsolete control over the market the big Western business opposes internal product competition. At IBM, the idea of two, let alone more divisions, calling on the same corporate client was anathema – especially if one was offering a cheaper solution. But what if cheaper is better?

If IT customers wanted one-stop shopping, the old ways would make more sense. But customers in all markets increasingly favour diversity. Businesses must become more diverse in management and in marketing to meet this fragmentation. The corporate centre can contribute nothing to market-centred businesses save a number of non-operational, but priceless elements. The first is to set – very preferably by broad consensus – the overall 'strategy', a word which covers both the choice of destination and the general means of getting there.

Within that framework, the centre sets minimum and very high standards; represents investors in seeing that each business is earning excellent returns on their money – and will continue to do so into the foreseeable future; facilitates ambitious plans with money, advice and connections (including interconnections with other group businesses); appoints excellent top managers, and insists that they recruit excellently; and looks after relations with outside agencies, including governments and other corporations, that really need handling centrally.

The list could go on. It's demanding enough already to provide plenty of occupation for men at the top – for which read 'the topless top'. Once the top people start giving orders to their appointees, the game is over. The bureaucratic silt builds up again; the best people leave in hope of finding a better environment; and the local initiative on which local success depends dries up.

As in the countries east of the Elbe, the political mould of the corporate world has been shattered by economic forces and social pressures. The great corporations were formed in eras when economies of scale were dominant, markets homogenous and competition primarily domestic. Fragmentation of markets that are now truly global demands a new corporate politics – but one that must undermine the power and privileges of today's top corporate politicians. For IBM and the rest, that will be no bad thing. Preserving the status quo will only lead to further disaster.

30

Who Killed IBM?
The Final Verdict

So who did kill IBM? As in an Agatha Christie novel, many suspects are assembled in the drawing room for the showdown. Which is the guilty party? The least culpable is the one most easily blamed: the technology. You can argue that the speed, force, depth and breadth of the second wave of computer technology would have swamped IBM in any circumstances. That was historical inevitability.

The little personal computer unveiled to such brilliant effect in 1981 was IBM's nemesis. Its primitive technology developed so rapidly that within a decade the baby would challenge all but its parent's most powerful computers – and leave them helplessly behind in cost. Whatever IBM's management had done, its mainframes and, not far behind, its minicomputers were bound to stagnate.

The essence of the new technology was ease of replication and communication. IBM strove to hold back the tide, but the technology could not be withstood. In a world of ridiculously cheap computing power, getting cheaper all the time; packaged software programs; and individual networks, nobody could maintain proprietary control. That meant, eventually, the loss of the account control that cemented the corporation – and ultimately IBM could do nothing to stem the loss.

The technology needed an accomplice: the IBM culture. The conspicuous end-product failures are bad enough – the four-year lag in PCs, the eleven-year lag in minis, the five-year lag in both laptops at one end and engineering workstations at the other. The corporate damage, long term and short, would have been limited if only IBM had kept abreast with mainstream technology in its product lines. Behind those painful delays lay a trail of missed deadlines, lost opportunities, mistakes and misunderstandings in many key technologies.

For all the protestations of its leaders, the modern IBM was never, first and foremost, a powerhouse of innovation. Its technological resources are immense, but its procedures and principles have retarded the progress of products to market. The culture was supposedly both customer-driven and innovation-led. In reality, the corporation was geared to eschewing risk and maintaining margins – whatever the technology might make possible, whatever the customer might demand.

On one argument, IBM's product lags were a deliberate and integral part of this overall policy. If you dominate a controlled market – in which IBM is as synonymous with computer as Kellogg's is with cornflakes – you can see the attraction of delay. If IBM shunned an emergent sector, its potentially disruptive growth would be stunted, possibly aborted. Even when launching the PC, was IBM seeking to create a market or control it?

The latter interpretation would explain why IBM underestimated initial demand for its PC so grossly – it could have been wishful thinking in reverse. But the customer had wishes, too. Once personal computing had been legitimised by IBM, the latent desire for computing on the desktop, under individual control and infinitely flexible, burst out of the closet.

The customer is also among the suspects. Loyalty to IBM was still strong beyond compare in the Nineties. The brand, thanks to sedulous marketing down the years, remained one of the world's best known and most respected – the only office equipment to rank with mighty consumer brands like Coca-Cola and McDonald's. But brands often maintain historic strength when current market penetration is shrinking fast. Even the most loyal customers will switch brands, for several reasons – some positive (lower prices, better performance, wider choice), some negative (bad service, poor quality).

IBM was once widely believed to bind customers to its products by superlative service. True, commentators also pointed to the 'FUD' factor – Fear, Uncertainty and Doubt. The fearful could reflect that 'nobody ever got fired for buying IBM'. The uncertain could reassure themselves by placing their computing futures in the hands of IBM. The doubtful were spared from the necessity of risking the company's money (and their own careers) on backing a non-IBM supplier or solution.

How much of IBM's hold on the market was positive, how much negative? The steady decline of the company's *Fortune* rating by its peers points to increasingly negative feelings. IBM's sales strategy was directed at the *Fortune* 500, America's leading corporations. The worsening appraisals presumably reflected falling satisfaction (or rising dissatisfaction) with IBM's handling of their own accounts.

The sharp increase in Digital's share of the corporate market with VAX machines was further evidence that IBM's hold over its largest and most preferred customers was weakening. Delays in delivering promised products (both hardware and software) must have added to the disillusion (and irritation) of IT managers. It doesn't matter whether the delays were inadvertent or deliberate. As a marketing ploy, premature announcement of pre-emptive products can be effective; but for every pre-empted competitor, a plus, there are many frustrated customers – thousands of minuses.

If the frustrated buyers were locked into IBM configurations, too bad. They had, willy-nilly, to wait. But the advent of compatibility, above all in PCs, removed the need to wait. And PC customers had no reason for fear, uncertainty or doubt. They bought on three counts – price, performance and product features. They could judge these perfectly well for themselves, or with the aid of a booming, expert specialist press – and IBM was too easily beaten on all three counts.

That was no accident. In one respect, IBM had been absolutely right in all its courtroom protestations in all those victorious lawsuits. The industry has always been a competitive battleground. The competitors, in seeking their own success, necessarily aimed to inflict maximum damage on IBM. For many years IBM was able to repel all would-be assassins. But their numbers kept on multiplying – not just mainline hardware rivals, but plug-compatible peripheral suppliers, leasing companies, added value retailers, software companies of all kinds, microprocessor manufacturers.

The monster grew far too many heads for Hercules to lop off. As one fell, anyway, a hundred sprouted in its place. This overflow of competitors suggests another suspect: the market. As the suppliers proliferated, so the economics deteriorated. In 1992, chairman John Akers could blame his company's operating losses (among other factors) on intense price-cutting in the PC market. Weakening prices across the board truly had undercut all his efforts to arrest decline.

The pattern of over-supply and commodity pricing has turned the PC dream market into a potential nightmare. But Compaq and Apple, IBM's main competitors, were both profitable in 1992. Unlike IBM, neither had other multi-billion dollar product lines which might have offset the problems in PCs. The market is an accessory after the fact, but can otherwise, on this evidence, be eliminated from the enquiry.

Did the murder stem from two traitors – was IBM stabbed in the back by two companies which grew rich on that back: Intel and Microsoft? By building their own businesses outside IBM, the pair automatically reduced IBM's market share. Every Intel 286, 386 and 486 chip sold to non-IBM customers, like every DOS operating system, was a loss to IBM. By 1992, Microsoft was in such open combat with IBM that, to some observers, the fateful decision to commission the PC's operating software from very young Mr Gates was the real villain.

Supposing that IBM had somehow maintained proprietary control over the operating system and the chips – would that have protected its future? The evidence of Apple doesn't encourage that theory. For all Apple's trials and tribulations, it sold the wholly incompatible Macintosh so successfully that, in the US market, it closed the gap with IBM – despite lower credibility with large corporate buyers. If cloning the IBM PC had been harder, other IBM attackers would have developed their own operating systems or taken out licences – perhaps, with help from the anti-trust authorities, licences from IBM.

As for the microprocessors, by 1992 cloners were working on Intel's Pentium chip before it had even reached the market. At best IBM could have delayed the inevitable. Sooner or later, the technological genius and entrepreneurial drive of the super-nerds would have broken the giant's hold. In the super-nerds' wake, the copyists would have come thundering through.

If a proprietary IBM had resisted or missed the technological trends (for instance, the miniaturisation that magically created laptops and palmtops), it would simply have created greater opportunities for others. Like the car-makers of Detroit, with their vain resistance to lower-profit, smaller cars, IBM couldn't hope to stop the future; not in a world where geographical and economic barriers to competition were breaking down universally.

Enter another suspect – the change from a cartelised world economy, controlled by economies of scale, to a global marketplace. Within that world arena, sourcing has become universal, and efficiencies, rather than scale economies, are decisive. There, the Asians, led by the Japanese, have murderous credentials. Japan's only truly successful end-product attack in computers has been in laptops. Even so, Japanese mastery of vital component technologies, from random access memories to flat screens, has undermined IBM's control of the market.

The vertical integration for which IBM was famous merely

condemned it to a proportion of costlier and inferior technologies. Put the other way, it enabled competitors to beat IBM on that vital trio of price, performance and product. The company's reaction to this looming threat, a $10 billion investment in automation, has only been touched on in this book. Like the similar programme at General Motors, it made the problem worse, lowering the productivity of capital, locking the corporation into long, unwanted product runs, and missing the true policy need.

The detective, like Hercule Poirot on the Orient Express, thus has too many suspects: the Technology, the Culture, the Customer, the Market, the Supplier turned Competitor, Globalisation itself. Like the train murderers, all of them stabbed IBM – but did so repeatedly. It wasn't the death of a thousand cuts, but a million. Yet none of the blows would have been fatal, save for self-inflicted wounds – there's a final suspect: Management.

Ineluctable external forces will always, at times, swamp the best of managements. But their supreme test, the proof of whether they truly are 'the best', comes in those times of tribulation. IBM's top management, by that criterion, failed relatively and absolutely. Performance deteriorated on every significant corporate measure, financial or non-financial, over the Akers years.

Reading the chairman's annual statements is to enter the 'all's for the best' world of Voltaire's Dr Pangloss. The repeated optimism in the face of mounting crisis amounts, on the most favourable interpretation, to massive self-deception. To argue that nothing within Armonk's power would have achieved better results is not acceptable. Managers are paid to succeed, not to fail.

The problems were (and are) hideously complex. IBM's top managers made them worse by the series of false starts along the road to radical reform. The famous military confusion – 'order, counter-order and disorder' – accurately describes the process that destabilised the corporation. It did so without arresting the decline in its competitive prowess. There were no compensatory benefits.

The dismissal of Akers, and the appointment of a new top management, removed one issue from the argument. The radical measures launched at end-1991, and prosecuted with some vigour thereafter, will be replaced in whole or part by new strategies. Whether or not they might have succeeded is an academic question. But without doubt, terrible damage has been inflicted which can't be repaired or reversed. Akers, a pre-eminent product of the IBM mould, found it too hard to recognise harsh realities that cut against the corporate grain.

The realities sprang from a common source. The slow down in mainframes and minicomputers; the sensational rise in power of personal computers at one end, and their descent into commodity status at the other; the astounding progress in miniaturisation; the collapse of proprietary systems and the rise of open ones; the newly asserted independence of customers; the challenge of the software and microprocessor firms – all these are symptoms of an irresistible upheaval. Changes in technology and changes in society are (as usual) feeding off each other.

By the millennium, and probably well before, the fate of IBM will be settled. It could become a shadow of its past – a basically centralised, bureaucratic, demoralised hulk, tied up in failed alliances, with a steadily leaking market share. At the opposite extreme, it could become a successful federation of genuinely independent states, each with their own spheres of competence and circles of influence. That would be the ultimate irony.

Throughout the Seventies, IBM devoted great energies to avoiding break-up by the Federal trustbusters. In its closing years, the Akers regime started to attempt a controlled break-up. In everything save equity ownership, the Akers plan would probably have been approved by the anti-trust authorities. The break-up they accepted in the contemporaneous case of American Telephone & Telegraph was similar. It forced the creation of the Baby Bells, which generated a near-threefold rise in value for shareholders from 1982 to 1992.

That represented $132.4 billion of wealth creation, six times the advance in the worth of IBM. Maybe turning IBM into a loose grouping of a dozen or so separately quoted companies would work the same magic. But the snags, as new chairman Lou Gerstner quickly discovered, are legion and literally large. If size is among the ailments that have enfeebled IBM's performance, break-up can't, of itself, cure the disease. The reason is simple.

The Akers re-division of the business is topped by four huge units. The mainframe-related operations, with sales of $22 billion, are bigger than United Technologies, which is sixteenth in the *Fortune* 500. The next three, ranging from $11.9 billion to $11.4 billion, are all larger than the great Motorola. This leading group of manufacturing and development businesses is followed by a second bunch which are also relatively big by industry standards.

One of these $2 billion-plus runners-up outranks disk drive makers Seagate (166th), another two are each bigger than Tandem (217th). This second set of software, peripheral, component, data transmissions and service companies are not viable independent competitors in their present shape. Either their businesses are too dependent on the captive markets of IBM, or they are not fully equipped for the rigours of the marketplace, or both.

The marketplace looms as an especially large problem given that Akers established four other companies in marketing and service. Two of them are gigantic (covering North America and Europe-plus), two merely huge (Asia and Latin America). Together, they account directly for the overwhelming bulk of all IBM sales. Setting these free would create 'hollow' corporations – making nothing themselves – and going far beyond any scale yet envisaged. Could they hope to compete successfully against smaller, tighter, integrated operations like NCR or Apple?

Their IBM suppliers would be in a comparable bind. Could they generate enough profit when so much added value would disappear into the pockets of the trading companies? Wouldn't IBM's problems of the Eighties and Nineties – the overlaps and excessive layers – be aggravated, rather than eased? Small wonder that a *Fortune* writer, David Kirkpatrick, made this comment: 'IBM faces practically every challenge known to management.'

In other words, so does Lou Gerstner. On the evidence of the fumbling of the Eighties, those challenges would certainly have defeated the best efforts of the Ancien Régime in the Nineties. The whole saga is reminiscent of the decline and fall of the Roman Empire. Its causes have never been finally determined – but it was irreversible and awesome. The wasteful excesses of Rome, the incursions of the barbarians, the economic cancer eating away at the empire's vitals, the incompetence of the emperors – it was all these things (which all have their IBM parallels) and none of them. The rise of Rome had set in train great, sweeping trends which its rulers were unable to comprehend fully or control entirely.

The grandeur of IBM, like the grandeur that was Rome, is now history. During that history, IBM played a glorious, magnificent, imperial part. No group of people anywhere in America or the world approached the immense contribution of the IBMers to the Age of Information. This deeply committed, worldwide community translated the technology into brilliant products, and placed them in the hands of users whose applications drove the entire global economy forward.

Possibly, an IBM was essential for the unfolding of the Age; possibly, its rapacity, the reverse side of its ambition, played a part similar to that of the Robber Barons. Their robbery created America's gigantic industrial wealth after the Civil War – possibly an indispensable, certainly an indefensible catalyst. But in the Nineties, IBM has lost its indispensable role. If it didn't exist, it wouldn't be necessary to invent it.

Can the new regime 'reinvent' the great corporation in

another, but still recognisable and successful form? Miracles can happen, even in management. Nobody can predict the outcome of the corporate upheavals inside IBM, which are continuing as this book is being written and read. If the reforms do succeed, that will be an achievement of unexampled brilliance. The future of the large corporation and, to a lesser extent, the fate of the West's advanced technology will both look far more secure.

The progress of that technology has been history's most fascinating display of human initiative, ingenuity and creativity. Even the ferment of the Italian Renaissance made less impact on human lives. For a long time, IBM seemed to embody all the hopes and fears raised by that progress. With the death of the old IBM in February 1992, the torch has passed, not only to its new leaders, but to others in many other companies. Their task is to build a new, multi-faceted, democratic order to replace and surpass the empire that, in the final analysis, killed itself.

Epilogue:

The Future of
the Dream

Commonly, those deeply immersed in an industry miss the moments of critical and absolute change. The obtuse Japanese customer who failed to understand the implications of Ted Hoff's microprocessor – the Intel device which made the PC possible – joined a long line of such failures. They include the General Electric president who ordered that no work be done on computers, and fired a man on the spot for developing one – even though the pioneer had won the Bank of America as a customer.

Later GE entered computers all the same and lost a fortune. Like other large electrical engineering firms, it had insuperable difficulty in adjusting to the new technology. The racing intellects of that technology's creators, however, have continually changed its shape and applications. Despite their past failures, GE and that Japanese client of Intel's (if it survived) are now enormous users and suppliers of data processing hardware and software.

The technology is widening the horizons of individuals and organisations in ways previously unimaginable. Managers of all types of business have been caught up in this revolution, from which new billions of sales and profits are waiting to be born. The future of business computing alone is still as rich and exciting as the prospects that opened before the two Watsons of IBM, and which they and their cohorts exploited so dynamically.

The graphical user interface (developed by Xerox, another of the giants which unaccountably muffed their computer chances), networks, open systems and many other advances are clearly changing management's world, as well as IBM's. Management's future must now take in 'virtual reality' (whose 3-D, living recreations of the real world certainly have business implications) and artificial intelligence (AI).

The so-called 'expert systems' of AI are already proving their business worth in many situations where experience can be codified and incorporated into rules of process. Expert systems will become both more expert and far more widely used. As it is, managers already have available, literally at their fingertips, remarkable powers that could radically change the way in which their minds control and direct organisations.

The ability now exists to achieve instant contact with colleagues and filed data all over the world, working to and from any location, and sharing the collaborative power of the network to create a unified, faster-moving and much more effective management. IBM was better placed than any company to use these tools. But their effective deployment depends on another revolution – from the top-down corporation, in which instructions flow downwards and very little comes back up, to the holistic organisation in which information and responsibility are shared from top to bottom, and also from bottom to top.

An Akers-style strategy of breaking up IBM into component parts, many of them still huge, can accomplish little without this literally fundamental upheaval in working and management methods. Such a change, however, is inimical to the born and bred IBMer, or to any corpocrat in any large unreformed organisation. At IBM (and analogies exist in nearly all other mega-corporations), all the logic pointed long ago to the new imperatives of management.

The aims are easy to list, hard to achieve: giving genuinely independent businesses their heads; allowing freer rein to internal competition; abandoning the impossible effort to lead across the board (which, in IBM's case, meant all three fields of information processing – hardware, software and microprocessors); and concentrating research and development on getting new and better products to market faster and better – with fewer Nobel prizes, but more best-sellers.

Such massive shifts are required from all large corporate groups. The new emphasis also demands being alert and hypersensitive to discoveries elsewhere. In America today (and probably in other countries), new insights must be waiting to be born. Their new and ramifying results must be as striking as any in the barely credible, hyper-drive past of information technology. It isn't a field in which it pays to be at all didactic. Talking about the hardware's continuing shrinkage, and its emergence as a piece of personal luggage, two authors had this to say: 'Computers seem to be heading this way, although currently portables are expensive and limited in their powers.' That statement was clearly being falsified even as it was being uttered, late in 1991. By 1992, IBM laptops were being offered at half-price – a mere £599 – even in the generally over-priced British market. As for being limited, laptops are now fully as powerful as most desktop machines, and who knows what the future will bring?

Even the scientists are not immune to future blindness. When Doug Engelbart, one of the great pioneers of personal computing, demonstrated his revolutionary concepts, the sceptics among his professional colleagues pointed to the demo's great cost, enormous use of computer power and wastefulness. Who wanted to employ such great resources 'simply to make computers easy to use'?

In fact, the ease-of-use issue still hung over the industry in the early Nineties, in executive suites and homes alike. The resulting unemployment or underemployment of computers has impeded their acceptance. But nothing can prevent their advance, especially as price gets lower, and use gets easier, year by year, even month by month. The pace of the computer's evolution has been and still is accelerating with unstoppable momentum.

Because of that sheer pace, the stunning history of the 'dream machine' has been studded with the errors of people who didn't see what was happening; saw, but didn't understand; understood, but didn't act. The manager of the future (in both senses) dare not repeat those failings. That would always have been more of a challenge for IBM than any other management in the world, given its size, scope and sunk investment.

One sceptical ex-IBMer believes that the sunk investment should literally be sunk, that IBM should take the largest write-off in financial history and wipe out $50 billion in assets (over half the end-1991 total). Much of that imposing sum has already been written off, anyway – not by IBM, and not from its balance sheet, but in reality and by history. Like the American polity in which it played so important a part, IBM was the creation of the war years and the wartime generations. IBM helped those generations to change the world – now the world has changed IBM.

Can IBM's own baby-boomers, under the outsider regime of Lou Gerstner, succeed where John Akers and his generation failed? Reinventing a giant corporation from the top is deeply unlikely to work: remaking, rethinking, reshaping one from bottom to top might succeed. The process would require newer men and women with newer ideas than vertically integrated colossi customarily breed – even in dire necessity. In any case, the necessities of IBM are not those of the US industry which it still leads.

Out there, beyond Armonk, the organisational forms are varied and adaptive, and iconoclasm rules. A well-placed IBMer, though, believes that the game is already lost; that the Japanese, by virtue of the technological fortresses they have built along almost very highway, have a power analogous to that of John D. Rockefeller. His Standard Oil Trust didn't own all the oil, but through the railroads and the pipelines it controlled all the access to markets.

America still dominates all the IT end-markets. But the industry no longer controls the access to marketable products. In the recent history of other markets attacked by the Japanese, that loss of control along the line has spelt eventual domination at its end. Somewhere along that line, managements have surrendered. Unable to beat the global competition, they have given away their markets, leaving Japan as virtually the sole supplier – as in TVs, VCRs, radios, faxes and microwaves.

Those products matter less. Information technology matters far more, for it is the blood in the veins and brains of the emerging society. For that reason, nobody should regret the passing of the old IBM. The triumphant survival of a monolithic, quasi-monopolistic computer giant would have seriously damaged the development of the most vibrant, diverse industry America has ever seen.

As this book has argued, that diversity provides the best reason for supposing that the US will retain its creative edge over the competition from the East. But there's a flip side. While the Americans have concentrated on the high ground, advancing the leading edge of existing technologies and discovering new ones, they have left too much low ground to Eastern competitors. The Eastern translation of American brilliance into mass commercial products has made remorseless progress into the middle and upper reaches of information technology.

The cause lies partly in a fundamental difference in approach between East and West. Where the Westerner is primarily interested in product, the Easterner emphasises process. Lester B Thurow, Dean of the Sloan School of Management at MIT, has pointed out that two-thirds of American research and development spending goes into new products, and only a third into process; the Japanese proportions are exactly the other way round. The payoff on process –

351

on making improved products in improving ways – has been miraculous.

In both cars and steel, American producers made the awful mistake of simply assuming that their manufacturing processes were more efficient than Japan's. The reverse was true, and by no small margin. The same weakness has been exploited by Asian makers of computers, components and peripherals. With superior production processes, the Asians have raised yields, quality and margins beyond the apparent reach of most American rivals.

This fascination with process explains why, in machinery for semiconductor production, once led effortlessly by firms like Perkins-Elmer, the Japanese swiftly took the lead. Very sensibly, the only US company still in the big league in this vital sector moved its epicentre to Japan. Today, that is the heartland of micro-electronic component manufacture. The micro-electronic valleys of America are now part of the picture, no longer the whole landscape.

This development might seem unimportant, considering that the rapid rise of Apple, Intel, Compaq and Microsoft and many others to international fame has not been matched in the East. In computer hardware alone, a dozen US manufacturers, out of the hundreds of entrepreneurs who have poured into the electronic valleys since the war, had passed a billion in sales by 1991. Yet that year Apple ($6.3 billion) and Intel ($4.8 billion) were easily the biggest of the newcomers. In global terms, most of the new boys were small fry.

Among *Fortune*'s Global 500 – the international élite – only Apple, Compaq, Sun, Seagate Technology and Intel had made the grade. And the old stagers were far ahead; companies like Motorola ($11.3 billion), Digital ($14 billion) and Hewlett-Packard ($14.3 billion), and, of course, IBM ($64.8 billion). Even the most successful newcomers gave little sign of reaching equal eminence, and too many others levelled off well below global scale.

Worse, as the Nineties developed, the industry was shrinking, and not only in numbers employed. Employment fell because of intense pressure on costs as margins tumbled. But company after company was also shrinking its ambitions. A previous chapter pointed out that IBM's marketing and services companies, if set free as independent units, would become 'hollow' corporations of unprecedented size. The whole US computer industry, though, is headed in the same hollow direction.

The word 'deconstruction' was used by *Business Week* to describe the process of cutting employment, closing facilities and abandoning activities in response to the tidal wave of change. According to McKinsey, at one point integrated makers of computer systems took four-fifths of all the industry's profits. Within a mere five years, that lion's share had shrunk to a miserable fifth. As cheap PCs took over from costly, high-margin mainframes and minis, half the industry's former profits were pocketed by customers who were no longer umbilically tied to single system suppliers.

At the same time, McKinsey's figures show, the share of firms supplying components, software and services rose from 20 per cent of profits to 31 per cent. Remaining a vertically integrated supplier is not an option under these pressures. Instead, companies can take one of two routes. One is break-up into many different, discrete businesses (the route favoured by Akers, whose president, Jack D. Kuehler, was talking in November 1992 of an eventual 'whole host of little companies under the IBM umbrella'). The other route is hollowing-out.

Thus Sun Microsystems, the star performer in Unix workstations, no longer runs its own distribution, or makes its own chips, or services its own machines, or manufactures its own components, or does anything else that others can do on its behalf. It designs chips, software and workstations, which it then markets. Sun is not alone. Unisys and Britain's ICL are other companies that have retreated massively from manufacturing to concentrate successfully on services and marketing.

From one aspect, this is a profound evolution that goes well beyond computers. The worldwide trend is towards a far higher degree of subcontracting as companies concentrate on their genuine core activities – the things that they do best. The European heavy engineering multinational, ABB, for example, cut HQ staff from 6,000 to 150 partly by setting up former head office departments as independent service companies. In theory, and often in practice, such greater visibility goes hand in hand with greater effectiveness.

Hollowing-out head office, though, isn't the same thing as hollowing-out the whole company. In computers, true, that began to happen inadvertently. If nearly every PC used the same chips and the same operating system at its heart, nearly every PC manufacturer was, to that extent, a hollow corporation. But what remaining role does the marketing-only company have in a high-tech world?

As in food retailing, the distributors must eventually take over the game. Why should you, as a retailer, sell an IBM, Compaq, or even perhaps, one day, a Sun, giving margins to the marketers, when you can pocket most of their profit yourself? If Sun can get Eastman Kodak to service its machines, somebody else can use the same strategy. The hollow companies can only preserve their strength and their fabulous sales per employee (Sun's are $280,000, 49 per cent better than IBM's) so long as they set the technological pace.

By definition, though, the technological lead must pass (indeed, has already passed) to the component and peripheral makers. Many have built stronger franchises than the systems suppliers who are their hosts. For instance, Hewlett-Packard has 43 per cent of a $5.4 billion US market for printers. Its major rivals come from Japan, whose strategy is perfectly plain – to achieve dominance in vital technologies, key components and high-selling peripherals. That will be the same dominance, spurred by intense domestic rivalry, that swept American and other Western companies out of other industries they had created and controlled.

Hollow companies offer no competition to this powerful strategy. The strongest model for the West is not Sun, but the microprocessor sub-industry. There the leader, Intel, is surrounded by aggressive challengers, some large and powerful (like IBM and Motorola), others small and climbing. The rivalry helps to drive the engine of progress, while many-sided competition virtually guarantees that no technological lead or market demand will be missed.

Once you could have said much the same of the radio and TV industry in America, and, for that matter, in Europe. Rivalry degenerated into complacency, and the greater part of a vast and viable market was lost. On the battlefield in personal computers, the big brand-name companies are assaulting each other's prices and profits to mutual damage. That is already leading to similar retreats. The labels on the boxes may stay American, or European, but on current trends few of the contents will be made in the West.

On a rosy reading, having 'a whole host of little companies' under the IBM umbrella could make a valuable contribution to arresting the relative decline of American information technology. As each IBM or ex-IBM unit fought for its own place in the sun, with lowered costs, competitive products and dedicated management, new energy would be injected into the 'free' sector of the industry. That is where the future plainly lies – with free suppliers which, like Intel and Microsoft, have untrammelled access to markets across the board and across the world.

But if the hollowing process continues, their Western customers will become expensive distributors. Computer services will be their largest source of revenue, and the industrial game will be lost. The auguries were already alarming as the Nineties began. Despite $80 billion of hardware sales, some ninety computer companies, or almost two-thirds of the industry, collectively lost money in 1991. Unless the hollow companies find and command productive technologies where they can achieve profitable world leadership in their own rights, their last state will be hollow indeed.

Co-operation and collaboration are needed as never before.

IBM not only acted as a whole combined, integrated industry in itself. It served as a target for all comers, unifying their efforts in the single cause of sabotaging IBM. That target no longer stands, and the cause is now nebulous: maintaining world leadership across a highly fragmented industry – the pre-eminent industry of the new millenium. Debilitating price wars, wasteful lawsuits, me-too product lines and cut-throat marketing campaigns will surely destroy a leadership they have already weakened.

Processes of relative decline take a long, long time. As General Motors sought to emerge from its deep abyss by 1992's shock changing of the guard, several observers recalled 'Engine' Charlie Wilson, President Eisenhower's Defence Secretary. A former head of GM, Wilson was misquoted for all eternity as saying, 'What's good for General Motors is good for America.' The misquote was deservedly criticised. But its reverse is undeniable – what was bad for GM truly was bad for the national economy.

The corporation's decline materialised in seemingly uncon-nected steps. At any stage, it was possible to believe, though with mounting difficulty, in renaissance and reform. The same phenomenon has been plainly visible at every point in the long march of IBM towards its fate. The downward steps, how-ever, were all connected – as this book has sought to show.

The consequent relative decline of IBM is now an accom-plished, irreversible fact. The threat to the entire marvellous industry, whose fate was once identical with IBM's, and no longer is, could still be met and conquered. The hour could be getting late. But what's good for the broadly defined com-puter industry would undoubtedly be good – very good – for the West.

Index

357

Index